Sock Yarn One-Skein Wonders

Sock Yarn One-Skein Wonders

Edited by JUDITH DURANT,
creator of the best-selling One-Skein Wonders series

The mission of Storey Publishing is to serve our customers by
publishing practical information that encourages
personal independence in harmony with the environment.

Edited by Gwen Steege
Technical editing by Edie Eckman
Art direction and book design by Mary Winkelman Velgos
Text production by Jennifer Jepson Smith

Photography by © Ira Garber Photography Inc., except for Mars Vilaubi, yarn cards
    (chapter openers and page edges) and pages 264 and 266
Photo styling by Caroline Woodward/Ennis Inc.
Illustrations by Alison Kolesar
Charts by Leslie Anne Charles

Indexed by Nancy D. Wood

Special thanks to WEBS of Northampton, Massachusetts, for loaning skeins of yarn, and The Porches Inn
of North Adams, Massachusetts, for letting us use the location in the photo shoots

Storey Publishing
210 MASS MoCA Way
North Adams, MA 01247
www.storey.com

Printed in China by R.R. Donnelley
10 9 8 7 6 5 4 3 2 1

LIBRARY OF CONGRESS CATALOGING-IN-PUBLICATION DATA

Sock yarn one-skein wonders / edited by Judith Durant.
    p. cm.
  Includes index.
  ISBN 978-1-60342-579-7 (pbk. : alk. paper)
  1. Knitting—Patterns. I. Durant, Judith.
TT825.S655 2010
746.43'2—dc22
                                2010022290

This book is dedicated to sock yarn stashers everywhere,
whose voracious desire for more has stimulated
the production of so much to choose from.

Contents

More than Just Socks! 9

From Head to Toe
(and Fingers, Too)

It's a Wrap!

Knits for Kids

Bag It and More

Appendix

More than Just Socks!

An Internet search for "sock yarn" yields almost half a million hits. And while that doesn't represent the actual number of brands available, it does represent a lot of information about yarn created for knitting one specific thing: socks.

So, what is sock yarn? On the most basic level, it's exactly what the name implies: yarn to knit socks with. While socks can be knit with finer yarns and heavier yarns, "sock yarn" most commonly refers to yarn that knits up between 6½ and 8 stitches per inch. But it's also much more than that.

Most yarn shops have an area reserved "solely" for sock yarn. There you'll find yarn that's been kettle-dyed, hand-dyed, and handpainted. You'll see solids, heathers, and self-patterning yarn ranging from bold stripes to intricate jacquards. Sock yarns are made from combinations of wool, cotton, alpaca, silk, bamboo, soy — even possum! — often with a bit of nylon added for extra strength. They come in skeins, balls, and pre-knitted sheets. And of course, sock yarn is available in at least a zillion colorways.

This begs another question: What are people doing with all that sock yarn? Another search, this time for "sock patterns," returns more than a million results. There are patterns for ankle socks, knee socks, and thigh-highs. You can knit sport socks and boot socks. You can find patterns for socks with none, one, or five articulated toes. Sock patterns range from the most basic models to the wildly ornate and are sized for babies, children, women, and men. You can knit them from the top down, from the bottom up, or from side to side. Knit them with four or five double-point needles. Knit them one at a time on two circular needles, or two at a time on one circular needle. Techniques, designs, and options abound.

Because so many knitters have caught sock fever, communities of sock knitters have formed all over the country and all over the Internet. There are sock clubs and sock blogs, even sock camps and a sock summit! Knitters come together in person or online to share their expertise and the news about books and yarns made just for them. If you peek into these groups, you'll find that they also share something else — stories about their stash. Knitters of all ages and backgrounds are right out there confessing that they're hoarders of sock yarn. And they're very good at justifying this habit: sock yarn "doesn't count" in one's stash. Since a pair of socks takes so little yarn, it's easy to pick some up with each trip to the yarn shop. One sock yarn groupie admitted having enough yarn to knit socks for an entire rugby team. Another 'fessed up to stashing enough for 180 pairs. There's even someone with a sock yarn stash and no idea how to knit socks.

Listen up, all you sockaholics. While you've clearly been doing a great job on your own obeying the voice that says, "Buy me," here are 101 more reasons to keep up the good work! For this collection our contributing designers created sock yarn projects for everything from scarves and shawls to mittens and gloves to bags and purses to baby and doll clothes to coffee and tea cozies to, yes, even socks. Plain and fancy, wool and cotton, you'll find something new to do with the next skein of sock yarn that calls your name.

o **Want to knit a child's sweater?** Check out Patches Baby Sweater (page 168) and Windowpane Cardigan (page 181), both featuring creative uses for self-patterning yarn.

o **Need a shawl or scarf for a special event?** Go to the Celeste Shawl (page 126), shaped for staying on the shoulders and featuring a beaded border, or the lovely and graceful Swan Shawl (page 137). The Lettuce Slide Scarf (page 117) offers a variety of wearing options.

o **You'll find bags to tote just about anything.** The Crocheted Market Bag (page 210) will carry groceries or yarn (sock or otherwise), and the Steppin' Out Wristlet (page 217) is perfect for a night on the town.

o **To keep your hands warm, fingerless mitts are all the rage,** and you'll find several styles, including Chevron Lace Fingerless Mitts (page 31) and Spring Garden Shorties (page 41).

o **Need more?** How about the French Press Snuggly (page 239) for keeping your coffee warm while you knit. And if that's not enough, check out the socks. The Sampler Socks (page 68) allow you to play with different patterns, Cable My Big Toes (page 79) are just right for wearing with flip-flops, and Sideways Socks (page 88) are just that — the vertical stripes are the result of working sideways "flat" on two straight needles.

So without further ado, here are more reasons than ever to stock up on sock yarn!

From
Head
to
Toe

(and Fingers too)

~~~~~~~~~~~~~~~~~~~~~~~

Hats and Caps

~~~~~~~~~~~~~~~~~~~~~~~

Mitts, Gloves, and Cuffs

~~~~~~~~~~~~~~~~~~~~~~~

Socks

~~~~~~~~~~~~~~~~~~~~~~~

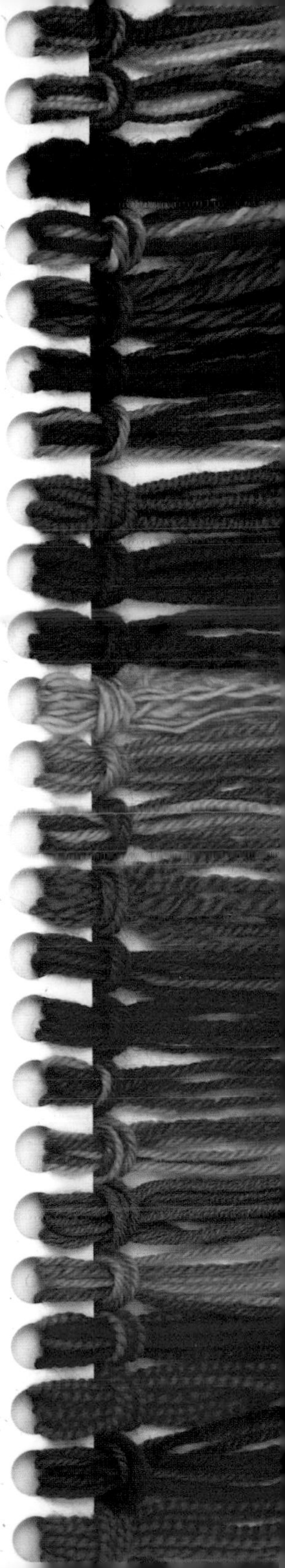

Moss Landing Hat

Designed by Sarah-Hope Parmeter

This beautiful hat of alternating lace and purled triangles provides just the right amount of warmth to ward off spring breezes and early-autumn gusts.

Knitting the Hat

○ Cast on 108 stitches. Place marker and join into a round, being careful not to twist the stitches.

KNITTING THE RIBBING

○ Work K1, P1 ribbing for 4 rounds.

○ Knit 1 round.

KNITTING THE BODY

○ Work Rounds 1–16 of Lacy Diamonds pattern three times.

DECREASING FOR THE CROWN

○ Round 1: P4, *K2tog, yo, K1, yo, ssk, P6, P2tog, s2kp, P2tog, P6, K2tog, yo, K1, yo, ssk, P7; repeat from * two more times, ending last repeat with P3. *You now have* 96 stitches.

○ Round 2: P4, *K5, P7, K1, P7, K5, P7; repeat from * two more times, ending last repeat with P3.

SIZES AND FINISHED MEASUREMENTS	Adult's small, approximately 18"/45.5 cm circumference
YARN	Schaefer Yarn Heather, 55% merino wool superwash/30% silk/15% nylon, 4 oz (113 g)/400 yds (366 m), Pomegranate
NEEDLES	US 4 (3.5 mm) circular needle 16"/40 cm long and set of four US 4 (3.5 mm) double-point needles *or size you need to obtain correct gauge*
GAUGE	23 stitches and 40 rounds= 4"/10 cm in Lacy Diamonds pattern
OTHER SUPPLIES	Stitch marker, tapestry needle

Pattern Essentials

LACY DIAMONDS

Round 1: P4, *K2tog, yo, K1, yo, ssk, P7; repeat from * eight more times, ending last repeat with P3.

Round 2: P4, *K5, P7; repeat from * eight more times, ending last repeat with P3.

Round 3: P3, *K2tog, yo, K3, yo, ssk, P5; repeat from * eight more times, ending last repeat with P2.

Round 4: P3, *K7, P5; repeat from * eight more times, ending last repeat with P2.

Round 5: P2, *K2tog, yo, K1, yo, s2kp, yo, K1, yo, ssk, P3; repeat from * eight more times, ending last repeat with P1.

Round 6: P2, *K9, P3; repeat from * eight more times, ending last repeat with P1.

Round 7: *P1, (K2tog, yo) twice, K3, (yo, ssk) twice; repeat from * to end of round.

Round 8: *P1, K11; repeat from * to end of round.

Round 9: *K1, yo, ssk, P7, K2tog, yo; repeat from * to end of round.

Round 10: K3, *P7, K5; repeat from * eight more times, ending last repeat with K2.

Round 11: K2, *yo, ssk, P5, K2tog, yo, K3; repeat from * eight more times, ending last repeat with K1.

Round 12: K4, *P5, K7; repeat from * eight more times, ending last repeat with K3.

Remove marker. Slip 1 stitch from right-hand needle to left-hand needle. Replace marker.

Round 13: *S2kp, yo, K1, yo, ssk, P3, K2tog, yo, K1, yo; repeat from * to end of round.

Round 14: K5, *P3, K9; repeat from * eight more times, ending last repeat with K4.

Round 15: K2, *(yo, ssk) twice, P1, (K2tog, yo) twice, K3; repeat from * eight more times, ending last repeat with K1.

Round 16: K6, *P1, K11; repeat from * eight more times, ending last repeat with K5.

Repeat Rounds 1–16 for pattern.

○ Round 3: P3, *K2tog, yo, K3, yo, ssk, P4, P2tog, K1, P2tog, P4, K2tog, yo, K3, yo, ssk, P5; repeat from * two more times, ending last repeat with P2. *You now have 90 stitches.*

○ Round 4: P3, *K7, P5, K1, P5, K7, P5; repeat from * two more times, ending last repeat with P2.

○ Round 5: P2, *K2tog, yo, K1, yo, s2kp, yo, K1, yo, ssk, P2, P2tog, K1, P2tog, P2, K2tog, yo, K1, yo, s2kp, yo, K1, yo, ssk, P3; repeat from * two more times, ending last repeat with P1. *You now have 84 stitches.*

○ Round 6: P2, *K9, P3, K1, P3, K9, P3; repeat from * two more times, ending last repeat with P1.

LACY DIAMONDS

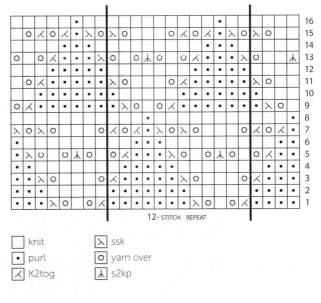

12-STITCH REPEAT

▢ knit	⟍ ssk
• purl	○ yarn over
⟋ K2tog	⋏ s2kp

○ Round 7: *P1, (K2tog, yo) twice, K3, (yo, ssk) twice, P2tog, K1, P2tog, (K2tog, yo) twice, K3, (yo, ssk) twice; repeat from * to end of round. *You now have* 78 stitches.

○ Round 8: *P1, K11, P3tog, K11; repeat from * to end of round. *You now have* 72 stitches.

○ Remove marker. Slip 1 stitch from right-hand needle to left-hand needle. Replace marker.

○ Round 9: *S2kp, P9; repeat from * to end of round. *You now have* 60 stitches.

○ Round 10: *K1, P9; repeat from * to end of round.

○ Remove marker. Slip 1 stitch from right-hand needle to left-hand needle. Replace marker.

○ Round 11: *S2kp, P7; repeat from * to end of round. *You now have* 48 stitches.

○ Round 12: *K1, P7; repeat from * to end of round.

○ Remove marker. Slip 1 stitch from right-hand needle to left-hand needle. Replace marker.

○ Round 13: *S2kp, P5; repeat from * to end of round. *You now have* 36 stitches.

○ Round 14: *K1, P5; repeat from * to end of round.

○ Remove marker. Slip 1 stitch from right-hand needle to left-hand needle. Replace marker.

○ Round 15: *S2kp, P3; repeat from * to end of round. *You now have* 24 stitches.

○ Round 16: *K1, P3; repeat from * to end of round.

○ Remove marker. Slip 1 stitch from right-hand needle to left-hand needle. Replace marker.

○ Round 17: *S2kp, P1; repeat from * to end of round. *You now have* 12 stitches.

○ Round 18: *K1, P1; repeat from * to end of round.

Finishing

○ Cut yarn, leaving a 12"/30.5 cm tail. Thread tail onto tapestry needle and draw through remaining stitches. Pull up snug and fasten off on inside. Weave in ends.

Ira Garber / John Tavares

Knot Head

Designed by Cheryl Oberle

Here's a cute topper that's perfect for cool autumn days. Knitted in the round in stockinette stitch, the hat features a rolled brim and long tabs that knot on top.

Knitting the Body

○ With circular needle, cast on 90 (100, 110) stitches. Place a marker (#1) and join into a round, being careful not to twist the stitches.

○ Round 1: K25, place marker (#2), K20 (25, 30), place marker (#3), K25, place marker (#4), K20 (25, 30).

○ Work even in stockinette stitch, slipping the markers on every round, until piece measures 10½" (10½", 11")/26.5 (26.5, 28) cm. *Note:* The bottom 2"/5 cm will roll to the outside and form the brim.

Shaping the Ties

○ Knit to marker #2. With straight needle, knit the next 25 stitches, turn. The first tie is knitted back and forth on these 25 stitches.

○ Beginning with a wrong-side row, work back and forth in stockinette stitch for 5 (7, 9) more rows.

○ Decrease Row (RS): K1, K2tog, knit to last 3 stitches, K2tog, K1.

SIZES AND FINISHED MEASUREMENTS	Woman's small (medium, large), approximately 16" (18", 20")/41 (45.5, 51) cm circumference
YARN	Weaving Southwest Superwash Sport Hand-dyed Tweed, 100% superwash merino wool, 4 oz (113 g)/375 yds (343 m), Camouflage
NEEDLES	US 5 (3.75 mm) circular needle 16"/40 cm long and US 5 (3.75 mm) straight needles *or size you need to obtain correct gauge*
GAUGE	22 stitches and 28 rounds = 4"/10 cm in stockinette stitch
OTHER SUPPLIES	Four stitch markers, tapestry needle

15

○ Continue in stockinette stitch and work the Decrease Row every fourth row nine more times, ending with a wrong-side row. *You now have 5 stitches.* Work the last 3 rows as follows:

○ Row 1: K1, K3tog, K1.

○ Row 2: Purl.

○ Row 3: K3tog.

○ Pull yarn through last stitch. Cut the yarn and weave in the end. With circular needle, slip next 20 (25, 30) stitches. With straight needle, knit the next 25 stitches (the stitches between markers #4 and #1). Work second tie as for first.

Joining the Crown

○ Place each of the remaining two sets of 20 (25, 30) stitches onto straight needles. With wrong sides together and using the circular needle, join stitches with three-needle bind off (see page 282).

Finishing

○ Weave in ends. Steam body lightly, avoiding rolled brim and ties. Bring ties together and tie into a knot, leaving 3"/7.5 cm tails.

Desiree's Hat

Designed by Marie R. Connolly

This simple hat is delightfully soft, knitted with a merino-cashmere blend. The ribbing can be turned up to form a brim or worn down for more ear coverage.

SIZES AND FINISHED MEASUREMENTS	Child's large/Adult's small, approximately 18"/45.5 cm circumference
YARN	Punta Del Este Mericash Solid, 80% merino/20% cashmere, 1.75 oz (50 g)/262.5 yds (240 m), Color 325
NEEDLES	US 4 (3.5 mm) circular needle 16"/40 cm long, set of four US 4 (3.5 mm) double-point needles, and US 3 (3.25 mm) circular needle 16"/40 cm long *or size you need to obtain correct gauge*
GAUGE	32 stitches and 38 rounds = 4"/10 cm in Diagonal Stripes pattern on larger needle
OTHER SUPPLIES	Stitch markers, tapestry needle
SPECIAL ABBREVIATIONS	**dec** decrease 1 stitch with slip, slip, knit or slip, slip, purl

Knitting the Hat

○ Using the smaller circular needle, cast on 120 stitches. Place a marker and join into a round, being careful not to twist the stitches. Work K2, P2 ribbing for 1¾"/4.5 cm, purling last 2 stitches together on last round of ribbing. *You now have* 119 stitches.

○ Change to larger circular needle and begin working the Diagonal Stripes pattern. Continue in pattern until piece measures 5"/12.5 cm from ribbing, ending with pattern Round 1.

DECREASING FOR THE CROWN

○ *Note:* With each decrease round there will be fewer knit stitches between the markers. Maintain pattern by continuing to work the purl stitches in a spiral as established.

Work ssk decrease when both stitches to be decreased are knit stitches; work ssp decrease when one of the stitches to be decreased is a purl stitch. Change to double-point needles when there are too few stitches for the circular needle.

o Round 1: *Work 10 stitches, dec, place marker; repeat from * eight times, work 9 stitches, dec. *You now have* 109 stitches.

o Round 2 and all even-numbered rounds: Work even in established pattern.

o Round 3: *Work 9 stitches, dec, slip marker; repeat from * eight times, work 8 stitches, dec. *You now have* 99 stitches.

o Round 5: *Work 8 stitches, dec, slip marker; repeat from * eight times, work 7 stitches, dec. *You now have* 89 stitches.

o Continue in this manner, maintaining Diagonal Stripes pattern and working decreases every other round just before each marker, until 19 stitches remain.

o Next Round: *K2 tog; repeat from * to last stitch, K1. *You now have* 10 stitches.

Finishing

o Cut yarn, leaving a 6"/15 cm tail. Thread tail onto tapestry needle and draw through remaining stitches. Pull up snug and fasten off on inside. Weave in ends.

Pattern Essentials
DIAGONAL STRIPES

Rounds 1 and 2: *K5, P1; repeat from * to last 5 stitches, K5.
Rounds 3 and 4: P1, *K5, P1; repeat from * to last 4 stitches, K4.
Rounds 5 and 6: K1, P1, *K5, P1; repeat from * to last 3 stitches, K3.
Rounds 7 and 8: K2, P1, *K5, P1; repeat from * to last 2 stitches, K2.
Rounds 9 and 10: K3, P1, *K5, P1; repeat from * to last stitch, K1.
Rounds 11 and 12: K4, P1, *K5, P1; repeat from * to end of round.
Repeat Rounds 1–12 for pattern.

DIAGONAL STRIPES

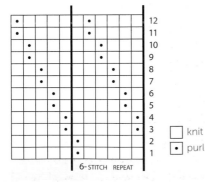

6-STITCH REPEAT

□ knit
• purl

Twist and Slouch

Designed by Kristina Taylor

This hat is made up of two conjoined parts: a stockinette stitch body knitted in the round and a garter stitch border worked back and forth. But for one inch of ribbing, no other purling is necessary!

Knitting the Hat

○ Using circular needle and a provisional method (see page 280), cast on 110 stitches. Place marker and join into a round, being careful not to twist the stitches.

○ Work K1, P1 ribbing for 1"/2.5 cm.

○ Next Row: *K11, M1; repeat from * to end of round. *You now have* 120 stitches.

○ Work stockinette stitch (knit every round) until piece measures 6"/15 cm from the cast-on edge.

DECREASING FOR THE CROWN

○ Round 1: *K10, K2tog; repeat from * to end of round. *You now have* 110 stitches.

○ Round 2 and all even-numbered rounds: Knit.

○ Round 3: * K9, K2tog; repeat from * to end of round. *You now have* 100 stitches.

○ Round 5: *K8, K2tog; repeat from * to end of round. *You now have* 90 stitches.

SIZES AND FINISHED MEASUREMENTS	To fit most adults, approximately 18"/46 cm circumference, unstretched
YARN	Mountain Colors Bearfoot, 60% superwash wool/25% mohair/15% nylon, 3.5 oz (100 g)/350 yds (320 m), Rosehip
NEEDLES	US 4 (3.5 mm) circular needle 16"/40 cm long and set of four US 4 (3.5 mm) double-point needles *or size you need to obtain correct gauge*
GAUGE	22 stitches and 32 rounds = 4"/10 cm in stockinette stitch
OTHER SUPPLIES	Stitch marker, scrap yarn for holder, tapestry needle

○ Continue in this manner, decreasing every other round, working 1 fewer stitch between the decreases and changing to double-point needles when there are too few stitches for the circular needle, until 20 stitches remain.

○ Round 21: *K2tog; repeat from *. *You now have* 10 stitches.

○ Round 22: Knit.

○ Round 23: Repeat Round 21. *You now have* 5 stitches.

○ Cut yarn leaving a 6"/15 cm tail. Thread tail onto tapestry needle and draw through remaining stitches. Pull up snug and fasten off on inside of hat.

KNITTING THE BANDEAU

○ Remove provisional cast on and place stitches on circular needle. With right side facing, attach yarn and begin working back and forth in rows.

○ Row 1: *K1 tbl; repeat from * to end of row, turn.

○ Row 2 (WS): Knit.

○ Row 3: Kfb, knit to last stitch, kfb.

○ Row 4: Knit.

○ Repeat Rows 3 and 4 until bandeau measures at least 24"/61 cm from tip to tip — the longer the bandeau, the larger the twist.

○ Knit 5 to 10 rows even. Bind off loosely.

Finishing

○ Weave in ends. Ties ends of bandeau into a knot.

Garbo's Turban

Designed by Judith Durant

Popular during the 1930s, '40s, and '50s, turbans are often associated with movie stars such as Greta Garbo, Gloria Swanson, and Audrey Hepburn. But they're also very practical, especially on a bad-hair day. This one is knitted in one long strip, then wrapped and sewn together.

19

SIZES AND FINISHED MEASUREMENTS	To fit most adults, approximately 22"/56 cm circumference
YARN	Cherry Tree Hill Supersock Solids, 100% superwash merino wool, 4 oz (113 g)/ 420 yds (384 m), Dove
NEEDLES	US 2 (2.75 mm) straight needles plus one extra for bind off *or size you need to obtain correct gauge*
GAUGE	48 stitches = 4"/10 cm in Rib pattern, unstretched
OTHER SUPPLIES	Scrap yarn for holder, head form (optional), tapestry needle

Pattern Essentials

RIB

Row 1 (RS): *K2, P2; repeat from * to last 2 stitches, K2.

Row 2: *P2, K2; repeat from * to last 2 stitches, P2.

Knitting the Turban

○ Cast on 34 stitches.

○ Row 1 (RS): *K2, P2; repeat from * to last 2 stitches, K2.

○ Row 2: *P2, K2; repeat from * to last 2 stitches, P2.

○ Row 3: K1, M1, K1, *P2, K2; repeat from * to last 4 stitches, P2, K1, M1, K1.

○ Row 4: P3, *K2, P2; repeat from * to last 5 stitches, K2, P3.

○ Row 5: K1, M1P, *K2, P2; repeat from * to last 3 stitches, K2, M1P, K1.

○ Row 6: P1, K1, *P2, K2; repeat from * to last 4 stitches, P2, K1, P1.

○ Row 7: K1, M1P, P1, *K2, P2; repeat from * to last 4 stitches, K2, P1, M1P, K1.

○ Row 8: P1, *K2, P2; repeat from * to last 3 stitches, K2, P1.

○ Continue in this manner, maintaining 1 stockinette edge stitch on each side and increasing in Rib pattern until you have 58 stitches, ending on a wrong-side row.

○ Work even in Rib pattern until piece measures 30"/76 cm from cast-on edge, ending on a wrong-side row.

KNITTING THE FRONT LOOP

○ Row 1: Work 25 stitches in Rib pattern as established and place on holder; bind off 8 stitches; work in rib as established to end of row.

○ Row 2: *P2, K2; repeat from * to last stitch, P1.

○ Row 3: Slip 1, *P2, K2; repeat from * to end of row.

○ Row 4: Repeat Row 2.

○ Repeat Rows 3 and 4 until piece measures 4½"/11.5 cm from bound-off stitches, ending on a wrong-side row.

○ Place held 25 stitches on needle. With a third needle and right sides together, use three-needle bind off (see page 282) to join the two sets of 25 stitches, forming a loop.

Wrapping the Turban

○ *Note:* This is best accomplished with a head form, but it is possible without one. Just be sure you pin everything in place and join row for row. You could also wrap a friend!

○ Holding loop at forehead, wrap the strip around the head over the left ear, around the back, and over the right ear. At the forehead, pass the end of the strip through the loop, and bring across the top of the head and to the back (Fig. 1). Pin the end of the strip to the edge that crosses the back of the head. Adjust the knitting and pin the edges together around the crown (Fig. 2). Carefully sew together invisibly with mattress stitch (see page 280).

Finishing

○ Weave in ends.

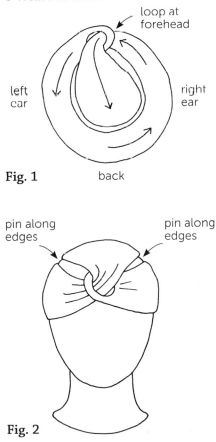

Fig. 1

Fig. 2

Rustica Cloche

Designed by Katherine Eng

This crocheted cloche features a lovely fold-up brim that is accented with glass beads. And the best part is the estimated stitching time — only three hours!

SIZES AND FINISHED MEASUREMENTS	To fit most adults, approximately 20"/51 cm circumference, unstretched
YARN	Red Heart Heart and Sole, 70% superwash wool/30% nylon, 1.75 oz (50 g)/213 yds (195 m), 3945 Rustica
CROCHET HOOK	Size G/6 (4 mm) or size you need to obtain correct gauge
GAUGE	Rounds 1–6 = 4"/10 cm
OTHER SUPPLIES	Thirty-two 5 mm blue triangle beads, size 10 (1.3 mm) steel crochet hook for beading, tapestry needle
SPECIAL ABBREVIATIONS	**HB (hook bead)** pick up bead onto small crochet hook, pick up stitch to be beaded, slide bead onto stitch, replace stitch on large hook

21

Pattern Essentials
SHELL
5 double crochet in 1 stitch or space

. . . .

Crocheting the Hat

o *Note:* Always join the last stitch of a round to the first stitch with a slip stitch. Work in specified stitches and spaces only, skipping over others.

o Setup: Ch 4 and join to form ring, ch 1.

o Round 1: (Sc, ch 2) in ring eight times; join, slipstitch in next ch-2 space, ch 1.

o Round 2: [(Sc, ch 2, sc) in ch-2 space, ch 1] eight times. Join, slipstitch in next ch-2 space, ch 1.

o Round 3: [(Sc, ch 2, sc) in ch-2 space, ch 2] eight times. Join, slipstitch in next ch-2 space, ch 1.

o Round 4: [(Sc, ch 2, sc) in ch-2 space, ch 3, skip next ch-2 space] eight times. Join, slipstitch in next ch-2 space, ch 1.

o Round 5: [(Sc, ch 2, sc) in ch-2 space, ch 1, (sc, ch 2, sc) in next ch-3 space, ch 1] around. Join, slipstitch in next ch-2 space, ch 1.

o Round 6: [(Sc, ch 2, sc) in ch-2 space, ch 1] 16 times. Join, slipstitch in next ch-2 space, ch 1.

o Round 7: [(Sc, ch 2, sc) in ch-2 space, ch 2] around. Join, slipstitch in next ch-2 space, ch 1.

o Round 8: [(Sc, ch 2, sc) in ch-2 space, ch 3, skip next ch-2 space] around. Join, slipstitch in next ch-2 space, ch 1.

o Round 9: Repeat Round 5.

o Rounds 10–13: [(Sc, ch 2, sc) in ch-2 space, ch 1] around. Join, slipstitch in next ch-2 space, ch 1.

o Rounds 14–26: [(Sc, ch 2, sc) in ch-2 space, ch 2] around. Join, slipstitch in next ch-2 space, ch 1.

o Round 27: Repeat Round 10.

o Round 28: Sc in first ch-2 space, ch 2, (sc in next ch-2 space, ch 2) around. Join, ch 1, turn.

Crocheting the Brim

o *Note:* The brim is worked with wrong side facing.

o Round 1: Sc in next ch-2 space, *shell in next ch-2 space, sc in next ch-2 space; repeat from *, ending with shell in last space. Join, ch 3 (counts as first dc of shell of next round).

o Round 2: 4 dc in same sc to complete shell, *sc in center dc of next shell, shell in next sc; repeat from *, ending last repeat with sc in center dc of last shell. Join to top of beginning ch-3, slip stitch to center dc of next shell, ch 1.

o Round 3: Sc in same dc. *Shell in next sc, sc in center dc of next shell; repeat from * around, ending with shell in last sc. Join to beginning sc, ch 3 (counts as first dc of shell of next round).

o Round 4: Repeat Round 2.

o Round 5: Repeat Round 3, omitting final ch-1.

o Round 6: HB, sc in first sc. *Ch 2, (sc, HB, sc) in center dc of next shell, ch 2, HB, sc in next sc; repeat from * around, ending with ch 2, (sc, HB, sc) in center dc of next shell, ch 2. Join to beginning sc. Fasten off.

Finishing

o Weave in ends. Turn brim up to right side.

Horizontal Rib Hat

Designed by Marci Blank

Self-patterning yarn takes on a whole new personality in this ribbed hat of garter and stockinette stitches. It's easy to make and wear, and you can experiment with all sorts of colorways!

SIZES AND FINISHED MEASUREMENTS	To fit most adults, approximately 22"/56 cm circumference, unstretched
YARN	Berroco Sox, 75% superwash wool/25% nylon, 3.5 oz (100 g)/440 yds (402 m), Color 1425
NEEDLES	US 6 (4 mm) circular needle 16"/40 cm long and set of four US 6 (4 mm) double-point needles *or size you need to obtain correct gauge*
GAUGE	16 stitches = 4"/10 cm in stockinette stitch (with yarn doubled)
OTHER SUPPLIES	Tapestry needle

23

Preparing the Yarn

o Yarn is used doubled throughout. You can either wind it into a center-pull ball and knit from the inside and outside of the ball at the same time or wind two balls of equal length and knit with one strand from each ball.

Knitting the Hat

o With circular needle, cast on 90 stitches. Join into a round, being careful not to twist the stitches.

o Rounds 1–8: Knit.

o Rounds 9–11: Purl.

o Rounds 12–17: Knit.

o Rounds 18–20: Purl.

o Repeat Rounds 12–20 two more times.

DECREASING FOR THE CROWN

o Keeping in pattern as established (knit 6 rounds, purl 3 rounds) and changing to double-point needles when there are too few stitches for the circular, shape the crown as follows.

o Decrease Round 1: *K7, K2tog; repeat from * to end of round. *You now have 80 stitches.*

o Knit 2 rounds.

o Decrease Round 2: *K8, K2tog; repeat from * to end of round. *You now have 72 stitches.*

o Knit 2 rounds.

o Decrease Round 3: *P7, P2tog; repeat from * to end of round. *You now have 64 stitches.*

o Purl 2 rounds.

o Decrease Round 4: *K6, K2tog; repeat from * to end of round. *You now have 56 stitches.*

o Knit 2 rounds.

o Decrease Round 5: *K5, K2tog; repeat from * to end of round. *You now have 48 stitches.*

o Knit 2 rounds.

o Decrease Round 6: *P4, P2tog; repeat from * to end of round. *You now have 40 stitches.*

o Purl 2 rounds.

o Decrease Round 7: *K3, K2tog; repeat from * to end of round. *You now have 32 stitches.*

o Knit 2 rounds.

o Decrease Round 8: *K2, K2tog; repeat from * to end of round. *You now have 24 stitches.*

o Knit 2 rounds.

o Decrease Round 9: *P1, P2tog; repeat from * to end of round. *You now have 16 stitches.*

o Purl 2 rounds.

o Final Decrease Round: *P2tog; repeat from * to end of round. *You now have 8 stitches.*

Finishing

o Cut yarn, leaving a 6"/15 cm tail. Thread tail onto tapestry needle and draw through remaining stitches. Pull up snug and fasten off. Weave in ends.

Emma's Star

Designed by Jennifer Chase-Rappaport

Emma or anyone else will be walking under a lucky star when wearing this beret. Knitted from the center of the star down to the brim, the beret works up quickly in this heavier-than-fingering-weight sock yarn.

SIZES AND FINISHED MEASUREMENTS	To fit large child/most adults, approximately 20"/51 cm circumference, unstretched
YARN	Hazel Knits Artisan Lively DK, 90% superwash merino/10% nylon, 5 oz (140 g)/ 275 yds (251.5 m), Color 217 Laguna
NEEDLES	US 4 (3.5 mm) circular needle 16"/40 cm long and set of five US 4 (3.5 mm) double-point needles *or size you need to obtain correct gauge*
GAUGE	22 stitches = 4"/10 cm in stockinette stitch
OTHER SUPPLIES	Stitch marker, tapestry needle

25

Knitting the Beret

○ Using the cable (see page 276) or knitted-on (see page 278) method, cast on 4 stitches onto one double-point needle. Kfb into each stitch. *You now have* 8 stitches. Distribute the stitches so there are 2 stitches on each of four needles. Place marker and join into a round, being careful not to twist the stitches.

○ Round 1: *Yo, K1; repeat from * to end of round. *You now have* 16 stitches.

○ Round 2 and all even-numbered rounds: Knit.

○ Round 3: *Yo, K2; repeat from * to end of round. *You now have* 24 stitches.

○ Round 5: *Yo, K3; repeat from * to end of round. *You now have* 32 stitches.

○ Round 7: *Yo, K4; repeat from * to end of round. *You now have* 40 stitches.

○ Rounds 9–16: Continue in this manner, knitting 1 more stitch between the yarn overs and working 1 round even between the increase rounds, until there are 8 stitches between the yarn overs. *You now have* 72 stitches.

○ Round 17: *Yo, K1, yo, K6, K2tog; repeat from * to end of round. *You now have* 80 stitches.

○ Round 19: *Yo, K3, yo, K5, K2tog; repeat from * to end of round. *You now have* 88 stitches.

○ Round 21: *Yo, K5, yo, K4, K2tog; repeat from * to end of round. *You now have* 96 stitches.

○ Round 23: *Yo, K7, yo, K3, K2tog; repeat from * to end of round. *You now have* 104 stitches.

○ Round 25: *Yo, K9, yo, K2, K2tog; repeat from * to end of round. *You now have* 112 stitches.

○ Round 27: *Yo, K11, yo, K1, K2tog; repeat from * to end of round. *You now have* 120 stitches.

○ Round 29: *Yo, K13, yo, K2tog; repeat from * to end of round. *You now have* 128 stitches.

○ Round 31: *Yo, K14, yo, K2tog; repeat from * to end of round. *You now have* 136 stitches.

○ Round 33: *Yo, K15, yo, K2tog; repeat from * to end of round. *You now have* 144 stitches.

○ Round 35: *Yo, K16, yo, K2tog; repeat from * to end of round. *You now have* 152 stitches.

○ Odd-numbered Rounds 37–45: *Yo, K2tog, K15, yo, K2tog; repeat from * to end of round.

DECREASING FOR THE BRIM

○ *Note:* These rounds will maintain the eyelet pattern while decreasing the circumference to the band.

○ Round 47: *Yo, K2tog, K13, K2tog, yo, K2tog; repeat from * to end of round. *You now have* 144 stitches.

○ Round 49: *Yo, K2tog, K12, K2tog, yo, K2tog; repeat from * to end of round. *You now have* 136 stitches.

○ Odd-Numbered Rounds 51–57: Continue in this manner, knitting 1 fewer stitch between the decreases and working 1 round even between the decrease rounds, until you have 104 stitches.

○ Next round: Knit.

Knitting the Band

○ Round 1: *K1, P1; repeat from * to end of round.

○ Repeat Round 1 until band measures 1"/2.5 cm or desired length.

Finishing

○ Bind off loosely. Weave in ends. Block over dinner plate to open the lace and shape the beret.

Hera Headband

Designed by Sarah-Hope Parmeter

The elaborate interwoven pattern on the Hera Head-band is worked with simple right and left crosses — you can leave your cable needle in your notions bag! This wool and silk sample was knitted by Chris Polak.

Knitting the Headband

o Cast on 12 stitches.

o Work Chart A once.

o Work Chart B once.

o Work Chart C once.

o Work Chart D once.

o Work Chart E once.

o Wrap the band around the wearer's head and measure the additional length required to make the ends meet but not overlap. (Band should be slightly snug.) Repeat Rows 25–34 of Chart E as necessary to make this length.

o Work Rows 25–34 once more for the button overlap as follows: On Rows 25 and 33, work the center 2 stitches as P2tog, yo to form the buttonholes. Bind off.

SIZES AND FINISHED MEASUREMENTS	Adjustable to fit all sizes
YARN	Curious Creek Omo, 50% merino wool/ 50% silk, 1.75 oz (50 g)/205 yds (186 m), Mysterious Night
NEEDLES	US 4 (3.5 mm) straight needles *or size you need to obtain correct gauge*
GAUGE	24 stitches = 4"/10 cm in stockinette stitch; 36 stitches = 4"/10 cm in pattern
OTHER SUPPLIES	Tapestry needle, two ½"/1.3 cm buttons
SPECIAL ABBREVIATIONS	**M1LP** make 1 left-leaning stitch purlwise (see page 279) **M1RP** make 1 right-leaning stitch purlwise (see page 279)

Finishing

○ Weave in ends. Sew buttons opposite buttonholes, spacing them 1"/2.5 cm apart.

Pattern Essentials

2-STITCH RIGHT CROSS

Knit the second stitch and leave it on the needle, then knit the first stitch and slip both stitches off the needle.

2-STITCH LEFT CROSS

Knit the second stitch through the back loop and leave it on the needle, then knit the first stitch and slip both stitches off the needle.

CHART A

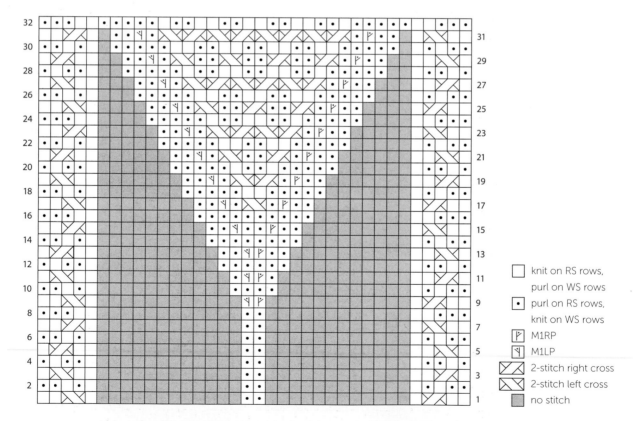

knit on RS rows, purl on WS rows

• purl on RS rows, knit on WS rows

⊵ M1RP

⊴ M1LP

2-stitch right cross

2-stitch left cross

no stitch

CHART B

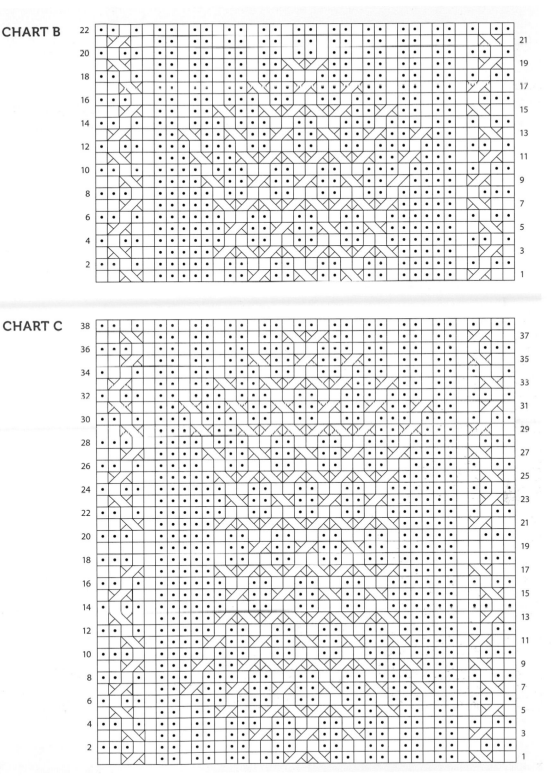

CHART C

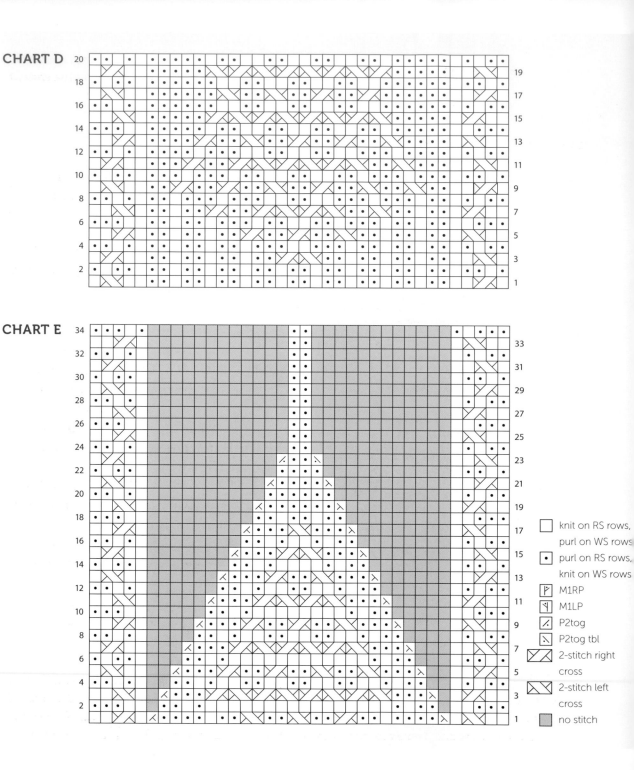

CHART D

CHART E

knit on RS rows,
purl on WS rows

• purl on RS rows,
knit on WS rows

M1RP

M1LP

P2tog

P2tog tbl

2-stitch right
cross

2-stitch left
cross

no stitch

Chevron Lace Fingerless Mitts

Designed by Lynne A. Evans

With an easy and fun-to-knit lace pattern, these unique mitts feature a picot cast on and a picot bind off. The lace is Flame Chevron from Barbara Walker's *A Second Treasury of Knitting Patterns.*

SIZES AND FINISHED MEASUREMENTS	Woman's small, approximately 7"/18 cm circumference
YARN	Premier Yarns Serenity Sock Weight, 50% superwash merino wool/25% bamboo/25% nylon, 1.75 oz (50 g)/230 yds (210 m), Color 10 Amethyst
NEEDLES	Set of four US 2 (2.75 mm) double-point needles *or size you need to obtain correct gauge*
GAUGE	36 stitches and 50 rounds= 4"/10 cm in stockinette stitch
OTHER SUPPLIES	Crochet hook size C/2 (2.75 mm), stitch marker, scrap yarn for holders, tapestry needle

KNITTING THE LEFT MITT

Knitting the Cuff

o Following the instructions for the Picot Crochet method on page 32, cast on 63 stitches, then place the loop from the crochet hook on the needle. *You now have* 64 stitches and 16 picots.

o Divide the stitches onto double-point needles so there are 32 stitches on Needle 1 and 16 stitches each on Needles 2 and 3. Join into a round, being careful not to twist the stitches.

o Work K2, P2 ribbing for 16 rounds. Note that the picots are at the ends of the pairs of knit stitches.

Beginning the Lace Pattern

o Following either the written instructions or the chart, work Rounds 1–24 of Chevron Lace pattern on Needle 1 while working stockinette stitch on Needles 2 and 3. Work Round 1 of Chevron Lace pattern one more time.

Knitting the Thumb Gusset

o Round 1: M1, place marker, work in patterns as established to end of round. *You now have* 65 stitches.

o Round 2: K1 (gusset stitch), slip marker, work in patterns as established to end of round.

o Round 3: M1, knit to marker, M1, slip marker, work in patterns as established to end of round.

o Round 4: Knit to marker, slip marker, work in patterns as established to end of round.

o Repeat Rounds 3 and 4 until there are 21 gusset stitches, ending on Round 4. Place 21 gusset stitches on holder.

o Rejoin into a round and continue in patterns as established until a total of two-and-one-half repeats of Chevron Lace pattern have been completed, ending on Round 12 of pattern.

Knitting the Ending Rib

○ Work K2, P2 ribbing for 6 rounds. Using the Picot Bind Off (see below), bind off all stitches.

Knitting the Thumb

○ Place 21 held gusset stitches onto two needles. With a third needle, pick up and knit (see page 280) 7 stitches in the space between the beginning and end of gusset stitches. *You now have* 28 stitches.

○ Work K2, P2 ribbing for 6 rounds. Using the Picot Bind Off, bind off all stitches.

KNITTING THE RIGHT MITT

○ Work cuff and beginning of lace pattern as for left mitt.

Knitting the Thumb Gusset

○ Round 1: Work in pattern as established on Needle 1, place marker, M1, knit to end of round. *You now have* 65 stitches.

○ Round 2: Work in pattern as established on Needle 1, slip marker, K1 (gusset stitch), place marker, work in pattern as established to end of round.

Pattern Essentials

PICOT CROCHET CAST ON

1. Make a slipknot on the crochet hook, leaving a 3"/ 7.5 cm tail.

2. Hold a knitting needle behind and perpendicular to the hook with yarn going from right to left behind the needle. Hook the yarn and pull a loop through the loop on the hook, forming a stitch on the needle. (See crochet over needle provisional cast on on page 280.)

3. Chain 3, slipstitch in fourth stitch from hook to form picot. Position the yarn so it comes from behind the knitting needle as for Step 2. Hook the yarn and pull a loop through the loop on the hook, forming a stitch on the needle.

4. Cast on 2 stitches as in Step 2.

Repeat Steps 2–4 for required number of stitches.

CHEVRON LACE

Round 1 and all odd-numbered rounds: Knit.

Round 2: K3, *ssk, K5, yo; repeat from * to last stitch, K1.

Round 4: K3, *ssk, K4, yo, K1; repeat from * to last stitch, K1.

Round 6: K3, *ssk, K3, yo, K2; repeat from * to last stitch, K1.

Round 8: K3, *ssk, K2, yo, K3; repeat from * to last stitch, K1.

Round 10: K3, *ssk, K1, yo, K4; repeat from * to last stitch, K1.

Round 12: K3, *ssk, yo, K5; repeat from * to last stitch, K1.

Round 14: K1, *yo, K5, K2tog; repeat from * to last 3 stitches, K3.

Round 16: K2, *yo, K4, K2tog, K1; repeat from * to last 2 stitches, K2.

Round 18: K3, *yo, K3, K2tog, K2; repeat from * to last stitch, K1.

Round 20: K4, *yo, K2, K2tog, K3; repeat from * to end of needle.

Round 22: K5, *yo, K1, K2tog, K4; repeat from * to last 6 stitches, yo, K1, K2tog, K3.

Round 24: K6, *yo, K2tog, K5; repeat from * to last 5 stitches, yo, K2tog, K3.

Repeat Rounds 1–24 for pattern.

PICOT BIND OFF

K1, *slipstitch on right-hand needle back to left-hand needle, cast on 3 with knitted-on method (see page 278), bind off 7; repeat from * until 1 stitch remains, fasten off this stitch.

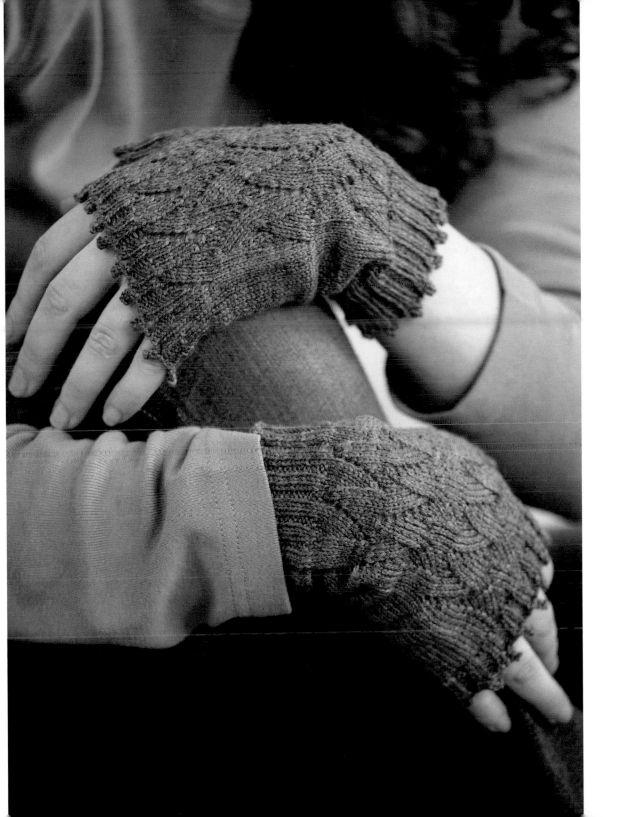

○ Round 3: Work in pattern as established on Needle 1, slip marker, M1, knit to marker, M1, slip marker, work in pattern as established to end of round.

○ Round 4: Work in pattern as established on Needle 1, slip marker, knit to end of round.

○ Repeat Rounds 3 and 4 until there are 21 gusset stitches, ending on Round 4. Place 21 gusset stitches on holder.

○ Rejoin into a round and continue in patterns as established until a total of two-and-one-half repeats of Chevron Lace pattern have been completed, ending on Round 12 of pattern.

○ Continue as for left mitt.

Finishing

○ Weave in ends. Block.

CHEVRON LACE

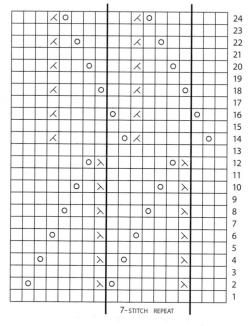

7-STITCH REPEAT

	knit
K2tog	K2tog
ssk	ssk
yo	yo

Golden Eyelet Cable Mitts

Designed by Cathleen Campbell

Cables and eyelets cover these fingerless mitts, and the thumb gusset springs from the middle of a cable. No right or left here, just put them on and go!

SIZES AND FINISHED MEASUREMENTS	Woman's medium–extra large (7"–8"/ 18–20.5 cm palm circumference), approximately 5½"/14 cm circumference, unstretched
YARN	Crystal Palace Panda Silk, 52% bamboo/ 43% superwash merino wool/5% combed silk, 1.75 oz (50 g)/204 yds (188 m), Color 3002 Butterscotch
NEEDLES	Set of five US 1 (2.25 mm) double-point needles *or size you need to obtain correct gauge*
GAUGE	36 stitches and 48 rounds = 4"/10 cm in stockinette stitch; 40 stitches and 56 rounds = 4"/10 cm in pattern, unstretched
OTHER SUPPLIES	Cable needle, stitch markers, scrap yarn for holders, tapestry needle
SPECIAL ABBREVIATIONS	**C6F** slip 3 stitches onto cable needle and hold in front, knit 3 from left-hand needle, knit 3 from cable needle

Knitting the Cuff

○ Cast on 60 stitches and divide onto four double-point needles so there are 12 stitches each on Needles 1 and 3 and 18 stitches each on Needles 2 and 4. Join into a round, being careful not to twist the stitches.

○ Work K2, P1 rib for 5 rounds.

Beginning the Cables and Lace

○ Work Rounds 1–20 of Cables and Lace pattern once, then work Rounds 1–18 once more. On last round, place markers after the eighth and tenth stitches.

Knitting the Thumb Gusset

○ Increase Round: Work in pattern as established to 2 stitches before marker, K2, slip marker, M1, knit to next marker, M1, slip marker, K2, work in pattern as established to end of round.

○ Next Round: Work in patterns as established, knitting the 2 stitches before and after the markers and the stitches between the markers.

○ Repeat these 2 rounds until there are 26 gusset stitches between the markers, ending with Round 1 of pattern.

○ Next Round: Work in pattern to marker, remove marker, K1, place next 24 gusset stitches on holder, K1, remove marker, work in pattern to end of round. *Note:* Pull the working yarn snug at gusset to close the gap.

○ Continue even in pattern until four repeats of pattern have been worked from the beginning.

○ Work K2, P1 rib for 5 rounds. Bind off in pattern.

Knitting the Thumb

o Place 24 held gusset stitches onto three double-point needles. Attach yarn and knit 1 round. Work K2, P1 rib for 4 rounds. Bind off in pattern.

Finishing

o Use tail at thumb gusset to close the gap. Weave in all ends.

CABLES AND LACE

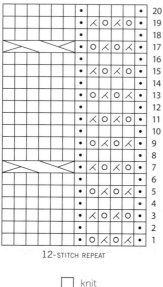

12-STITCH REPEAT

knit
purl
K2tog
yo
C6F

Pattern Essentials

CABLES AND LACE

Round 1: *P1, (K2tog, yo) twice, P1, K6; repeat from * to end of round.

Round 2 and all even-numbered rounds: *P1, K4, P1, K6; repeat from * to end of round.

Round 3: *P1, (yo, K2tog) twice, P1, K6; repeat from * to end of round.

Rounds 5, 9, and 13: Repeat Round 1.

Round 7: *P1, (yo, K2tog) twice, P1, C6F; repeat from * to end of round.

Rounds 11, 15, and 19: Repeat Round 3.

Round 17: P1, (K2tog, yo) twice, P1, C6F; repeat from * to end of round.

Round 20: *P1, K4, P1, K6; repeat from * to end of round.

Repeat Rounds 1–20 for pattern.

"Woven" Fingerless Gloves

Designed by Laura Hein Eckel

These ambidextrous finger-less mitts are knitted in a very flexible "woven" pattern, which makes them suitable for many sizes of hands. You'll want to knit these in many different colors!

Knitting the Cuff

○ Cast on 56 stitches and divide evenly onto four double-point needles. Join into a round, being careful not to twist the stitches.

○ Work K2, P2 rib for 15 rounds.

○ Work Rounds 1–8 of Woven Stitch pattern, then work Rounds 1–4 once more.

Knitting the Thumb Gusset

○ Round 1: M1, K2, M1, place marker, P2, continue in pattern as established to end of round.

○ Rounds 2 and 3: Knit to marker, slip marker, continue in pattern as established to end of round.

○ Round 4: M1, knit to marker, M1, slip marker, continue in pattern as established to end of round.

SIZES AND FINISHED MEASUREMENTS	To fit most adults, approximately 6"/15 cm circumference, unstretched
YARN	Koigu Wool Designs Premium Merino, 100% merino wool, 1.75 oz (50 g)/175 yds (160 m), Color 2323
NEEDLES	Set of five US 2 (2.75 mm) double-point needles *or size you need to obtain correct gauge*
GAUGE	37 stitches and 52 rounds = 4"/10 cm in Woven Stitch pattern
OTHER SUPPLIES	Stitch marker, scrap yarn for holders, tapestry needle

Pattern Essentials
WOVEN STITCH

Rounds 1–3: *K2, P6; repeat from * to end of round.

Round 4: Knit.

Rounds 5–7: P4, *K2, P6; repeat from * to last 4 stitches, K2, P2.

Round 8: Knit.

Repeat Rounds 1–8 for pattern.

. . . .

WOVEN STITCH

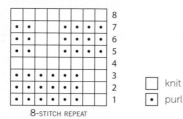

knit

• purl

8-STITCH REPEAT

○ Repeat Rounds 2–4 until there are 20 stitches before the marker.

○ Work Rounds 2 and 3 once more.

Knitting the Hand

○ Place first 20 stitches on hold for the thumb. Cast on 2 stitches, continue in pattern as established to end of round.

○ Continue in pattern as established for 16 rounds, ending on a knit round.

○ Work 8 rounds of K2, P2 rib. Bind off.

Knitting the Thumb

○ Place 20 held thumb stitches on needles. Attach yarn at beginning of gusset and K20, pick up and knit (see page 280) 4 stitches into 2 cast-on stitches. *You now have 24 stitches.* Work 10 rounds of K2, P2 rib.

Finishing

○ Bind off. Weave in ends.

Beaded Fingerless Mitts

Designed by Marji LaFreniere

These delightful mitts are all the more so with the addition of seed beads to the cables! The beads are knitted right in, and the cuff, thumb, and finger edges are picot trimmed.

. . . .

Pattern Essentials
BEADED CABLE RIBBING

Rounds 1 and 2: *P2, K2; repeat from * to end of round.

Round 3: *P2, KB1, K1; repeat from * to end of round.

Round 4: *P2, knit second stitch tbl and leave on needle, knit first stitch tbl and slip both stitches from needle; repeat from * to end of round.

Repeat Rounds 1–4 for pattern.

. . . .

SIZES AND FINISHED MEASUREMENTS	Woman's small, approximately 6½"/16.5 cm circumference
YARN	Koigu Painter's Palette Premium Merino, 100% merino wool, 1.75 oz (50 g)/175 yds (160 m), Color P105
NEEDLES	Sets of five US 2 (2.75 mm) and US 1 (2.25 mm) double-point needles *or size you need to obtain correct gauge*
GAUGE	34 stitches and 46 rounds= 4" (10 cm) in Beaded Cable Ribbing pattern, blocked, on larger needles
OTHER SUPPLIES	Big eye beading needle, approximately 400 (15 g) size 8° seed beads, stitch markers, scrap yarn for holders, tapestry needle
SPECIAL ABBREVIATIONS	**KB1** knit 1 bead by knitting the stitch then sliding a bead up to the work and pushing it through to the right side **M1LP** make 1 left-leaning stitch purlwise (see page 279) **M1RP** make 1 right-leaning stitch purlwise (see page 279)

KNITTING THE RIGHT MITT

○ Thread the yarn onto the big eye beading needle and string half the beads onto the yarn. Push the beads down along the yarn and bring them up as needed.

Knitting the Cuff

○ With smaller needle, cast on 52 stitches. Divide evenly onto four double-point needles. Join into a round, being careful not to twist the stitches.

○ Rounds 1–5: Knit.

○ Round 6: *K2tog, yo; repeat from * to end of round.

o Change to larger needles.

o Rounds 7–11: Knit.

o Next Round: Knit each stitch together with 1 cast-on stitch, being sure to line the stitches up straight.

o Work Rounds 1–4 of Beaded Cable Ribbing for 2½"/ 6.5 cm, ending with Round 1.

Knitting the Thumb Gusset

o Setup Round: P1, place marker, P1, K2, P1, place marker, P21 (reverse stockinette), work Beaded Cable Ribbing as established on 26 stitches. Repeat this round two more times, slipping markers as you come to them.

o Round 1: P1, slip marker, P1, M1RP, K2, M1LP, P1, slip marker, continue in patterns as established to end of round.

o Rounds 2 and 3: Work even in patterns as established, working the 2 stitches at the center of the gusset as a beaded cable as established and the remaining stitches between markers in reverse stockinette stitch.

o Repeat Rounds 1–3, working the increases after the first purl stitch and before the last purl stitch inside the markers, until you have 18 thumb gusset stitches between the markers, and ending on Round 3 of Beaded Cable Ribbing.

Knitting the Hand

o Next Round: Work to marker, place 18 thumb gusset stitches on holder, cast on 5 stitches, P1, pass the fifth cast-on stitch over this purl stitch, continue in patterns as established to end of round. *You now have* 52 stitches.

o On the next Round 1 of Beaded Cable Ribbing, reestablish the pattern on all stitches. Work even in pattern until there are 4 beaded rounds above the thumb, ending with Round 1 of pattern.

Knitting the Edging

o Rounds 1–3: Knit.

o Round 4 (Picot Round): *K2, yo; repeat from * to end of round.

o Change to smaller needle.

o Rounds 5–7: Knit.

o Bind off loosely. Fold edge to inside along Picot Round and stitch loosely to inside.

Knitting the Thumb

o Place 18 held thumb stitches on two needles. With right side facing, P8, work 2 in beaded cable as established, P8. Pick up and purl (see page 280) 5 stitches in cast-on stitches, P1, pass fifth picked-up stitch over this purl stitch. *You now have* 22 stitches. Work these stitches in patterns as established for 4 to 6 rounds, ending with Round 1 of Beaded Cable Ribbing. Work picot edging as for end of hand.

KNITTING THE LEFT MITT

o Work as for right mitt, but begin Beaded Cable Ribbing with K2 instead of P2.

Knitting the Thumb Gusset

o Setup Round: K2, (P2, K2) six times, P21, place marker, P1, K2, P1, place marker, P1.

o Continue as for right mitt, reversing shaping.

Finishing

o Weave in ends. Block.

Spring Garden Shorties

Designed by Cathleen Campbell

Double vertical decreases and yarn overs form the lovely diamond lace pattern in these ambidextrous mitts. The stitch pattern is a repeat of fourteen stitches for the cuff, increasing to a repeat of fifteen stitches.

SIZES AND FINISHED MEASUREMENTS	Woman's large, approximately 7½"/19 cm circumference, unstretched
YARN	Crystal Palace Panda Soy, 60% bamboo/ 22% soy/18% elastic, 1.75 oz (50 g)/185 yds (169 m), Color 2101 Provence
NEEDLES	Set of five US 1.5 (2.5 mm) double-point needles *or size you need to obtain correct gauge*
GAUGE	33 stitches and 42 rounds = 4"/10 cm in Diamond Lace pattern
OTHER SUPPLIES	Scrap yarn for holders, tapestry needle

41

Pattern Essentials

DIAMOND LACE
(WORKED OVER A MULTIPLE OF 14 [15] STITCHES)

Note: Slip all stitches purlwise with yarn in back.

Setup Round 1: *K1 (2), yo, K5, s2kp, K5, yo: repeat from * to end of round.

Setup Round 2, Round 2, and all even-numbered rounds: Knit.

Round 1: *K2 (3), yo, K4, s2kp, K4, yo, K1; repeat from * to end of round.

Round 3: *K3 (4), yo, K3, s2kp, K3, yo, K2; repeat from * to end of round.

Round 5: *K4 (5), yo, K2, s2kp, K2, yo, K3; repeat from * to end of round.

Round 7: *K5 (6), yo, K1, s2kp, K1, yo, K4; repeat from * to end of round.

Round 9: *K6 (7), yo, s2kp, yo, K5; repeat from * to end of round.

Round 11: *K4 (5), K2tog, yo, K1, slip 1, K1, yo, ssk, K3; repeat from * to end of round.

Round 13: *K3 (4), K2tog, yo, K2, slip 1, K2, yo, ssk, K2; repeat from * to end of round.

Round 15: *K2 (3), K2tog, yo, K3, slip 1, K3, yo, ssk, K1; repeat from * to end of round.

Round 17: *K1 (2), K2tog, yo, K4, slip 1, K4, yo, ssk; repeat from * to end of round.

Round 18: Knit.

Repeat Rounds 1–18 for 14-stitch (15-stitch) pattern as directed.

DIAMOND LACE

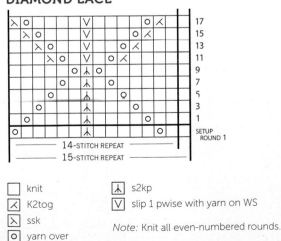

SETUP ROUND 1

17
15
13
11
9
7
5
3
1

— 14-STITCH REPEAT —
— 15-STITCH REPEAT —

☐ knit
◩ K2tog
◪ ssk
◎ yarn over

⋏ s2kp
▽ slip 1 pwise with yarn on WS

Note: Knit all even-numbered rounds.

Getting Started

○ Cast on 56 stitches and divide evenly onto four double-point needles. Join into a round, being careful not to twist the stitches.

○ Purl 1 round.

○ Knit 1 round.

Beginning the Lace Pattern

○ Work Setup Rounds 1 and 2 of 14-stitch Diamond Lace pattern once, then work Rounds 1–18 once.

○ Work Rounds 1 and 2 of 14-stitch Diamond Lace pattern once more.

○ Increase Round: Work Round 3 of pattern, but work M1 at the beginning of each repeat. *You now have 60 stitches.*

○ Work Round 5 of 15-stitch Diamond Lace pattern.

Knitting the Thumb Gusset

○ Round 1: Yo, K2, yo, work next 13 stitches in established 15-stitch Diamond Lace pattern (omitting first 2 stitches of chart), work remainder of round in established 15-stitch Diamond Lace pattern.

○ Round 2: Knit.

○ Round 3: Yo, K4, yo, work in established pattern to end of round.

○ Repeat Rounds 2 and 3, knitting 2 more stitches between the yarn overs on each increase round, until there are 20 gusset stitches between the yarn overs, ending with Round 7 of Diamond Lace pattern.

Knitting the Hand

○ K1, place next 20 stitches on hold for the thumb, knit to end of round, closing gap at gusset.

○ Continuing with Round 9 of 15-stitch Diamond Lace pattern on all stitches, work Diamond Lace pattern until there are four complete repeats from the cast-on edge. Purl 1 round. Bind off.

Knitting the Thumb

○ Place 20 held thumb stitches on needles. Attach yarn at beginning of gusset and K20, pick up and knit (see page 280) 2 stitches at thumb gap. *You now have* 22 stitches. Knit 5 rounds more. Purl 1 round.

Finishing

○ Bind off. Use tail at thumb to close gap. Weave in ends.

Floral Fingerless Gloves

Designed by Caroline Perisho

These sweet and romantic mitts are reminiscent of a spring bouquet. The flowers are knitted separately and accented with beads, and a quill lace pattern is used for the cuff.

SIZES AND FINISHED MEASUREMENTS	Woman's small (medium, extra large), approximately 6½" (7", 8")/16.5 (18, 20.5) cm circumference
YARN	ShibuiKnits Sock, 100% superwash merino, 1.75 oz (50 g)/191 yds (175 m), Color 3930
NEEDLES	Set of five US 2 (2.75 mm) double-point needles for gloves *or size you need to obtain correct gauge* and two US 1 (2.25 mm) needles for flowers
GAUGE	30 stitches and 46 rounds = 4"/10 cm in stockinette stitch on larger needles
OTHER SUPPLIES	Stitch markers, scrap yarn for holders, tapestry needle, sewing needle and coordinating thread, 18 small glass beads

KNITTING THE RIGHT GLOVE

Knitting the Cuff

○ Cast on 48 (54, 60) stitches and divide evenly onto four double-point needles. Join into a round, being careful not to twist the stitches. Work Rounds 1 and 2 of Quill Lace pattern seven times, increasing 1 stitch on last round. *You now have* 49 (55, 61) stitches. Work stockinette stitch for 3 rounds.

Knitting the Thumb Gusset

○ Round 1: K24 (27, 30), place marker, M1L, K1, M1R, place marker, knit to end of round.

○ Rounds 2 and 3: Knit.

○ Round 4: Knit to marker, slip marker, M1L, knit to next marker, M1R, slip marker, knit to end of round.

○ Rounds 5 and 6: Knit.

○ Round 7: K7 (9, 11), work Vase chart over next 9 stitches, knit to marker, slip marker, M1L, knit to next marker, M1R, knit to end of round.

○ Rounds 8 and 9: K7 (9, 11), work Vase chart over next 9 stitches, knit to end of round.

○ Repeat Rounds 7–9 until there are 15 (19, 23) stitches between the markers, continuing in stockinette stitch when Round 18 of Vase chart is complete.

Knitting the Hand

○ Work as established to marker, remove marker, place gusset stitches on holder, remove second marker, cast on 1 stitch, knit to end of round. *You now have* 49 (55, 61) stitches. Continue working stitches as established, until piece measures 4"/10 cm from cuff.

○ Next Round: Knit, decreasing 7 stitches evenly spaced. *You now have* 38 (48, 54) stitches.

○ Bind off with the I-cord method as follows: Using cable cast on (see page 276), cast on 3 stitches. *Slip 3 stitches to left-hand needle, K2, K2tog tbl. Repeat from * to end of round. Bind off last 3 stitches.

Knitting the Thumb

○ With right side facing, pick up and knit (see page 280) 1 stitch between hand and gusset, knit 15 (19, 23) thumb stitches, pick up and knit 1 stitch between gusset and hand. *You now have* 17 (21, 25) stitches. Divide stitches onto three double-point needles. Join into a round and work in stockinette stitch for 1"/2.5 cm. Bind off with I-cord method as for end of hand.

Making the Flowers

○ Complete five petals (see page 47). Arrange the petals with the bind-off tails at the center of the flower. Using the tails and a tapestry needle, join petals side to side along the edges for a few stitches. Weave in ends, leaving one tail to attach flower to glove. Thread remaining tail onto tapestry needle and attach flower to glove at desired position on back of hand. Use remaining tail to embroider a "stem" that goes to the vase by sewing under one-half of each stitch in a gentle curve. Repeat for two more flowers.

Finishing

○ Weave in ends. Use sewing needle and thread to attach three beads to the center of each flower.

KNITTING THE LEFT GLOVE

○ Work as for right glove to the thumb gusset.

Knitting the Thumb Gusset

○ Round 1: K48 (54, 60), place marker, M1L, K1, M1R, place marker.

○ Rounds 2 and 3: Knit.

○ Round 4: Knit to marker, slip marker, M1L, knit to next marker, M1R, slip marker.

○ Rounds 5 and 6: Knit.

○ Round 7: K8 (9, 10), work Vase chart over next 9 stitches, knit to marker, slip marker, M1L, knit to next marker, M1R, slip marker.

○ Rounds 8 and 9: K8 (10, 12), work Vase chart over next 9 stitches, knit to end of round.

○ Repeat Rounds 7–9 until there are 15 (19, 23) stitches between the markers, continuing in stockinette stitch when Round 18 of Vase chart is complete.

○ Continue as for right glove.

QUILL LACE

6-STITCH REPEAT

VASE CHART

9-STITCH PANEL

☐ knit

• purl

○ yarn over

人 s2kp

Pattern Essentials

QUILL LACE

Round 1: Knit.

Round 2: *K1, yo, K1, s2kp, K1, yo; repeat from * to end of round.

Repeat Rounds 1 and 2 for pattern.

FLOWER PETALS

Cast on 2 stitches.

Row 1: Kfb, K1. *You now have* 3 stitches.

Row 2 and all even-numbered rows through Row 8: Knit.

Row 3: K1, M1, K1, M1, K1. *You now have* 5 stitches.

Row 5: Knit.

Row 7: Ssk, K1, K2tog. *You now have* 3 stitches.

Row 9: Ssk, K1. *You now have* 2 stitches.

Row 10: K2tog.

Bind off, leaving a 6"/15 cm tail. Weave cast-on tail into back of petal.

Repeat four times for each flower.

Scottish Fleet Mittens

Designed by Terry Liann Morris

Simple knit-and-purl patterning complements the moderately self-striping sock yarn used here — the stripes don't overwhelm the texture. Many men like the geometric patterns of traditional Gansey sweaters, which influenced this design.

KNITTING THE RIGHT MITTEN

Knitting the Cuff

○ Loosely cast on 56 (60, 64) stitches. Divide evenly onto four needles. Place marker to indicate beginning of round and join into a round, being careful not to twist the stitches.

○ Purl 3 rounds.

○ Work K2, P2 rib until cuff measures 3"/7.5 cm from beginning, increasing 5 stitches evenly spaced in last round. *You now have* 61 (65, 69) stitches.

○ Purl 3 rounds.

SIZES AND FINISHED MEASUREMENTS	Woman's medium/Man's small (Woman's large/Man's medium, Woman's extra large/Man's large) approximately 7" (7½", 8")/18 (19, 20.5) cm circumference
YARN	Regia 4 fädig Line Steps Color, 75% wool/25% polyamide, 3.5 oz (100 g)/460 yds (420 m), Color #5365
NEEDLES	Set of five US 1 (2.25 mm) double-point needles *or size you need to obtain correct gauge*
GAUGE	32 stitches and 48 rounds = 4"/10 cm in stockinette stitch
OTHER SUPPLIES	Stitch markers, scrap yarn for holder, tapestry needle

Knitting the Thumb Gusset

o Round 1. K3 (4, 5), work Scottish Fleet pattern over next 25 stitches, knit to end of round.

o Round 2: K3 (4, 5), work pattern over next 25 stitches, K2 (3, 4), place marker, M1, K1, M1, place marker, knit to end of round. *You now have 63 (67, 71) stitches.*

o Round 3: Work in established patterns to marker, knit to end of round.

o Round 4: Work in established patterns to marker, slip marker, M1, knit to next marker, M1, slip marker, knit to end of round. *You now have 65 (69, 73) stitches.*

o Rounds 5 and 6: Repeat Round 3.

o Repeat Rounds 4–6 until there are 19 (21, 23) stitches between the gusset markers, ending having worked Round 6.

Dividing for the Thumb

o Work in established patterns to marker, remove marker, place next 19 (21, 23) thumb stitches on holder, cast on 1 with backward-loop method (see page 276), remove marker, knit to end of round.

Knitting the Hand

o Continue in patterns as established until piece measures 5½" (5¾", 6¼"/14 (14.5, 16) cm from beginning of Scottish Fleet pattern.

Pattern Essentials
SCOTTISH FLEET
(WORKED OVER 25 STITCHES)

Round 1: P2, K1 tbl, P1, K1, P1, K1 tbl, K11, K1 tbl, P1, K1, P1, K1 tbl, P2.

Round 2: P2, K1 tbl, P3, K1 tbl, K5, P1, K5, K1 tbl, P3, K1 tbl, P2.

Round 3: P2, K1 tbl, P1, K1, P1, K1 tbl, K4, P3, K4, K1 tbl, P1, K1, P1, K1 tbl, P2.

Round 4: P2, K1 tbl, P3, K1 tbl, K3, P2, K1, P2, K3, K1 tbl, P3, K1 tbl, P2.

Round 5: P2, K1 tbl, P1, K1, P1, K1 tbl, K2, P2, K3, P2, K2, K1 tbl, P1, K1, P1, K1 tbl, P2.

Round 6: P2, K1 tbl, P3, K1 tbl, K1, P2, K5, P2, K1, K1 tbl, P3, K1 tbl, P2.

Round 7: P2, K1 tbl, P1, K1, P1, K1 tbl, P2, K7, P2, K1 tbl, P1, K1, P1, K1 tbl, P2.

Round 8: Repeat Round 6.

Round 9: Repeat Round 5.

Round 10: Repeat Round 4.

Round 11: Repeat Round 3.

Round 12: Repeat Round 2.

Repeat Rounds 1–12 for pattern.

SCOTTISH FLEET

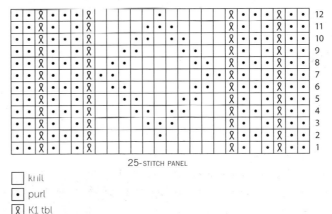

25-STITCH PANEL

☐ knit

· purl

R K1 tbl

DECREASING FOR THE TOP

o Round 1: K1, ssk, K0 (1, 2), work in established pattern over next 25 stitches, K0 (1, 2) K2tog, K1, place marker, K1, ssk, knit to last 3 stitches, K2tog, K1. *You now have 57 (61, 65) stitches.*

o Round 2: Work even in established pattern.

o *Note:* Decreases will consume stitches from Scottish Fleet pattern. Continue in pattern as established, maintaining 2 stitches on either side of markers in stockinette stitch.

o Round 3: *K1, ssk, work in established pattern to 3 stitches before marker, K2tog, K1, slip marker; repeat from *. *You now have* 53 (57, 61) stitches.

o Repeat Rounds 2 and 3 two more times. *You now have* 45 (49, 53) stitches.

o Repeat Round 3 only until 13 stitches remain.

o Next Round: K1, ssk, knit to 4 stitches before marker, K3tog, K1, slip marker, K1, ssk, knit to 3 stitches before marker, K2tog, K1. *You now have* 8 stitches.

o Place the first 4 stitches on one needle and the last 4 on another needle. Graft stitches together with Kitchener stitch (see page 278).

Knitting the Thumb

o Place 19 (21, 23) held gusset stitches onto two needles. With a third needle, pick up and knit (page 280) 3 stitches in the gap at base of thumb, place marker. *You now have* 22 (24, 26) stitches.

o Divide stitches evenly onto three needles. Join into a round and work stockinette stitch until thumb measures 1¾" (2", 2")/4.5 (5, 5) cm.

DECREASING FOR THE TOP

o Round 1: *K2tog, K5 (6, 6); repeat from * two times, K1 (0, 2). *You now have* 19 (21, 23) stitches.

o Rounds 2 and 4: Knit.

o Round 3: *K2tog, K4 (5, 5); repeat from * two times, K1 (0, 2). *You now have* 16 (18, 20) stitches.

o Round 5: *K2tog, K3 (4, 4); repeat from * two times, K1 (0, 2). *You now have* 13 (15, 17) stitches. Continue to decrease 3 stitches in this manner every round two (two, three) more times. *You now have* 7 (9, 8) stitches.

o Break yarn, leaving an 8"/20.5 cm tail. Thread tail onto tapestry needle and draw through remaining stitches. Pull up snug and fasten off.

KNITTING THE LEFT MITTEN

o Work cuff as for right hand.

Knitting the Thumb Gusset

o Round 1: K33 (36, 39), work pattern over next 25 stitches, knit to end of round.

o Round 2: K30 (32, 34), place marker, M1, K1, M1, place marker, K2 (3, 4), work pattern over next 25 stitches, knit to end of round. *You now have* 63 (67, 71) stitches.

o Round 3: Knit to marker, slip marker, knit to next marker, slip marker, K2 (3, 4), work pattern over next 25 stitches, knit to end of round.

o Round 4: Knit to marker, slip marker, M1, knit to next marker, M1, slip marker, work in established patterns to end of round. *You now have* 65 (69, 73) stitches.

o Rounds 5 and 6: Repeat Round 3.

o Repeat Rounds 4–6 until there are 19 (21, 23) stitches between the gusset markers, ending having worked Round 6. *You now have* 61 (65, 69) stitches.

Dividing for the Thumb

o Knit to marker, remove marker, place next 19 (21, 23) thumb stitches on holder, cast on 1 with backward-loop method, remove marker, work in established patterns to end of round.

Knitting the Hand

o Continue in patterns as established until piece measures 5½" (5¾", 6¼")/14 (14.5, 16) cm from beginning of Scottish Fleet pattern.

DECREASING FOR THE TOP

o Round 1: K1, ssk, K24 (26, 28), K2tog, K1, place marker, K1, ssk, K0 (1, 2), work in established pattern over next 25 stitches, K0 (1, 2), K2tog, K1. *You now have* 57 (61, 65) stitches.

o Round 2: Work even in established patterns.

o *Note:* Decreases will consume stitches from Scottish Fleet pattern. Continue in pattern as established, maintaining 2 stitches on either side of markers in stockinette stitch.

o Round 3: *K1, ssk, work in established pattern to 3 stitches before marker, K2tog, K1, slip marker; repeat from *. *You now have* 53 (57, 61) stitches.

o Repeat Rounds 2 and 3 two more times. *You now have* 45 (49, 53) stitches.

o Repeat Round 3 only until 13 stitches remain.

o Next Round: K1, ssk, knit to 3 stitches before marker, K2tog, K1, slip marker, K1, ssk, knit to 4 stitches before marker, K3tog, K1. *You now have* 8 stitches.

o Place the first 4 stitches on one needle and the last 4 on another needle. Graft stitches together with Kitchener stitch (see page 278).

Knitting the Thumb

o Work thumb as for right mitten.

Finishing

o Weave in ends. Block.

Mitered Squares Gloves

Designed by Kathleen Taylor

Sized to fit most adult women, these gloves are perfect for self-patterning, heavy fingering- or light sport-weight sock yarn. The mitered-square cuffs are worked flat and seamed. The rest of the glove is worked in the round. You can cut and choose sections of yarn so that the fingers match or let the colors fall as they may.

SIZES AND FINISHED MEASUREMENTS	Woman's small/medium, approximately 6½"/16.5 cm circumference, unstretched
YARN	Twisted Fiber Art Playful, 100% superwash merino wool, 4.2 oz (120 g)/350 yds (320 m), Scorched/Organic Stripe
NEEDLES	US 3 (3.25 mm) straight needles and set of four US 3 (3.25 mm) double-point needles *or size you need to obtain correct gauge*
GAUGE	30 stitches and 40 rounds = 4"/10 cm in stockinette stitch
OTHER SUPPLIES	Tapestry needle, stitch markers, scrap yarn for holders

Knitting the Cuffs

○ *Note:* If you want the gloves to match, divide the yarn into two equal balls and begin both gloves at the same place in the color repeat.

○ Row 1: Following the instructions for Basic Mitered Square/Square 1 and Mitered Square 2 and Remaining First-Row Squares on page 54, work five mitered squares.

○ Row 2: Following the instructions for Mitered Square 1/ Second Row and Mitered Square 2 and Remaining Second-Row Squares, work five mitered squares.

○ Row 3: Work as for Row 2.

KNITTING THE EDGING

○ With right side facing, pick up and knit (see page 280) 48 stitches along bottom edge of cuff. Knit 3 rows. Bind off, leaving a 10"/25.5 cm tail. Thread tail onto tapestry needle and sew side seam.

Knitting the Gloves

○ With right side facing and beginning at the seam, pick up and knit 48 stitches along upper edge of cuff. Divide onto three double-point needles and place marker for beginning of round.

○ Rounds 1–4: Knit.

Knitting the Thumb Gusset

○ Round 1: M1, K1, M1, place marker, knit to end of round. *You now have* 50 stitches.

○ Round 2: Knit.

○ Round 3: M1, knit to next marker, M1, slip marker, knit to end of round. *You now have* 52 stitches.

○ Repeat Rounds 2 and 3 until there are 17 stitches between markers.

○ Knit 4 rounds.

Knitting the Hand

○ Round 1: Place 17 thumb gusset stitches on holder, cast on 1, rejoin and knit to end of round. *You now have* 48 stitches.

○ Rounds 2–13: Knit.

Setting Up for the Fingers

○ Knit 24 and place these stitches on one needle. Place remaining 24 stitches on another needle. Working from the thumb side, place first 6 stitches from each needle on one holder for index finger. Repeat twice more for middle and ring fingers, placing each set of 12 stitches on separate holders. *You now have* 6 stitches on each needle.

Knitting the Little Finger

○ Beginning at outside of hand, K6, cast on 3, K6. *You now have* 15 stitches. Distribute stitches for knitting in the round. Work even in stockinette stitch for 2"/5 cm or desired length.

○ Next Round: *K2tog; repeat from * to last stitch, K1. Cut yarn, leaving a 6"/15 cm tail. Thread tail onto tapestry needle and draw through remaining stitches. Pull up snug and fasten off on inside.

Knitting the Ring Finger

○ Place 6 front stitches on one needle and 6 back stitches on another needle. With third needle, join yarn and pick up and knit 2 stitches at the base of

the previous finger, K6, cast on 2 in the gap between the front and back stitches, K6. *You now have* 16 stitches. Distribute stitches for knitting in the round. Work even in stockinette stitch for 2¾"/7 cm or desired length.

○ Next Round: *K2tog; repeat from *. *You now have* 8 stitches. Finish as for little finger.

Knitting the Middle Finger

○ Work as for ring finger until piece measures 3"/7.5 cm or desired length. Finish as for ring finger.

Knitting the Index Finger

○ Work as for ring finger (but pick up and knit 3 stitches at the base of previous finger and do not cast on any

53

Pattern Essentials

BASIC MITERED SQUARE/SQUARE 1

With straight needles, cast on 19 stitches.

Row 1 (WS): K9, P1, K9, turn.

Row 2: K7, K2tog, K1, K2tog, K7, turn. *You now have* 17 stitches.

Row 3 and all odd-numbered wrong-side rows through Row 17: Knit to center stitch, purl the center stitch, knit to end of row.

Row 4: K6, K2tog, K1, K2tog, K6, turn. *You now have* 15 stitches.

Row 6: K5, K2tog, K1, K2tog, K5, turn. *You now have* 13 stitches.

Continue in this manner, knitting 1 fewer stitch before and after the decreases, until you have 5 stitches.

Row 16: K2tog, K1, K2tog, turn. *You now have* 3 stitches.

Row 18: Skp. Do not turn. *You now have* 1 stitch.

MITERED SQUARE 2 AND REMAINING FIRST-ROW MITERED SQUARES

With 1 remaining stitch on needle and right side facing, pick up and knit (see page 280) 9 stitches down left side of Square 1, cast on 9 stitches. *You now have* 19 stitches.

Work as for Basic Square, cutting yarn only after completing last square in the row and pulling the tail through the remaining stitch.

MITERED SQUARE 1/SECOND ROW

Cast on 10 stitches. With right side facing, pick up and knit 9 stitches along top of first square of first row. *You now have* 19 stitches. Work as for Basic Square.

MITERED SQUARE 2 AND REMAINING SECOND-ROW SQUARES

With 1 remaining stitch on needle and right side facing, pick up and knit 9 stitches down left side of Square 1 of second row, pick up and knit 9 stitches along top of Square 2 of first row. *You now have* 19 stitches. Work as for Basic Mitered Square/Square 1, cutting yarn only after completing last square in the row and pulling the tail through the remaining stitch.

new stitches) until piece measures 2½"/6.5 cm or desired length. Finish as for little finger.

Knitting the Thumb

○ Place 17 held thumb stitches on needles. With right side facing, pick up and knit 3 stitches at base of hand. *You now have* 20 stitches. Distribute stitches for knitting in the round. Work even in stockinette stitch for 1½"/4 cm or desired length.

○ Decrease Round: *K2tog; repeat from * to end of round. *You now have* 10 stitches.

○ Next Round: Knit.

○ Repeat Decrease Round. *You now have* 5 stitches. Finish as for other fingers.

Finishing

○ Weave in ends, using tails from fingers to close up gaps between the fingers if necessary. Wash and block.

Handful-of-Color Mittens

Designed by Gwen Steege

These classic mittens are knit using Best Foot Forward, a new sock yarn designed by Kristin Nicholas. Watching the bold colors develop their stripes and patterns makes the knitting go fast. The all-purl section after the cast on automatically creates a rolled cuff. For an exactly matched pair, begin the second mitten by drawing out whatever length of yarn is necessary to bring you to the same color sequence that began your first mitten. You'll find that you can match up your stripes to determine where to begin the gusset and top shaping.

SIZES AND FINISHED MEASUREMENTS	Woman's small/medium, approximately 6½"/16.5 cm circumference
YARN	Nashua Best Foot Forward, 75% wool/ 25% nylon, 3.5 oz (100 g)/459 yd (420 m), Color 7327
NEEDLES	One set of five US 1 (2.25 mm) double-point needles *or size you need to obtain correct gauge*
GAUGE	32 stitches = 4" (10 cm) in stockinette stitch
OTHER SUPPLIES	Stitch marker, scrap yarn, tapestry needle

Knitting the Cuff

o Setup: Cast on 56 stitches. Divide stitches evenly onto four needles. Join into a round, being careful not to twist the stitches.

o Purl each round until piece measures 1¼"/3 cm from cast-on edge.

o Next Rounds: Knit each round until piece measures 3½"/9 cm from cast-on edge.

Knitting the Thumb Gusset

o Round 1: Kfb twice, place marker, knit to end of round.

o Rounds 2–4: Knit.

o Round 5: Kfb, knit to 1 stitch before marker, kfb, slip marker, knit to end of round.

o Rounds 6–29: Repeat Rounds 2–5 until there are 18 thumb gusset stitches.

o Round 30: Place the 18 thumb stitches on scrap yarn. Cast on 2 stitches, then knit to end of round. *You now have 56 stitches.*

Knitting the Hand

o Next Rounds: Knit each round until mitten measures 10"/25.5 cm from the cast-on edge.

o Next Round: *K25, K2tog, K1; repeat from * to end of round. *You now have 54 stitches.*

DECREASING FOR THE TOP

o Round 1: *K4, ssk; repeat from * to end of round. *You now have 45 stitches.*

o Rounds 2 and 3: Knit.

o Round 4: *K3, ssk; repeat from * to end of round. *You now have 36 stitches.*

o Rounds 5 and 6: Knit.

o Round 7: *K2, ssk; repeat from * to end of round. *You now have 27 stitches.*

o Rounds 8 and 9: Knit.

o Round 10: *K1, ssk; repeat from * to end of round. *You now have 18 stitches.*

o Rounds 11 and 12: Knit.

o Round 13: *Ssk; repeat from * to end of round. *You now have 9 stitches.*

o Cut yarn leaving an 8"/20.5 cm tail. Thread the tail through a tapestry needle and draw the tail through the remaining stitches twice, slipping them off the needle the second time around. Draw the stitches up and fasten the yarn off on the inside.

Knitting the Thumb

o Place 18 held stitches onto two double-point needles. With a third needle, pick up and knit (see page 280) 2 stitches between thumb stitches and first cast-on stitch on hand, pick up and knit the 2 cast-on stitches, pick up another stitch between last cast-on stitch and thumb stitches. *You now have 23 stitches.*

o Next Rounds: Knit each round until thumb measures 2"/5 cm.

o Next Round: *K3, ssk; repeat from * to last 3 stitches, K1, ssk. *You now have 18 stitches.*

o Next Round: *K1, ssk; repeat from * to end of round. *You now have 12 stitches.*

o Next Round: *Ssk; repeat from * to end of round. *You now have 6 stitches.*

o Cut yarn and finish as for mitten top.

o Repeat for the second mitten. Remember to begin the color sequence at the same point as on the first mitten, if you want identical mittens.

Socrates Gloves

Designed by Edie Eckman

These gloves are a nice introduction to glove knitting as the lacy stitch pattern is fairly easy and is complete before the fingers are knit. For even easier knitting, omit the stitch pattern entirely and work all stitches in stockinette stitch.

KNITTING THE RIGHT GLOVE

Knitting the Cuff

○ Cast on 48 stitches. Place marker and join into a round, being careful not to twist the stitches. Work in K1, P1 rib until piece measures 1½"/4 cm.

○ K2, work Round 1 of Fagoted Rib pattern over next 19 stitches, knit to end of round.

○ Continue in established pattern until piece measures 2½"/6.5 cm from cast-on edge.

SIZES AND FINISHED MEASUREMENTS	Woman's medium, approximately 7"/18 cm palm circumference
YARN	Alpaca With A Twist Socrates, 30% baby alpaca/30% merino wool/20% bamboo/20% nylon, 3.5 oz (100 g)/400 yds (365 m), Color 2016 Laura's Purple
NEEDLES	Set of four US 4 (3.5 mm) double-point knitting needles *or size you need to obtain correct gauge*
GAUGE	28 stitches and 38 rounds = 4"/10 cm in stockinette stitch
OTHER SUPPLIES	Stitch markers, scrap yarn for holders, tapestry needle
SPECIAL ABBREVIATIONS	**M1L** make 1 left (see page 279) **M1R** make 1 right (see page 279)

Shaping the Thumb Gusset

○ Round 1: Work in established pattern over 23 stitches, place marker, K2, place marker, work in established pattern to end of round.

○ Round 2: Work to marker, slip marker, M1R, K2, M1L, slip marker, work to end of round.

○ Rounds 3 and 4: Work even in established patterns.

○ Repeat Rounds 2–4 until there are 18 stitches between markers.

○ Work even until gusset measures 2½"/6.5 cm, working all stitches in stockinette stitch when 29 rounds of Fagoted Rib pattern are complete.

Pattern Essentials

FAGOTED RIB

Round 1: *K1, yo, K2tog, P1; repeat from * to last 3 stitches, K1, yo, K2tog.

Rounds 2 and 4: K3, *P1, K3; repeat from * to end of round.

Round 3: *Ssk, yo, K1, P1; repeat from * to last 3 stitches, ssk, yo, K1.

Rounds 5–24: Repeat Rounds 1–4.

Rounds 25–26: Repeat Rounds 1–2.

Round 27: K4, (ssk, yo, K1, P1) two times, ssk, yo, knit to end of round.

Round 28: K4, (K3, P1) two times, knit to end of round.

Round 29: K9, yo, K2tog, knit to end.

FAGOTED RIB

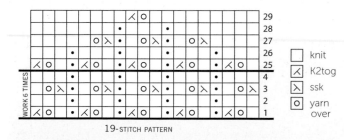

19-STITCH PATTERN

knit
K2tog
ssk
yarn over

○ Next Round: Work to marker, remove marker, place thumb gusset stitches onto a length of scrap yarn, remove marker, cast on 2 stitches over gap left by gusset, knit to end of round. *You now have* 48 stitches.

○ Continue to work even until piece measures 6¼"/16 cm from cast-on edge.

Knitting the Little Finger

○ K6, place next 36 stitches onto a length of scrap yarn, cast on 4 stitches over gap, knit remaining 6 stitches, and join into a round. *You now have* 16 stitches. Knit until finger measures 2½"/6.5 cm or desired length.

○ To make top of finger: *K2tog; repeat from * until 4 stitches remain. Cut yarn, leaving a 4"/10 cm tail. Thread tail onto tapestry needle and draw through remaining stitches. Pull up snug and fasten off.

Setting Up for Remaining Fingers

○ Put held stitches back on needles. Beginning at the center of the cast-on stitches at base of little finger, join yarn, pick up and knit (see page 280) 2 stitches, K36, pick up and knit 2 stitches from base of little finger. *You now have* 40 stitches. Knit 5 rounds.

Knitting the Ring Finger

o K7, place next 26 stitches onto a length of scrap yarn, cast on 4 stitches over the gap, knit remaining 7 stitches. *You now have* 18 stitches. Knit until finger measures 2½"/6.5 cm or desired length.

o To make top of finger: *K2tog; repeat from * until 5 stitches remain. Finish as for little finger.

Knitting the Middle Finger

o Put first and last 6 stitches from holder onto separate needles. Beginning at the center of the cast-on stitches at the base of the ring finger, pick up and knit 2 stitches, knit next 6 stitches, cast on 4 stitches over the gap, knit last 6 stitches, pick up and knit 2 stitches from base of ring finger. *You now have* 20 stitches. Knit until finger measures 2¾"/7 cm or desired length.

o Shape top of finger and finish as for ring finger.

Knitting the Index Finger

o Place remaining 14 held stitches back on needles. Beginning at the center of the cast-on stitches at the base of the middle finger, pick up and knit 2 stitches, knit remaining 14 stitches, pick up and knit 2 stitches from base of middle finger. *You now have* 18 stitches. Complete as for ring finger.

Knitting the Thumb

o Place 18 held stitches back on needles. Pick up and knit 2 stitches from cast-on stitches at thumb gusset, K18. *You now have* 20 stitches. Knit for 1¾"/4.5 cm more, or to desired length.

o Shape top of thumb and finish as for ring finger.

KNITTING THE LEFT GLOVE

o Work cuff as for right glove.

o K26, work Round 1 of Fagoted Rib over next 19 stitches, knit to end of round.

o Work in established pattern until piece measures 2½"/6.5 cm from beginning. Work thumb gusset, fingers, and thumb as for right glove.

Finishing

o Weave in all loose ends, using tails to close gaps at base of thumb and fingers.

Lily Cuffs

Designed by Nichole Reese

Upside down, downside up — anything goes with these versatile cuffs! The cabled rib expands to create a one-size-fits-most design, and you should have enough yarn to make them longer if you like.

Knitting the Cuffs

○ Cast on 48 stitches. Divide evenly onto four double-point needles. Place marker and join into a round, being careful not to twist the stitches. Work K1, P1 ribbing for 1"/2.5 cm.

○ Next Round: *K1, P1, K1, [M1, (P1, K1) 3 times] seven times, M1, P1, K1, P1. *You now have* 56 stitches.

○ Work Rounds 1–10 of Cabled Rib pattern six times.

Knitting the Ruffle

○ Round 1: *Kfbf, P1; repeat from * to end of round. *You now have* 112 stitches.

○ Rounds 2–4: *K3, P1; repeat from * to end of round.

○ Round 5: *Kfb, K1, kfb, P1; repeat from * to end of round. *You now have* 168 stitches.

○ Rounds 6–10: *K5, P1; repeat from * to end of round.

SIZES AND FINISHED MEASUREMENTS	To fit most adults, approximately 5"/12.5 cm circumference, unstretched
YARN	Cascade Heritage, 75% superwash merino wool/25% nylon, 3.5 oz (100 g)/ 437 yds (400 m), Color 5614 Lilac
NEEDLES	Set of five US 2.5 (3 mm) double-point needles *or size you need to obtain correct gauge*
GAUGE	42 stitches and 42 rounds = 4"/10 cm in Cabled Rib pattern, unstretched
OTHER SUPPLIES	Stitch marker, cable needle, tapestry needle
SPECIAL ABBREVIATIONS	**C4B** slip next 2 stitches to cable needle and hold in back, knit 2 from left needle, knit 2 from cable needle **C4F** slip next 2 stitches to cable needle and hold in front, knit 2 from left needle, knit 2 from cable needle **kfb** knit into the front and back of next stitch (1 stitch increased) **kfbf** knit into the front, back, and front of the next stitch (2 stitches increased)

Finishing

o Bind off. Weave in ends.

Pattern Essentials

CABLED RIB

Rounds 1–4: *K2, P1, K4, P1; repeat from * to end of round.

Round 5: *K2, P1, C4F, P1; repeat from * to end of round.

Rounds 6–9: Repeat Round 1.

Round 10: *K2, P1, C4B, P1; repeat from * to end of round.

Repeat Rounds 1–10 for pattern.

CABLED RIB

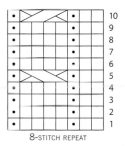

8-STITCH REPEAT

☐ knit
▪ purl
⬗ C4B
⬗ C4F

Eyelet and Feather Socks

Designed by Ann McClure

These socks, knitted from the top down, have the gusset decreases on the bottom of the foot, allowing the pattern to continue uninterrupted onto the instep.

SIZES AND FINISHED MEASUREMENTS	Woman's medium, approximately 8"/20.5 cm circumference, unstretched
YARN	Lucy Neatby Cat's Pajamas, 80% merino wool/10% cashmere/10% nylon, 3.5 oz (100 g)/274 yds (300 m), Fiery Fuchsia
NEEDLES	Set of five US 1.5 (2.5 mm) double-point needles *or size you need to obtain correct gauge*
GAUGE	14-stitch repeat = 2"/5 cm in Eyelet and Feather pattern
OTHER SUPPLIES	Stitch markers, tapestry needle

Pattern Essentials

EYELET AND FEATHER

Round 1 and all odd-numbered rounds: Knit.

Round 2: *Yo, ssk, K9, K2tog, yo, K1; repeat from * to end of round.

Round 4: *Yo, K1, ssk, K7, K2tog, K1, yo, K1; repeat from * to end of round.

Round 6: *Yo, K2, ssk, K5, K2tog, K2, yo, K1; repeat from * to end of round.

Round 8: *Yo, K3, ssk, K3, K2tog, K3, yo, K1; repeat from * to end of round.

Round 10: *Yo, K4, ssk, K1, K2tog, K4, yo, K1; repeat from * to end of round.

Round 12: *Yo, K5, sk2p, K5, yo, K1; repeat from * to end of round.

Repeat Rounds 1–12 for pattern.

EYELET AND FEATHER

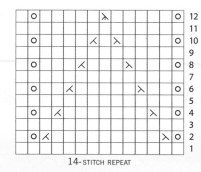

14-STITCH REPEAT

	knit
⟋	K2tog
⟍	ssk
O	yarn over
⟑	s2kp

Knitting the Cuff

○ Cast on 56 stitches and divide evenly onto four double-point needles. Join into a round, being careful not to twist the stitches.

○ Rounds 1–15: *K2, P2; repeat from * to end of round.

Knitting the Leg

○ Work Rounds 1–12 of Eyelet and Feather pattern four times.

Setting Up for the Heel

○ Knit 28 stitches onto one needle for the heel; leave remaining 28 stitches on hold for the instep. Turn.

Knitting the Heel Flap

○ Row 1 (WS): Slip 1, purl to end of row.

○ Row 2: *Slip 1, K1; repeat from * to end of row.

○ Repeat Rows 1 and 2 thirteen more times, then work Row 1 once more for a total of 29 rows.

Turning the Heel

○ Row 1 (RS): Slip 1, K16, ssk, K1, turn.

○ Row 2: Slip 1, P7, P2tog, P1, turn.

○ Row 3: Slip 1, K8, ssk, K1, turn.

○ Row 4: Slip 1, P9, P2tog, P1, turn.

○ Continue in this manner, working 1 more stitch before the decrease on every row, until all stitches have been worked and 18 stitches remain.

Knitting the Gusset

O With right side facing and using needle that holds heel stitches (Needle 1), K18, place marker, pick up and knit (see page 280) 15 stitches along side of heel flap. Work 28 held instep stitches in pattern as established onto Needles 2 and 3. With Needle 4, pick up and knit 15 stitches along other side of heel flap, place marker, knit 9 heel stitches from Needle 1. The round begins at center of sole.

O *You now have* 76 stitches: 24 stitches each on Needles 1 and 4 and 14 stitches each on Needles 2 and 3.

O Round 1: On Needle 1, knit to last 3 stitches, K2tog, yo, K1; on Needles 2 and 3, work instep stitches in pattern as established; on Needle 4, yo, ssk, knit to end.

O Rounds 2, 4, 6, 8, and 10: On Needle 1, knit to marker, slip marker, ssk, knit to end; on Needles 2 and 3, work in established pattern; on Needle 4, knit to 2 stitches before marker, K2tog, slip marker, knit to end.

O Round 3: On Needle 1, knit to last 4 stitches, K2tog, K1, yo, K1; on Needles 2 and 3, work in established pattern; on Needle 4, yo, K1, ssk, knit to end of needle.

O Round 5: On Needle 1, knit to last 5 stitches, K2tog, K2, yo, K1; on Needles 2 and 3, work in established pattern; on Needle 4, yo, K2, ssk, knit to end of needle.

O Round 7: On Needle 1, knit to last 6 stitches, K2tog, K3, yo, K1; on Needles 2 and 3, work in established pattern; on Needle 4, yo, K3, ssk, knit to end of needle.

O Round 9: On Needle 1, knit to last 7 stitches, K2tog, K4, yo, K1; on Needles 2 and 3, work in established pattern; on Needle 4, yo, K4, ssk, knit to end of needle.

O Round 11: On Needle 1, knit to last 8 stitches, K2tog, K5, yo, K1; on Needles 2 and 3, work instep stitches in pattern as established; on Needle 4, yo, K5, ssk, knit to end of needle.

O Round 12: Repeat Round 2.

O Repeat Rounds 1–8. *You now have* 56 stitches.

Knitting the Foot

O Remove markers. Work even in patterns as established until foot measures 2"/5 cm less than desired finished length.

Shaping the Toe

O Round 1: Knit.

O Round 2: Knit to last 3 stitches on Needle 1, K2tog, K1; on Needle 2, K1, ssk, knit to end of needle; on Needle 3, knit to last 3 stitches, K2tog, K1; on Needle 4, K1, ssk, knit to end of needle.

O Repeat Rounds 1 and 2 eight more times. *You now have* 20 stitches. Knit 5 stitches from Needle 1 onto Needle 4; slip 5 stitches from Needle 3 onto Needle 2.

Finishing

O Use Kitchener stitch (page 278) to graft the two sets of 10 stitches together. Weave in ends. Block.

Butterfly Garden Socks

Designed by Kerin Dimeler-Laurence for Knit Picks

Watch the instep cable metamorphose into a butterfly while knitting these delightful toe-up socks. These are not for the faint of cable!

SIZES AND FINISHED MEASUREMENTS	Woman's medium, approximately 7"/18 cm circumference
YARN	Knit Picks Stroll Tonal, 75% superwash merino wool, 25% nylon, 3.5 oz (100 g)/ 462 yds (422.5 m), Springtime
NEEDLES	Set of five US 2 (2.75 mm) double-point needles *or size you need to obtain correct gauge*
GAUGE	32 stitches and 40 rounds = 4"/10 cm in stockinette stitch
OTHER SUPPLIES	Stitch marker, cable needle, tapestry needle
SPECIAL ABBREVIATIONS	*Note:* See chart symbol key on page 67 for cable and twist instructions **WT** wrap and turn (see page 282)

Knitting the Toe

○ Using backward-loop method (see page 276), cast on 10 stitches and knit these stitches. Turning work so the cast-on edge is on top and working yarn is at the right, pick up and knit (see page 280) into each cast-on stitch. Divide stitches evenly onto four double-point needles, 5 instep stitches each on Needles 1 and 2, 5 sole stitches each on Needles 3 and 4.

○ Round 1: On Needle 1, K1, M1L, knit to end of needle; on Needle 2, knit to last stitch, M1R, K1; on Needle 3, repeat Needle 1; on Needle 4, repeat Needle 2.

○ Rounds 2 and 3: Repeat Round 1. *You now have 32 stitches.*

○ Round 4: Knit.

○ Round 5: Repeat Round 1.

○ Repeat Rounds 4 and 5 six more times, then work Round 4 once. *You now have* 60 stitches: 30 instep stitches and 30 sole stitches.

Knitting the Foot

○ Knit 10 instep stitches, place marker, work Instep chart over 10 stitches, knit 10 instep stitches, work 30 sole stitches in stockinette stitch. Continue in patterns as established until foot measures about 2"/ 5 cm less than desired finished length.

Knitting the Heel Bottom

○ Work the instep stitches in pattern on Needles 1 and 2 and note which pattern round you last worked. Leave these stitches on hold while you work the heel. Slip stitches from Needles 3 and 4 onto one needle.

HEEL (PART ONE)

○ Row 1: K28, WT.

○ Row 2: P26, WT.

○ Row 3: Knit to stitch before the wrap, WT.

○ Row 4: Purl to stitch before the wrap, WT.

○ Repeat Rows 3 and 4 until there are 10 unwrapped stitches in center of needle.

○ Row 3: Knit to first wrapped stitch, pick up both wraps and knit them together with the stitch, WT.

○ Row 4: Purl to first wrapped stitch, pick up both wraps and purl them together with the stitch, WT.

○ Repeat Rows 3 and 4 until you have worked all double-wrapped stitches.

REJOINING THE ROUND

○ Next Round: Knit to single-wrapped stitch, pick up the wrap and knit it together with the stitch; on next needles (now Needles 1 and 2), continue in pattern as established on instep stitches; with next needle (now Needle 3), pick up the wrap of the next stitch and knit it together with the stitch, K14; with last needle (now Needle 4) K15. *You now have 15 sole stitches each on Needles 3 and 4 and 15 instep stitches each on Needles 1 and 2.*

Knitting the Leg

○ Continue in pattern as established on instep stitches and work stockinette stitch on sole stitches until two more pattern repeats are completed, ending with Round 6 of pattern.

KNITTING THE ANKLE CHART

○ Work Rounds 1–11 of Ankle chart on front *and* back of leg.

○ Purl 1 round.

HEEL (PART TWO)

○ Row 1: Knit to the first wrapped stitch, pick up wrap and knit it together with the stitch, WT. *Note:* This stitch will have two wraps.

○ Row 2: Purl to the first wrapped stitch, pick up wrap and purl it together with the stitch, WT. *Note:* This and all subsequent wrapped stitches except the 2 end stitches will have two wraps.

KNITTING THE BUTTERFLY CHART

○ Establish pattern: *P2, work Round 1 of Butterfly chart over next 26 stitches, P2; repeat from * once.

○ Continue in established pattern through Round 36 of Butterfly chart.

○ Purl 3 rounds.

Knitting the Picot Edging

○ Rounds 1–5: Knit.

○ Round 6 (Eyelet Round): *K2tog, yo; repeat from * to end of round.

○ Rounds 7–10: Knit.

○ Bind off loosely, leaving a 20"/51 cm tail. Fold fabric to inside along Eyelet Round. Thread tail onto tapestry needle and invisibly sew bound-off edge to inside.

Finishing

○ Weave in ends. Block.

ANKLE

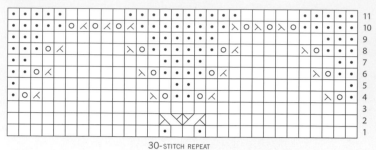

30-STITCH REPEAT

BUTTERFLY

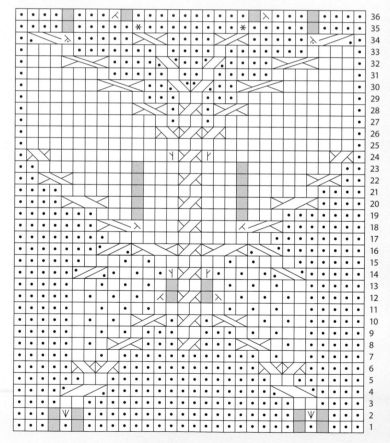

INSTEP

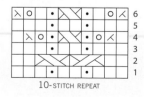

10-STITCH REPEAT

☐ knit

• purl

⊠ K2tog

⊠ ssk

○ yarn over

✳ **MK (make knot)** K3 into next stitch, turn, P3, turn, slip 2 together knitwise, K1, p2sso

Ɏ **M1L** make 1 left-leaning stitch (see page 279)

Y **M1R** make 1 right-leaning stitch (see page 279)

1/1LT knit the second stitch through the back loop and leave it on the needle, then knit the first stitch and slip both stitches off the needle

1/1RT knit the second stitch and leave it on the needle, then knit the first stitch and slip both stitches off the needle.

C4L slip 2 stitches to cable needle and hold in front, K2 from left-hand needle, K2 from cable needle

C4LP slip 2 stitches to cable needle and hold in front, P2 from left-hand needle, K2 from cable needle

C4RP slip 2 stitches to cable needle and hold in back, K2 from left-hand needle, P2 from cable needle

C4R slip 2 stitches to cable needle and hold in back, K2 from left-hand needle, K2 from cable needle

V **CDI** centered double increase (K1 tbl, K1) into 1 stitch, insert left-hand needle from left to right under vertical strand between 2 stitches just made, K1 tbl into this strand

C1/1LP slip 1 stitch to cable needle and hold in front, P1 from left-hand needle, K1 from cable needle

C1/1RP slip 1 stitch to cable needle and hold in back, K1 from left-hand needle, P1 from cable needle

C1/2L slip 1 stitch to cable needle and hold in front, K2 from left hand needle, K1 from cable needle

C1/2R slip 2 stitches to cable needle and hold in back, K1 from left-hand needle, K2 from cable needle

C1/2RP slip 2 stitches to cable needle and hold in back, K1 from left-hand needle, P2 from cable needle

C1/3R slip 3 stitches to cable needle and hold in back, K1 from left-hand needle, K3 from cable needle

C1/2LP slip 1 stitch to cable needle and hold in front, P2 from left-hand needle, K1 from cable needle

C1/3L slip 1 stitch to cable needle and hold in front, K3 from left-hand needle, K1 from cable needle

D1/3RT slip 3 stitches to cable needle and hold in back, K1 from left-hand needle, (K1, K2tog) from cable needle

D1/3LT slip 1 stitch to cable needle and hold in front, (K2tog, K1) from left-hand needle, K1 from cable needle

D1/3RTP slip 3 stitches to cable needle and hold in back, K1 from left-hand needle, (P1, P2tog) from cable needle

D1/3LTP slip 1 stitch to cable needle and hold in front, (P1, P2tog) from left-hand needle, K1 from cable needle

☐ no stitch

Sampler Socks

Designed by Dorothy E. Ratigan

Don't be a clone — design your own! Socks are a great place for trying out new stitch patterns, and there's no rule saying that the socks must be identical. So go ahead and experiment with your own stitches and repeats — with 56 stitches, as in these socks, you may use patterns with multiples of 2, 4, 7, or 8 stitches.

KNITTING THE FIRST SOCK

Knitting the Leg

O Using long-tail method (see page 278) and straight needle, cast on 56 stitches. Purl 1 row. With the purl side of cast-on facing, divide the stitches evenly onto four double-point needles. Place a marker and join into a round, being careful not to twist the stitches.

SIZES AND FINISHED MEASUREMENTS	Woman's medium/large, Man's small/medium, approximately 8"/20.5 cm circumference
YARN	Schaefer Yarn Nichole, 80% extrafine merino wool superwash/20% nylon, 5 oz (142 g)/405 yds (370 m), One-of-a-kind color
NEEDLES	Set of five US 3 (3.25 mm) double-point needles *or size you need to obtain correct gauge*
GAUGE	28 stitches and 38 rounds = 4"/10 cm in stockinette stitch
OTHER SUPPLIES	One US 4 (3.5 mm) straight needle for cast on, stitch marker, tapestry needle

Pattern Essentials

CUFF (BOTH SOCKS)

Round 1: Knit.

Round 2: Purl.

Repeat these 2 rounds five times.

Knit 6 rounds.

Work 3 dividing rounds: purl, knit, purl.

SOCK 1, PATTERN 1
(MULTIPLE OF 2 STITCHES)

Rounds 1 and 2: Knit.

Round 3: *K2tog; repeat from * to end of round.

Round 4: *K1, M1; repeat from * to end of round.

Repeat Rounds 1–4 until you decide to change.

Work 3 dividing rounds: purl, knit, purl.

SOCK 1, PATTERN 2
(MULTIPLE OF 4 STITCHES)

Round 1: *K2, slip 2 purlwise wyif; repeat from * to end of round.

Round 2: Knit.

Round 3: *Slip 2 purlwise wyif, K2; repeat from * to end of round.

Round 4: Knit.

Repeat Rounds 1–4 until you decide to change.

Work 3 dividing rounds: purl, knit, purl.

SOCK 1, PATTERN 3
(MULTIPLE OF 2 STITCHES)

Rounds 1 and 2: Knit.

Rounds 3 and 5: *Yo, K2; repeat from * to end of round.

Rounds 4 and 6: *Slip 1 purlwise, K1, yo, pass the slipped stitch over the K1 and the yo; repeat from * to end of round.

Repeat Rounds 1–6 until piece measures 7¼"/18.5 cm.

Work Rounds 1 and 2 once more.

Work 3 dividing rounds: purl, knit, purl.

SOCK 2, PATTERN 1
(MULTIPLE OF 2 STITCHES)

Round 1: Purl.

Round 2: Knit.

Round 3: Purl.

Round 4: *Yo, skp; repeat from * to end of round.

Repeat Rounds 1–4 until you decide to change.

Work 3 dividing rounds: purl, knit, purl.

SOCK 2, PATTERN 2
(MULTIPLE OF 4 STITCHES)

Rounds 1 and 2: *K2, P2; repeat from * to end of round.

Rounds 3 and 4: *P2, K2; repeat from * to end of round.

Repeat Rounds 1–4 for pattern until you decide to change.

Work 3 dividing rounds: purl, knit, purl.

SOCK 2, PATTERN 3
(MULTIPLE OF 2 STITCHES)

Round 1: *Yo, K2; repeat from * to end of round.

Note: To work Round 2, shift the stitches by slipping the first stitch of each needle to the previous needle.

Round 2: *P3, pass third stitch over the first 2 stitches; repeat from * to end of round.

Round 3: *K2, yo; repeat from * to end of round.

Round 4: Repeat Round 2.

Repeat Rounds 1–4 until you decide to change.

Work 3 dividing rounds: purl, knit, purl.

SOCK 2, PATTERN 4
(MULTIPLE OF 2 STITCHES)

Round 1: *K1, slip 1 purlwise wyif; repeat from * to end of round.

Round 2: Knit.

Round 3: *Slip 1 purlwise wyif, K1; repeat from * to end of round.

Round 4: Knit.

Repeat Rounds 1–4 until piece measures 7½"/19 cm.

Work 3 dividing rounds: purl, knit, purl.

○ Work Sock 1, Patterns 1–3 until leg measures 7½"/19 cm or desired leg length to top of heel, ending on an even-numbered round followed by 3 dividing rounds.

Knitting the Heel Flap

○ Place 14 stitches each from Needles 3 and 4 plus the last stitch from Needle 2 onto one needle for the heel. Leave remaining 27 stitches on hold for the instep. With wrong side facing, K29.

○ *Note:* Slip all stitches purlwise.

○ Row 1 (RS): *Slip 1, K1; repeat from * to last stitch, slip 1 wyif.

○ Row 2: K28, P1.

○ Repeat Rows 1 and 2 seventeen more times. *You now have* 18 chain stitches along each side of the heel.

Turning the Heel

○ Row 1 (RS): K16, K2tog, K1, turn.

○ Row 2: Slip 1, P4, ssp, P1, turn.

○ Row 3: Slip 1, K5, K2tog, K1, turn.

○ Row 4: Slip 1, P6, ssp, P1, turn.

○ Continue in this manner, working 1 more stitch before the decrease on every row, until all stitches have been worked and 17 heel stitches remain. End on a right-side row, slipping the last stitch of this row.

Knitting the Gussets

○ *Note:* Knit through both loops of slipped chain stitches.

○ With the same needle that holds the heel stitches, pick up and knit (see page 280) 18 chain stitches along one side of the heel flap. Knit the held instep stitches on the next two needles. With the fourth needle, pick up and knit 18 chain stitches along the other side of the heel flap, then knit 9 heel stitches onto this needle. *You now have* 80 stitches arranged as follows:

> ○ Needle 1: 26 stitches
>
> ○ Needle 2: 14 stitches
>
> ○ Needle 3: 13 stitches
>
> ○ Needle 4: 27 stitches

Shaping the Gussets

○ Round 1: Knit to last 2 stitches on Needle 1, ssk; knit instep stitches; K2tog at the beginning of Needle 4, knit to end of round.

○ Round 2: Knit.

○ Repeat Rounds 1 and 2 until 14 stitches remain on Needle 1 and 15 stitches remain on Needle 4. Slip 1 stitch from Needle 4 to Needle 3. *You now have* 56 stitches, 14 on each needle.

Knitting the Foot

○ Continue working in stockinette stitch until foot measures 7"/18 cm from back of heel or 2"/5 cm less than desired finished measurement.

Shaping the Toe

○ Round 1: Knit to last 2 stitches on Needle 1, ssk; K2tog at beginning of Needle 2, knit to end; knit to last 2 stitches on Needle 3, ssk; K2tog at beginning of Needle 4, knit to end of round.

o Round 2: Knit.

o Repeat Rounds 1 and 2 until 4 stitches remain on each needle.

o Knit 4 stitches from Needle 1 onto Needle 4. Slip 4 stitches from Needle 3 onto Needle 2.

Finishing

o Use Kitchener stitch (see page 278) to graft the two sets of 8 stitches together.

o Weave in ends. Wash and block.

KNITTING THE SECOND SOCK

Knitting the Leg

o Using long-tail method (see page 278) and straight needle, cast on 56 stitches. Purl 1 row. With the purl side of cast on facing, divide the stitches evenly onto four double-point needles. Place a marker and join into a round, being careful not to twist the stitches.

o Work Sock 2, Patterns 1–4 until leg measures 7½"/19 cm or desired leg length to top of heel, ending on an even-numbered round followed by 3 dividing rounds.

o Complete as for first sock.

Bridal Socks

Designed by Kerri A. Shank

Flicks of silver in this sock yarn make it appropriate for the most special occasions. These lovely socks feature a ribbed leg with lace insets, and the patterns continue along the instep to the toe shaping.

SIZES AND FINISHED MEASUREMENTS	Woman's medium, approximately 7"/18 cm circumference
YARN	Kraemer Sterling, 63% superwash merino/20% silk/15% nylon/2% silver, 3.5 oz (100 g)/420 yds (384 m), Natural
NEEDLES	Set of five US 3 (3.25 mm) double-point needles *or size you need to obtain correct gauge*
GAUGE	30 stitches and 37 rounds = 4"/10 cm in stockinette stitch
OTHER SUPPLIES	Tapestry needle

Knitting the Cuff

o Cast on 64 stitches and divide evenly onto four double-point needles. Join into a round, being careful not to twist the stitches.

o Round 1: *P1, K1; repeat from * to end of round.

o Repeat Round 1 until cuff measures 1"/2.5 cm.

Knitting the Leg

o Setup Round: On Needle 1, K4, M1, K4, (P1, K1) four times; on Needle 2, (P1, K1) four times, K4, M1, K4; on Needles 3 and 4, continue in established P1, K1 rib. *You now have* 17 stitches each on Needles 1 and 2 and 16 stitches each on Needles 3 and 4.

Pattern Essentials

LACE CLOCK

Round 1: Ssk, (K1, yo) two times, K3, K2tog.

Round 2 and all even-numbered rounds through Round 8: Knit.

Round 3: Ssk, yo, K3, yo, K2, K2tog.

Round 5: Ssk, K3, yo, K1, yo, K1, K2tog.

Round 7: Ssk, K2, yo, K3, yo, K2tog.

Repeat Rounds 1–8 for pattern.

SLIP-STITCH RIB

Round 1: *P1, Slip 1 purlwise wyib; repeat from *.

Round 2: *P1, K1 tbl; repeat from *.

○ On Needle 1, work Round 1 of Lace Clock pattern over 9 stitches, then Round 1 of Slip-Stitch Rib over 8 stitches; on Needle 2, work Round 1 of Slip-Stitch Rib over 8 stitches, then Round 1 of Lace Clock pattern over 9 stitches; on Needles 3 and 4, work Round 1 of Slip-Stitch Rib.

○ Continue in patterns as established, repeating Rounds 1–8 of Lace Clock pattern and Rounds 1–2 of Slip-Stitch Rib, until piece measures 6"/15 cm from cast-on edge.

Knitting the Heel Flap

○ Setup Row (RS): Work in established patterns on Needles 1 and 2. Leave these stitches on hold for instep. Work stitches on Needles 3 and 4 onto one needle as follows: *K1 tbl, K1; repeat from * to end of Needle 4 stitches, turn.

○ Row 1 (WS): *Slip 1 purlwise wyif, P1; repeat from * to end of row.

○ Row 2: Slip 1 purlwise wyib, *K1 tbl, K1; repeat from * to last stitch, K1.

○ Row 3: Slip 2 purlwise wyif, *P1, slip 1 purlwise wyif; repeat from * to last 2 stitches, P2.

○ Row 4: Slip 1 purlwise wyib, *K1, K1 tbl; repeat from * to last stitch, K1.

○ Repeat Rows 1–4 six more times, then work Rows 1–3 once more.

Turning the Heel

○ Row 1 (RS): Slip 1 purlwise wyib, K17, ssk, K1, turn.

○ Row 2: Slip 1 purlwise wyif, P5, P2tog, P1, turn.

○ Row 3: Slip 1 purlwise wyif, knit to 1 stitch before the gap, ssk, K1, turn.

○ Row 4: Slip 1 purlwise wyif, purl to 1 stitch before the gap, P2tog, P1, turn.

○ Repeat Rows 3 and 4 until all stitches have been worked and ending with a wrong-side row. *You now have* 18 heel stitches.

Knitting the Gusset

○ With right side facing and using needle that holds heel stitches (Needle 1), K18, pick up and knit (see page 280) 15 stitches along side of heel flap. Work 34 held instep stitches in pattern as established onto Needles 2 and 3. With Needle 4, pick up and knit 15 stitches along other side of heel flap, knit 9 heel stitches from Needle 1. The round begins at center of sole.

○ *You now have* 82 stitches: 24 stitches each on Needles 1 and 4 and 17 stitches each on Needles 2 and 3.

○ Round 1: Knit to last 3 stitches on Needle 1, K2tog, K1; on Needles 2 and 3, work instep stitches in pattern as established; on Needle 4, K1, ssk, knit to end of round.

○ Round 2: Knit stitches on Needles 1 and 4, work instep stitches in patterns as established on Needles 2 and 3.

○ Repeat Rounds 1 and 2 seven more times. *You now have* 66 stitches.

Knitting the Foot

○ Work even in patterns as established until foot measures 8"/20.5 cm from back of heel or 1¾"/4.5 cm less than desired finished length.

Shaping the Toe

○ Discontinue lace and rib patterns and work all stitches in stockinette stitch.

○ Round 1: Knit to last 3 stitches on Needle 1, K2tog, K1; on Needle 2, K1, ssk, knit to end of needle; on Needle 3, knit to last 3 stitches, K2tog, K1; on Needle 4, K1, ssk, knit to end of needle.

○ Round 2: Knit.

○ Repeat Rounds 1 and 2 seven more times. *You now have* 34 stitches.

○ Repeat Round 1 only until 10 stitches remain.

Finishing

○ Cut yarn leaving a 6"/15 cm tail. Thread tail onto tapestry needle and draw through remaining stitches. Pull up snug and fasten off. Weave in ends.

SLIP-STITCH RIB

2-
STITCH
REPEAT

LACE CLOCK

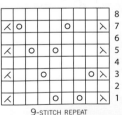

9-STITCH REPEAT

	knit		yarn over
•	purl	V	slip 1 pwise with
⊼	K2tog		yarn on WS
⊠	ssk	⅋	K1 tbl

Lacy Summer Footlets

Designed by Betsy McCarthy

These lacy ribbed "footlets" are cute and comfortable to wear. The yarn is silky and cool for summer, and it offers lots of stretch for a good fit.

SIZES AND FINISHED MEASUREMENTS	Woman's medium, approximately 8"/20.5 cm circumference
YARN	Crystal Palace Panda Silk, 52% bamboo/43% superwash merino/5% combed silk, 1.75 oz (50 g)/204 yds (187 m), Mint Cream
NEEDLES	Set of five US 1 (2.25 mm) double-point needles *or size you need to obtain correct gauge*
GAUGE	36 stitches and 50 rounds = 4"/10 cm in stockinette stitch
OTHER SUPPLIES	Stitch markers, tapestry needle

Knitting the Cuff

○ Cast on 60 stitches and divide onto double-point needles so there are 14 stitches on Needle 1, 15 stitches on Needles 2 and 3, and 16 stitches on Needle 4. Join into a round, being careful not to twist the stitches.

○ Work K1, P1 rib for 6 rounds.

Knitting the Heel Flap

○ Working with 31 heel stitches on Needles 3 and 4 only, turn so wrong side is facing and slip all stitches onto one needle.

○ Row 1 (WS): Slip 1 purlwise, P30.

○ Row 2: *Slip 1 purlwise wyib, K1; repeat from * to last stitch, K1.

○ Repeat Rows 1 and 2 until piece measures 2½"/6.5 cm from rib, ending with a right-side row.

Turning the Heel

○ Row 1 (WS): Slip 1, P15, P2tog, P1, turn.

○ Row 2: Slip 1, K2, ssk, K1, turn.

○ Row 3: Slip 1, P3, P2tog, P1, turn.

○ Row 4: Slip 1, K4, ssk, K1, turn.

○ Continue in this manner, working 1 more stitch before the decrease on every row, until all stitches have been worked, ending with a right-side row. *You now have* 17 stitches.

Knitting the Gussets

○ With right side facing and using needle that holds heel stitches (Needle 1), pick up and knit (see page 280) 20 stitches along side of heel flap. Knit

29 held instep stitches onto Needle 2. With Needle 3, pick up and knit 20 stitches along other side of heel flap, K8 from Needle 1. *You now have 86 stitches arranged as follows:*

- Needle 1: 29 stitches
- Needle 2: 29 stitches
- Needle 3: 28 stitches

o Place marker for beginning of round.

o Round 1:
- Needle 1: Knit to last 3 stitches, K2tog, K1.
- Needle 2: Work Round 1 of Summer Lace pattern.
- Needle 3: K1, ssk, knit to end of round.

o Round 2:
- Needle 1: Knit.
- Needle 2: Work the next round of Summer Lace pattern as established.
- Needle 3: Knit.

o Repeat Rounds 1 and 2 working patterns as established until 60 stitches remain.

Knitting the Foot

o Continue working the sole in stockinette stitch and the instep in Summer Lace pattern as established until foot measures 1½"/4 cm less than desired finished length, ending with Round 8 of Summer Lace pattern. Move 1 stitch from Needle 1 (sole) to Needle 2 (instep).

- Needle 1: 15 stitches
- Needle 2: 30 stitches
- Needle 3: 15 stitches

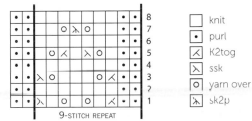

- -

Pattern Essentials

SUMMER LACE

Round 1: *P2, K2tog, K1, yo, K1, yo, K1, ssk; repeat from * to last 2 stitches, P2.

Round 2 and all even-numbered rounds: *P2, K7; repeat from * to last 2 stitches, P2.

Round 3: *P2, K2tog, yo, K3, yo, ssk; repeat from * to last 2 stitches, P2.

Round 5: *P2, K1, yo, ssk, K1, K2tog, yo, K1; repeat from * to last 2 stitches, P2.

Round 7: P2, K2, yo, sk2p, yo, K2; repeat from * to last 2 stitches, P2.

Round 8: Repeat Round 2.

Repeat Rounds 1–8 for pattern.

- -

SUMMER LACE

9-STITCH REPEAT

	knit
•	purl
⋌	K2tog
⋋	ssk
o	yarn over
⋏	sk2p

Shaping the Toe

o Round 1:
- Needle 1: Knit to last 3 stitches, K2tog, K1.
- Needle 2: K1, ssk, knit to last 3 stitches, K2tog, K1.
- Needle 3: K1, ssk, knit to end of round.

o Round 2: Knit.

o Repeat Rounds 1 and 2 five more times. *You now have* 36 stitches.

o Repeat Round 1 five times. *You now have* 16 stitches.

o Knit 4 stitches from Needle 1 onto Needle 3.

Finishing

o Graft toe stitches together with Kitchener stitch (see page 278). Weave in ends. Block.

SIZES AND FINISHED MEASUREMENTS	Woman's medium, approximately 8"/20.5 cm circumference
YARN	Malabrigo Sock Kettle Dyed, 100% super-wash merino wool, 3.5 oz (100 g)/440 yds (402 m), Color 37 Lettuce
NEEDLES	Set of five US 2 (2.75 mm) double-point needles *or size you need to obtain correct gauge*
GAUGE	32 stitches and 48 rounds = 4"/10 cm in stockinette stitch
OTHER SUPPLIES	Cable needle, tapestry needle
SPECIAL ABBREVIATIONS	**C4B** slip 2 stitches onto cable needle and hold in back, knit 2 from left-hand needle, knit 2 from cable needle **C4F** slip 2 stitches onto cable needle and hold in front, knit 2 from left-hand needle, knit 2 from cable needle **LT** knit second stitch tbl and leave on needle, knit first stitch, slip both stitches off needle **RT** knit 2 together and leave on needle, insert needle between the stitches and knit the first stitch again, slip both stitches off needle **WT** wrap and turn (see page 282)

Vidia Socks

Designed by Rebecca Mercier

These oh-so-feminine and oh-so-soft socks used about 80 grams of a 100-gram skein. They are knitted from the toe up and feature a figure-8 cast on, short-row heel, and different patterns on the front and back.

Knitting the Toe

○ Using the figure-8 (see page 277) or method of choice, cast on 16 stitches. Knit 1 round, dividing the stitches evenly onto four needles. Knit 1 more round.

○ Increase Round:

> ○ Needle 1 (instep): K1, M1R, knit to end.
>
> ○ Needle 2 (instep): Knit to last stitch, M1L, K1.
>
> ○ Needle 3 (sole): Same as Needle 1.
>
> ○ Needle 4 (sole): Same as Needle 2.

○ Repeat this Increase Round three more times. *You now have 32 stitches.*

○ Next Round: Knit.

○ Next Round: Repeat Increase Round.

○ Repeat these 2 rounds until you have 64 stitches.

o Next Round: K1, M1R, knit to end of round. *You now have* 65 stitches: 33 instep stitches and 32 sole stitches

Knitting the Foot

o Following Chart A, work pattern on instep stitches and knit all sole stitches. Work Rounds 1–12 once, then repeat Rounds 13–24 until foot measures 8"/20.5 cm or 2"/5 cm less than desired finished length, ending last round at end of Needle 2. Make a note of the last round completed.

Knitting the Heel

o Leaving 33 instep stitches on hold, work back and forth on 32 sole stitches, as follows.

HEEL (PART ONE)

o Row 1: K30, WT.

o Row 2: P28, WT.

o Row 3: Knit to stitch before the wrap, WT.

o Row 4: Purl to stitch before the wrap, WT.

o Repeat Rows 3 and 4 until there are 12 unwrapped stitches in center of needle.

HEEL (PART TWO)

o Row 1: Knit to the first wrapped stitch, pick up wrap and knit it together with the stitch, WT. *Note:* This stitch will have two wraps.

o Row 2: Purl to the first wrapped stitch, pick up wrap and purl it together with the stitch, WT. *Note:*

This and all subsequent wrapped stitches except the 2 end stitches will have two wraps.

o Row 3: Knit to first wrapped stitch, pick up both wraps and knit them together with the stitch, WT.

o Row 4: Purl to first wrapped stitch, pick up both wraps and purl them together with the stitch, WT.

o Repeat Rows 3 and 4 until you have worked all double-wrapped stitches.

o Next Round: Knit to single-wrapped stitch, pick up the wrap and knit it together with the stitch, knit in pattern as established on instep stitches, pick up the wrap of the next stitch and knit it together with the stitch, knit to end of round. You are now at the end of Needle 4.

Knitting the Leg

o If necessary, work a few rounds of Chart A as established for the foot so that you end with Round 18 or 24.

o Next Round: Work pattern as established on instep stitches and follow Chart B to work pattern on back of leg. Continue as established until sock measures about 2"/5 cm less than desired finished length, ending front of leg with Rounds 25–30 and back of leg with Rounds 1–6.

Knitting the Cuff

o Setup Round: K1, P2tog, *K1, P1; repeat from * to end of round. *You now have* 64 stitches.

o Rounds 1–15: *K1, P1; repeat from * to end of round.

Finishing

o Bind off loosely as follows: K1, P1, slip these 2 stitches back to left-hand needle, P2tog, *K1, slip 2 stitches back to left-hand needle, K2tog; P1, slip 2 stitches back to left-hand needle, P2tog; repeat from * until all stitches are bound off. Weave in ends.

CHART A

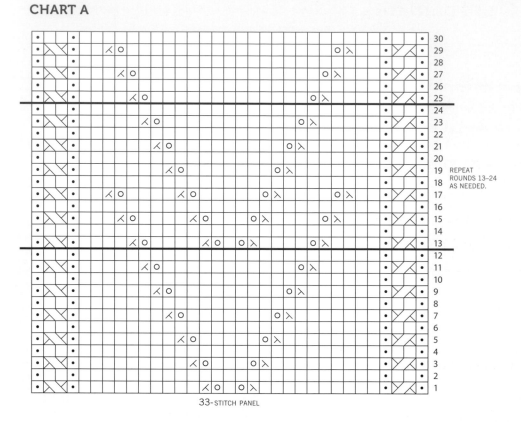

REPEAT
ROUNDS 13–24
AS NEEDED.

33-STITCH PANEL

CHART B

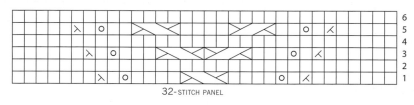

32-STITCH PANEL

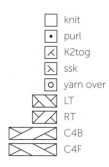

☐	knit
•	purl
⟋	K2tog
⟍	ssk
○	yarn over
	LT
	RT
	C4B
	C4F

Cable My Big Toes

Designed by Hélène Rush

Now you can wear your flip-flops and show your stripes at the same time! This clever pattern has a cable running down the length of the leg, through the foot, and ending at the tip of the big toe.

KNITTING THE RIGHT SOCK

Knitting the Cuff

○ Cast on 72 stitches. Divide evenly onto four double-point needles and join into a round, being careful not to twist the stitches.

○ Round 1: *K2, P2; repeat from * to end of round.

○ Repeat Round 1 until cuff measures 2"/5 cm

Knitting the Leg

○ *Note:* Round begins at inside of leg.

○ Round 1: Knit all stitches on Needles 1, 2, and 3. On Needle 4, K1, work Round 1 of Braided Cable pattern.

SIZES AND FINISHED MEASUREMENTS	To fit most adults, approximately 8"/20.5 cm circumference
YARN	Knit One, Crochet Too Ty-Dy Socks, 80% wool/20% nylon, 3.5 oz (100 g)/436 yds (399 m), Color 1520 Arizona
NEEDLES	Set of five US 1 (2.25 mm) double-point needles *or size you need to obtain correct gauge*
GAUGE	36 stitches and 52 rounds = 4"/10 cm in stockinette stitch
OTHER SUPPLIES	Cable needle, scrap yarn for holders, stitch marker, tapestry needle
SPECIAL ABBREVIATIONS	**C6B (cable 6 right)** slip 3 stitches to cable needle and hold in back, knit 3 from left needle, knit 3 from cable needle **C6F (cable 6 left)** slip 3 stitches to cable needle and hold in front, knit 3 from left needle, knit 3 from cable needle

o Continue in patterns as established until piece measures 6"/15 cm from beginning, ending with Round 4 or 8 of Braided Cable pattern.

Knitting the Heel Flap

o Row 1 (RS): Slip 1, K35; turn, placing remaining 36 stitches on hold for instep.

o Row 2: Slip 1, P35.

o Row 3: *Slip 1, K1; repeat from * to end of row.

o Repeat Rows 2 and 3 seventeen more times, then work Row 2 once more. Heel flap measures about 2" (5 cm).

Turning the Heel

o Row 1: Slip 1, K21, K2tog, K1, turn.

o Row 2: Slip 1, P9, P2tog, P1, turn.

o Row 3: Slip 1, K10, K2tog, K1, turn.

o Row 4: Slip 1, P11, P2tog, P1, turn.

o Continue in this manner, working 1 more stitch before the decrease on every row until all stitches are worked. *You now have* 22 heel stitches.

- - - - - - - - - - - - - - -

Pattern Essentials

BRAIDED CABLE
(OVER 17 STITCHES)

Rounds 1–3: K1, P3, K9, P3, K1.
Round 4: K1, P3, C6F, K3, P3, K1.
Rounds 5–7: Repeat Round 1.
Round 8: K1, P3, K3, C6B, P3, K1.
Repeat Rounds 1–8 for pattern.

- - - - - - - - - - - - - - -

Knitting the Gusset

o With right side facing and using needle that holds heel stitches (Needle 1), K22 heel stitches, pick up and knit (see page 280) 18 stitches along side of heel flap, M1 in corner. Work 36 held instep stitches in pattern as established onto Needles 2 and 3. With Needle 4, M1 in corner, pick up and knit 18 stitches along other side of heel flap, knit 11 heel stitches from Needle 1.

o The round begins at center of sole. *You now have* 96 stitches, with 30 stitches each on Needles 1 and 4 and 18 stitches each on Needles 2 and 3.

o Round 1: Knit to last 2 stitches on Needle 1, K2tog; on Needles 2 and 3, work instep stitches in pattern as established; on Needle 4, ssk, knit to end of round.

o Round 2: Knit stitches on Needles 1 and 4, work instep stitches in patterns as established on Needles 2 and 3.

o Repeat Rounds 1 and 2 ten more times. *You now have* 74 stitches.

Knitting the Foot

o Work even in patterns as established until foot measures 7"/18 cm from back of heel or desired length to base of big toe.

Shaping the Toes

o Setup Round: K16. The round now begins at this point (outside of foot).

o Next Round: Knit 20 (now Needle 1); place next 27 stitches on holder for big toe; on Needle 2, cast on 3 stitches, K3, place marker, K8; on Needle 3, knit remaining 16 stitches.

o *You now have* 50 stitches: 20 stitches on Needle 1, 14 stitches on Needle 2, and 16 stitches on Needle 3.

o Knit 3 rounds.

o Decrease Round: Knit to last 2 stitches on Needle 3, slip last stitch from Needle 1 to Needle 3, sk2p.

o Repeat the Decrease Round seven more times. *You now have* 34 stitches.

o Next Round: Knit to 1 stitch before marker on Needle 2, remove marker, sk2p, knit to last 2 stitches on Needle 3, sk2p using first stitch of next round. *You now have 30 stitches.*

o Next Round: Knit to 1 stitch before decrease of previous round on Needle 2, sk2p, knit to last 2 stitches, sk2p, using first stitch of next round. *You now have 26 stitches.*

o Repeat this round once more. *You now have 22 stitches.*

o Slip 2 stitches from Needle 2 to Needle 1, slip 5 stitches from Needle 3 to Needle 2. Join 11 instep stitches and 11 sole stitches together with Kitchener stitch (see page 278).

Knitting the Big Toe

o Attach yarn and pick up and knit 3 stitches from the cast-on stitches; work in established pattern on 27 held toe stitches. *You now have 30 stitches.*

o Arrange the stitches onto three double-point needles and continue in pattern as established until toe measures ¼"/0.5 cm less than desired finished length.

SHAPING THE TOE TOP

o Round 1: *K2tog, K2; repeat from * to last 2 stitches K2. *You now have 23 stitches.*

o Round 2: *K2tog, K1; repeat from * to last 2 stitches, K2. *You now have 16 stitches.*

o Round 3: *K2tog; repeat from *. *You now have 8 stitches.*

o Cut yarn leaving a 6"/15 cm tail. Thread tail onto tapestry needle and draw through remaining stitches. Pull up snug and fasten off. Weave in ends.

KNITTING THE LEFT SOCK

o Work cuff as for right sock.

Knitting the Leg

o On Needle 1, work Braided Cable pattern on 17 stitches, K1, knit all stitches on Needles 2, 3, and 4.

o Continue in patterns as established to end of leg, ready to begin heel.

Knitting the Heel Flap

o Row 1: Work in pattern as established on 36 instep stitches and place on hold, K36, turn.

o Beginning with Row 2, work heel flap as for right sock.

o Continue as for right sock until ready to work big toe.

Shaping the Toes

o Setup Round: On Needle 1, K8, place marker, K3, place next 27 stitches on holder for big toe, cast on 3 stitches; on Needle 2, K20. The round now begins here (outside of foot).

o *You now have 50 stitches: 16 stitches on Needle 1, 14 stitches on Needle 2, and 20 stitches on Needle 3.*

o Complete toes as for left sock, reversing all shaping.

BRAIDED CABLE

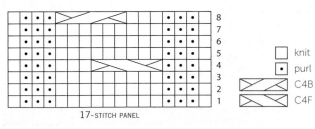

17-STITCH PANEL

☐ knit
• purl
C4B
C4F

Busy Bee Socks

Designed by Kerin Dimeler-Laurence for Knit Picks

SIZES AND FINISHED MEASUREMENTS	Woman's medium, approximately 7½"/19 cm circumference
YARN	Knit Picks Stroll Tonal, 75% superwash merino wool/25% nylon, 3.5 oz (100 g)/462 yds (422 m), Golden Glow
NEEDLES	Set of five US 2 (2.75 mm) double-point needles *or size you need to obtain correct gauge*
GAUGE	30 stitches and 42 rounds = 4"/10 cm in stockinette stitch
OTHER SUPPLIES	Cable needle, tapestry needle
SPECIAL ABBREVIATIONS	**1/1LT** knit the second stitch through the back loop and leave it on the needle, then knit the first stitch and slip both stitches off the needle **1/1RT** knit the second stitch and leave it on the needle, then knit the first stitch and slip both stitches off the needle **C4F (cable 4 front)** slip next 2 stitches onto cable needle and hold in front, knit 2 from left-hand needle, knit 2 from cable needle **C4B (cable 4 back)** slip next 2 stitches onto cable needle and hold in back, knit 2 from left-hand needle, knit 2 from cable needle **C6F (cable 6 front)** slip 3 stitches to cable needle and hold in front, knit 3 from left-hand needle, knit 3 from cable needle **PU dropped yos** insert right-hand needle under 5 loose strands of dropped yarn overs and draw a loop through; place on left-hand needle **T4B (twist 4 back)** slip next 2 stitches to cable needle and hold in back, knit 2 from left-hand needle, purl 2 from cable needle **T4F (twist 4 front)** slip 2 stitches on cable needle and hold in front, purl 2 from left-hand needle, knit 2 from cable needle **WT (wrap and turn)** see page 282

There's a lot to love about these socks! Knitted from the toe up, the instep and leg combine a honeycomb cable with columns of twisted stitches. Then the cuff combines horizontal rib with a "busy bee" pattern. A joy to knit and to wear.

Pattern Essentials

BEEHIVE

Rounds 1 and 2: Knit.

Rounds 3–6: Purl.

Repeat Rounds 1–6 for pattern.

BUSY BEE

Rounds 1: P2, K5, ssk, K4, P2.

Round 2: P2, K3, K2tog, yo two times, ssk, K3, P2.

Round 3: P2, K2, K2tog, yo three times, drop all yarn overs from previous round, ssk, K2, P2.

Round 4: P2, K1, K2tog, yo four times, drop all yarn overs from previous round, ssk, K1, P2.

Round 5: P2, K2tog, yo four times, drop all yarn overs from previous round, ssk, P2.

Round 6: P2, K1, drop all yarn overs from previous round, cast on 4 stitches onto right-hand needle with cable or backward-loop method (see page 276), insert right-hand needle from front to back under 4 loose strands of dropped yarn overs and draw through a loop onto right-hand needle, cast on 4 more stitches onto right-hand needle with cable or backward-loop method, K1, P2.

Knitting the Toe

○ *Note:* Socks may be knit on two circular needles or on double-point needles. If using double-point needles, you will have to rearrange your stitches to complete some of the cable crossings.

○ Using backward-loop method (see page 276), cast on 10 stitches and knit these stitches. Turning work so the cast-on edge is on top and working yarn is at the right, pick up and knit (see page 280) into each cast-on stitch. Divide stitches evenly onto four double-point needles: 5 instep stitches each on Needles 1 and 2, 5 sole stitches each on Needles 3 and 4.

○ Round 1: On Needle 1, K1, M1L, knit to end of needle; on Needle 2, knit last stitch, M1R, K1; on Needle 3, repeat Needle 1; on Needle 4, repeat Needle 2.

○ Rounds 2 and 3: Repeat Round 1. *You now have* 32 stitches.

○ Round 4: Knit.

○ Round 5: Repeat Round 1.

○ Repeat Rounds 4 and 5 six more times, then work Round 4 once. *You now have* 60 stitches: 30 instep stitches and 30 sole stitches.

Knitting the Foot

○ Following Honeycomb chart on instep stitches and working sole in stockinette stitch, work even until foot measures about 2"/5 cm less than desired finished length.

Knitting the Heel Bottom

○ Work the instep stitches in pattern on Needles 1 and 2 and note which pattern round you last worked. Leave these stitches on hold while you work the heel. Slip stitches from Needles 3 and 4 onto one needle.

HEEL (PART ONE)

○ Row 1: K28, WT.

○ Row 2: P26, WT.

○ Row 3: Knit to stitch before the wrap, WT.

○ Row 4: Purl to stitch before the wrap, WT.

○ Repeat Rows 3 and 4 until there are 10 unwrapped stitches in center of needle.

HEEL (PART TWO)

○ Row 1: Knit to the first wrapped stitch, pick up wrap and knit it together with the stitch, WT. *Note:* This stitch will have two wraps.

○ Row 2: Purl to the first wrapped stitch, pick up wrap and purl it together with the stitch, WT. *Note:* This and all subsequent wrapped stitches except the 2 end stitches will have two wraps.

○ Row 3: Knit to first wrapped stitch, pick up both wraps and knit them together with the stitch, WT.

○ Row 4: Purl to first wrapped stitch, pick up both wraps and purl them together with the stitch, WT.

○ Repeat Rows 3 and 4 until you have worked all double-wrapped stitches.

REJOINING THE ROUND

○ Next Round: On Needle 1, knit to single-wrapped stitch, pick up the wrap and knit it together with the stitch; on Needles 2 and 3, continue in pattern as established on instep stitches; with Needle 4, pick up the wrap of the next stitch from Needle 1 and knit it together with the stitch, K14. *You now have* 15 sole stitches each on Needles 1 and 4 and 15 instep stitches each on Needles 2 and 3.

Knitting the Leg

o Continue in pattern as established on instep stitches and work stockinette stitch on sole stitches until one more full pattern repeat is completed, ending with Round 12 of pattern.

o Work Rounds 1–12 of Honeycomb chart on all stitches three times.

Knitting the Cuff

o Work Rounds 1–6 of Beehive pattern three times, then work Rounds 1 and 2 once more.

o Work Rounds 1–6 of Busy Bee pattern, working the 15-stitch repeat four times in each round.

o Work Rounds 1–6 of Beehive pattern three times, then purl 7 rounds.

Finishing

o Bind off loosely. Weave in ends. Block.

BUSY BEE

HONEYCOMB

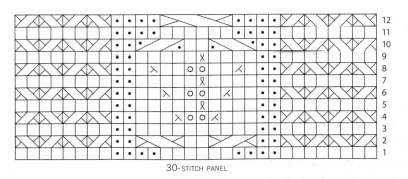

30-STITCH PANEL

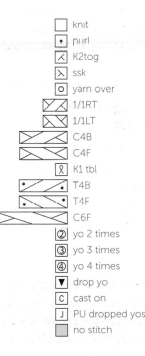

☐ knit
• purl
☒ K2tog
☒ ssk
○ yarn over
⧄ 1/1RT
⧅ 1/1LT
C4B
C4F
⚡ K1 tbl
T4B
T4F
C6F
② yo 2 times
③ yo 3 times
④ yo 4 times
▼ drop yo
C cast on
J PU dropped yos
▦ no stitch

Bohusian Socks

Designed by Mary Alice Baker

These socks come from a unique skein of yarn — one end is painted with the deepest teal, evergreen, turquoise, and purple, the other end is semisolid black. Working from the inside and outside of a center-pull ball enables you to work the two colors simultaneously.

SIZES AND FINISHED MEASUREMENTS	Child's large (Woman's medium), approximately 6½" (8½")/16.5 (21.5) cm circumference
YARN	KamaSuutra Fiber Arts Opposites Attract, 100% superwash merino wool, 3.6 oz (103 g)/505 yds (462 m), Congress of Crows
NEEDLES	Set of five US 1.5 (2.5 mm) double-point needles *or size you need to obtain correct gauge*
GAUGE	34 stitches and 48 rounds = 4"/10 cm in stockinette stitch; 36 stitches and 72 rounds = 4"/10 cm in Bohus Color pattern
OTHER SUPPLIES	Tapestry needle
SPECIAL ABBREVIATIONS	**A** yarn from colorful end of ball **B** yarn from black end of ball

Knitting the Leg

o *Note:* Throughout pattern, slip all stitches purlwise with yarn in back.

o With A, cast on 120 (160) stitches and divide evenly onto four double-point needles. Join into a round, being careful not to twist the stitches.

o Round 1: Knit.

o Round 2: *K2tog; repeat from * to end of round. *You now have* 60 (80) stitches.

o Rounds 3–8: Knit.

o Rounds 9–13: *K1, P1; repeat from * to end of round.

o Repeat Rounds 1–10 of Bohus Color pattern until piece measures 4½"/11.5 cm or desired length, ending with Round 2 or 7. Record the round number.

Knitting the Heel Flap

o Working 30 (40) heel stitches only, work back and forth with color A or color B. Hold remaining stitches (instep) on their needles until needed again.

o Row 1: *Slip 1, K1; repeat from * to end of row.

o Row 2: *Slip 1, purl to end of row.

o Repeat Rows 1 and 2 seventeen (nineteen) times more.

Turning the Heel

o Row 1: K17 (22), ssk, K1, turn.

o Row 2: Slip 1, P5, P2tog, P1, turn.

o Row 3: Slip 1, knit to stitch before the gap, ssk, K1, turn.

o Row 4: Slip 1, purl to stitch before the gap, P2tog, P1, turn.

o Repeat Rows 3 and 4 until all stitches have been worked and you have 18 (22) stitches.

o Knit 1 row.

Knitting the Gussets

o With right side facing and using needle that holds heel stitches (Needle 1), pick up and knit (see page 280) 18 (20) stitches along side

Pattern Essentials
BOHUS COLOR

Round 1: With B *K1, slip 1; repeat from * to end of round.

Round 2: *P1, slip 1; repeat from * to end of round.

Rounds 3–5: Knit.

Round 6: With A *slip 1, K1; repeat from * to end of round.

Round 7: *Slip 1, P1; repeat from * to end of round.

Rounds 8–10: Knit.

Repeat Rounds 1–10 for pattern.

DECREASING FOR THE TOE

○ *Note:* The toe is worked in stockinette stitch. You may use either A or B, depending on remaining yarn amounts.

○ Round 1: Knit to last 3 stitches on Needle 1, K2tog, K1; on Needle 2, K1, ssk, knit to end of needle; on Needle 3, knit to last 3 stitches, K2tog, K1; on Needle 4, K1, ssk, knit to end of round.

○ Round 2: Knit.

○ Repeat Rounds 1 and 2 seven more times. *You now have* 28 (48) stitches.

○ Repeat Round 1 three (eight) more times. *You now have* 16 stitches.

○ Knit 4 stitches from Needle 1 onto Needle 4. Slip 4 stitches from Needle 3 onto Needle 2.

Finishing

○ Use Kitchener stitch (see page 278) to graft the two sets of 8 stitches together.

○ Weave in ends. Block.

of heel flap. Knit held instep stitches (continuing with pattern Round 3 or 8) onto Needles 2 and 3. With Needle 4, pick up and knit 18 (20) stitches along other side of heel flap, K9 (11) from Needle 1. *You now have* 84 (102) stitches arranged 27-15-15-27 (31-20-20-31). The round now begins at the center of the heel.

○ Round 1: Knit to last 3 stitches on Needle 1, K2tog, K1; work instep stitches in pattern as established on Needles 2 and 3; K1, ssk at beginning of Needle 4, knit to end of round.

○ Round 2: Knit stitches on Needles 1 and 4, work instep stitches in pattern as established on Needles 2 and 3.

○ Repeat Rounds 1 and 2 until 60 (80) stitches remain.

Knitting the Foot

○ Continue working the sole in stockinette stitch and the instep in pattern until foot measures 6½" (7½")/ 16.5 (19) cm from heel flap or 1½" (2")/4 (5) cm less than desired finished length.

87

Sideways Socks

Designed by Judith Durant

Take a new angle on self-striping yarn by running the stripes vertically. Because this yarn has a bit of elastic in it, the knitting will stretch in both directions. The sock begins with a provisional cast on, is knitted flat, and is then joined at the center back with Kitchener stitch. Stitches are picked up along each end of the resulting tube for the toe and the cuff.

SIZES AND FINISHED MEASUREMENTS	Woman's medium/large, approximately 8"/20.5 cm circumference
YARN	Lana Grossa Fantasy Stretch, 41% cotton/ 39% superwash wool/13% polyamide/ 7% elastic, 3.5 oz (100 g)/503 yds (460 m), Color 8337
NEEDLES	US 1.5 (2.5 mm) straight or circular needle and set of five US 1.5 (2.5 mm) double-point needles *or size you need to obtain correct gauge*
GAUGE	26 stitches and 36 rows = 4"/10 cm in stockinette stitch
OTHER SUPPLIES	Size C/2 (2.75 mm) crochet hook, smooth scrap yarn for cast on and holders, stitch marker, tapestry needle

Knitting the First Half of the Leg

○ *Note:* The sock leg begins at the center front with a provisional cast on. To ensure you get symmetrical, matching socks, pick up the cast on for the second half of the sock at the same place in the yarn's pattern repeat that you cast on. Then be sure the toes and cuffs start at the same place for both socks.

○ With scrap yarn and using the crochet-over-the-needle provisional method (see page 280), cast on 81 stitches. With working yarn, knit 1 row, placing a marker between the 40th and 41st stitches. Work back and forth in stockinette stitch for 2"/5 cm, ending with a wrong-side row.

SHAPING THE HEEL

○ Row 1: Knit to marker, M1, slip marker, K1, M1, knit to end of row.

○ Row 2: Purl.

○ Repeat Rows 1 and 2 twelve more times. *You now have* 107 stitches. Place stitches on hold.

Knitting the Second Half of the Leg

○ Remove the provisional cast on and place 81 stitches on needle. Join yarn and work as for the first half of the leg, leaving stitches on needle.

Joining the Leg

○ Using Kitchener stitch (see page 278), graft the stitches together at the center back, forming a tube.

Knitting the Toe

○ With right side facing and beginning at center front of tube, use double-point needles to pick up and knit (see page 280) 72 stitches evenly around opening, arranging stitches so there are 18 stitches on each of four needles.

o Round 1: Knit to last 3 stitches on Needle 1, K2tog, K1; on Needle 2, K1, ssk, knit to end of needle; on Needle 3, knit to last 3 stitches, K2tog, K1; on Needle 4, K1, ssk, knit to end of round.

o Round 2: Knit.

o Repeat Rounds 1 and 2 nine more times. *You now have* 32 stitches.

o Work Round 1 four times. *You now have* 16 stitches.

o Knit 4 stitches from Needle 1 onto Needle 4. Slip the stitches from Needle 2 to Needle 3. Use Kitchener stitch to join the two sets of 8 stitches together.

Knitting the Cuff

o With right side facing and beginning at center back of tube, use double-point needles to pick up and knit 72 stitches evenly around opening, arranging stitches so there are 18 stitches on each of four needles. Work K1, P1 rib for 1½"/4 cm. Bind off loosely.

Finishing

o Weave in all ends.

It's a **Wrap!**

ᴜᴜᴜᴜᴜᴜᴜᴜᴜᴜᴜᴜᴜᴜᴜᴜ

Scarves and Neck Warmers

ᴜᴜᴜᴜᴜᴜᴜᴜᴜᴜᴜᴜᴜᴜᴜᴜ

Shawls

ᴜᴜᴜᴜᴜᴜᴜᴜᴜᴜᴜᴜᴜᴜᴜᴜ

Shimmy and Shrug

ᴜᴜᴜᴜᴜᴜᴜᴜᴜᴜᴜᴜᴜᴜᴜᴜ

School at Play Scarf

Designed by Sharon A. Winsauer

Fish are romping along this scarf, which is a unique blend of baby alpaca, merino, bamboo, and nylon. They'll swim upstream on half the scarf and downstream on the other!

Knitting the Scarf

○ *Note:* In Row 3 and Row 13 there is an unmatched yarn over in the center of the fish's tail. This stitch is removed with a decrease in Rows 5 and 15.

○ Loosely cast on 43 stitches.

○ Row 1 (WS): Knit.

○ Row 2: K1, *yo, K2tog; repeat from *.

○ Row 3: Purl.

○ Work Rows 1–40 of chart nine times.

○ Next row (RS): K1, *yo, K2tog; repeat from *.

○ Next row: Knit.

○ Loosely bind off knitwise.

Finishing

○ Weave in ends. Block, pinning through yarn overs at the points along the edges.

FINISHED MEASUREMENTS	Approximately 7"/18 cm wide and 48"/122 cm long
YARN	Alpaca With A Twist Socrates, 30% baby alpaca/30% merino wool/20% bamboo/20% nylon, 3.5 oz (100 g)/400 yds (366 m), Color 4017 Macaw
NEEDLES	US 4 (3.5 mm) straight needles *or size you need to obtain correct gauge*
GAUGE	24 stitches and 32 rows = 4"/10 cm in stockinette stitch, blocked
OTHER SUPPLIES	Tapestry needle

SCHOOL AT PLAY CHART

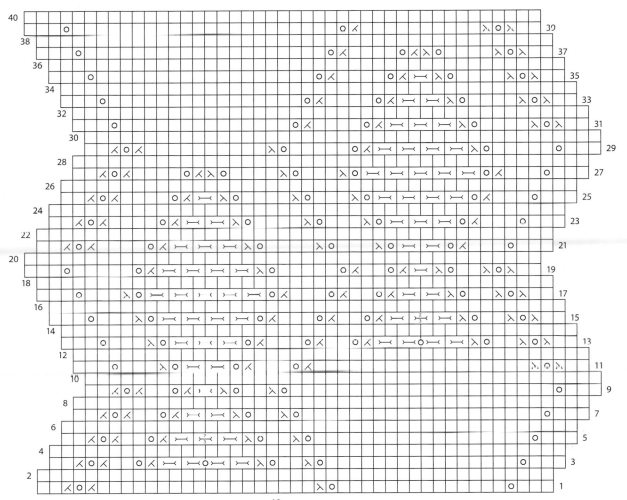

43-STITCH PANEL

Pattern Essentials

MAKE 2 FROM 2

K2tog, leaving stitches on needle, K2tog tbl, drop both stitches from needle.

MAKE 2 FROM 3

K3tog, leaving stitches on needle, K3tog tbl, drop all 3 stitches from needle.

☐	knit
⟋	K2tog
⟍	ssk
○	yarn over
⊢⊣	make 2 from 2
⅔⊣	make 2 from 3

93

The Ericka Scarf

Designed by Gina House

This simple, open lace pattern is easy to knit and works up quickly. It also looks great on both sides! The scarf can be long and narrow or shorter and wider. Each version uses one skein of yarn.

Pattern Essentials

LACE

Row 1: K3, *yo, slip 1, K2, pass slipped stitch over 2 knit stitches; repeat from * to last 3 stitches, K3.

Row 2: K3, purl to last 3 stitches, K3.

Knitting the Scarf

○ Cast on 51 (75) stitches loosely.

○ Knit 4 rows.

○ Work Rows 1 and 2 of Lace pattern until scarf measures 55" (37")/139.5 (94) cm, ending with Row 1.

○ Knit 4 rows.

○ Bind off loosely.

Finishing

○ Weave in ends. Block to open up lacework.

94

FINISHED MEASUREMENTS	Approximately 8" (10½")/20.5 (26.5) cm wide and 60" (44")/152.5 (112) cm long
YARN	Noro Kuryeon Sock Yarn, 70% wool/30% nylon, 3.5 oz (100 g)/459 yds (420 m), Color S40 (Color S92)
NEEDLES	US 6 (4 mm) straight needles *or size you need to obtain correct gauge*
GAUGE	30 stitches = 4"/10 cm in Lace pattern
OTHER SUPPLIES	Tapestry needle

Candleglow Scarf

Designed by Jessica X. Wright-Lichter

Knitted in gorgeously warm yellow tones, the checkerboard mesh pattern resembles flickering candle flames. The corded ribbing provides a nice, firm edge.

Knitting the Scarf

○ Cast on 56 stitches. Work Corded Ribbing for 7 rows.

○ Decrease Row (WS): Work 5 stitches in pattern as established, place marker, P2tog, *P2, P2tog; repeat from * to last 5 stitches, place marker, work 5 stitches in pattern as established. *You now have* 44 stitches.

WORKING CHECKERBOARD MESH:

○ Keeping the first and last 5 stitches in Corded Ribbing pattern as established, follow the chart or written instructions to work Rows 2–20 of Checkerboard Mesh over 34 stitches between the borders. Work Rows 1–20 of Checkerboard Mesh 25 times, then work Row 1 once more.

○ Increase Row (RS): K1, ssk, M1, P2, slip marker, *M1, K3; repeat from * to 4 stitches before marker, M1, K4, M1, slip marker, P2, ssk, M1, K1. *You now have* 56 stitches.

○ Beginning with Row 2 of pattern, work Corded Ribbing for 6 more rows.

○ Bind off in pattern.

Finishing

○ Weave in ends. Block to measurements.

FINISHED MEASUREMENTS	Approximately 6½"/16.5 cm wide and 53"/134.5 cm long
YARN	Madelinetosh Tosh Sock, 100% superwash merino wool, 4.4 oz (125 g)/395 yds (361 m), Gilded
NEEDLES	US 2 (2.75 mm) straight needles *or size you need to obtain correct gauge*
GAUGE	26 stitches = 4"/10 cm in pattern
OTHER SUPPLIES	Stitch markers, tapestry needle

Pattern Essentials

CORDED RIBBING

Row 1 (RS): K1, *ssk, M1, P2; repeat from * to last 3 stitches, ssk, M1, K1.

Row 2: K1, P2, *ssk, M1, P2; repeat from * to last stitch, K1.

CHECKERBOARD MESH

Row 1 and all other odd-numbered WS rows: Purl.

Row 2 (RS): K4, *yo, ssk, K1, (K2tog, yo) twice, K3; repeat from * to end of row.

Row 4: *K3, (yo, ssk) twice, K1, K2tog, yo; repeat from * to last 4 stitches, K4.

Row 6: K2, *(yo, ssk) three times, K4; repeat from * to last 2 stitches, yo, ssk.

Row 8: K1, *(yo, ssk) four times, K2; repeat from * to last 3 stitches, yo, ssk, K1.

Row 10: Repeat Row 6.

Row 12: Repeat Row 4.

Row 14: Repeat Row 2.

Row 16: K2tog, yo, *K4, (K2tog, yo) three times; repeat from * to last 2 stitches, K2.

Row 18: K1, K2tog, yo, *K2, (K2tog, yo) four times; repeat from * to last stitch, K1.

Row 20: Repeat Row 16.

Repeat Rows 1–20 for pattern.

CHECKERBOARD MESH

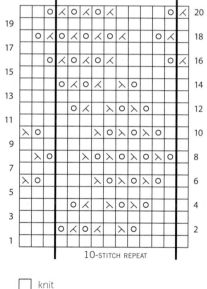

10-STITCH REPEAT

☐ knit
☒ K2tog
☒ ssk
☐ yarn over

Easy Lace Scarf

Designed by Marci Blank

FINISHED MEASUREMENTS	Approximately 8"/20.5 cm wide and 64"/162.5 cm long
YARN	Plymouth Italian Collection Sockotta, 45% cotton/40% superwash wool/15% nylon, 3.5 oz (100 g)/414 yds (379 m), Color 0003
NEEDLES	US 8 (5 mm) straight needles *or size you need to obtain correct gauge*
GAUGE	20 stitches = 4"/10 cm in pattern
OTHER SUPPLIES	Tapestry needle

Because of its airiness, the simple lace pattern used for this scarf lends itself well to a subtly variegated sock yarn. The beige, brown, and black version shown here will go with many outfits!

97

Pattern Essentials

EASY LACE

Row 1 (RS): K4, *(K2tog) twice, (yo, K1) three times, yo, (ssk) twice, K1; repeat from * to last 3 stitches, K3.

Row 2: K4, P35, K4.

Repeat Rows 1–2 for pattern.

Knitting the Scarf

○ Cast on 43 stitches.

○ Knit 6 rows.

○ Begin Easy Lace pattern and work until piece measures 63½"/161.5 cm or desired length.

○ Knit 6 rows.

Finishing

○ Bind off loosely. Weave in ends.

EASY LACE

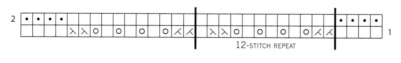

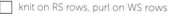

☐   knit on RS rows, purl on WS rows

▪   purl on RS rows, knit on WS rows

K2tog

ssk

○   yarn over

Roses for Rosa Scarf

Designed by Judith Durant

Schaefer Yarns has a line of colorways named for remarkable women in history. This scarf is knitted with the color Rosa Parks, and the roses are a tribute to her courage.

FINISHED MEASUREMENTS	Approximately 4½"/11.5 cm wide and 50"/127 cm long
YARN	Schaefer Yarn Anne, 60% superwash merino wool/25% mohair/15% nylon, 4 oz (113.5 g)/560 yds (512 m), Rosa Parks
NEEDLES	US 2 (2.75 mm) straight needles and set of five US 2 (2.75 mm) double-point needles *or size you need to obtain correct gauge*
GAUGE	35 stitches = 4"/10 cm in pattern
OTHER SUPPLIES	Tapestry needle

Pattern Essentials

BASIC FAGOTING

Row 1: *Yo, K2tog; repeat from * to end of row.

Repeat Row 1 for pattern.

Knitting the Scarf

○ Cast on 40 stitches. Knit 10 rows. Work Basic Fagoting pattern until piece measures 48"/122 cm or desired length. Knit 10 rows. Bind off.

Knitting the Roses (make 12)

○ Cast on 8 stitches. Divide onto four double-point needles and join into a round, being careful not to twist the stitches. Knit 1 round.

○ Round 1: *Yo, K1; repeat from * to end of round. *You now have* 16 stitches.

○ Round 2 and all even-numbered rounds: Knit.

○ Round 3: Repeat Round 1. *You now have* 32 stitches.

○ Round 5: *Yo, K2tog; repeat from * to end of round.

○ Round 7: Repeat Round 1. *You now have* 64 stitches.

○ Round 9: Repeat Round 5.

○ Round 11: Repeat Round 1. *You now have* 128 stitches.

○ Round 12: Knit. Bind off.

Finishing

○ Sew roses to both sides of garter stitch borders, aligning the centers and tacking down as desired. Weave in ends.

Vine Lace Scarf

Designed by Marin J. Melchior

This simple lace scarf is worked in two pieces and joined at the center with Kitchener stitch. It uses a nice open lace that can be worked by a beginning knitter and also enjoyed by a more experienced one. This scarf is knitted with O-Wool Legacy DK, which comes in lovely landscape-inspired colors.

- 2 from left to Right
- needle thru both, wrap
yarn around back needle
(2 loops behind)

Pattern Essentials

VINE LACE

Rows 1 and 3 (WS): Slip 1, purl to end of row.

Row 2: Slip 1, K2, *yo, K2, ssk, K2tog, K2, yo, K1; repeat from * to last stitch, K1.

Row 4: Slip 1, K1, *yo, K2, ssk, K2tog, K2, yo, K1; repeat from * to last 2 stitches, K2.

. . . .

Knitting the Scarf

○ Cast on 31 stitches and purl 1 row. Work Vine Lace pattern until piece measures 33"/84 cm, ending with a wrong-side row. Place stitches on hold. Knit another piece the same as the first and join them together with Kitchener stitch (see page 278).

Finishing

○ Weave in ends, wash, and block.

VINE LACE

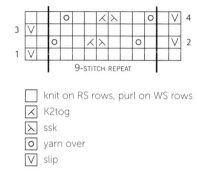

9-STITCH REPEAT

☐ knit on RS rows, purl on WS rows
◿ K2tog
◺ ssk
○ yarn over
V slip

FINISHED MEASUREMENTS	Approximately 6"/15 cm wide and 66"/167.5 cm long
YARN	Vermont Organic Fiber Company O-Wool Legacy DK, 100% certified organic merino wool, 3.5 oz (100 g)/305 yds (280 m), Color 3212 Sprig
NEEDLES	US 8 (5 mm) straight needles *or size you need to obtain correct gauge*
GAUGE	20 stitches = 4" (10 cm) in Vine Lace pattern
OTHER SUPPLIES	Scrap yarn for holders, tapestry needle

Autumn Rose Neck Wrap

Designed by Reneé Barnes

Large and small layered flowers grace the ends of this crocheted warmer. There's a "keyhole" in one end of the scarf to thread the other end through for snugness.

FINISHED MEASUREMENTS	Approximately 4"/10 cm wide and 33"/84 cm long, exclusive of flowers and leaves
YARN	Universal Pace, 75% superwash wool/ 25% polyamide, 1.75 oz (50 g)/220 yds (200 m), Color 09 Persimmon
CROCHET HOOK	US F/5 (3.75 mm) *or size you need to obtain correct gauge*
GAUGE	Three pattern repeats = 5"/12.5 cm
OTHER SUPPLIES	Tapestry needle
SPECIAL ABBREVIATIONS	**dc2tog (double crochet 2 together)** (yarn over, insert hook into next stitch and pull up a loop, yarn over and pull through 2 loops) two times, yarn over and pull through all 3 loops on hook. **dc4tog (double crochet 4 together)** (yarn over, insert hook into next stitch and pull up a loop, yarn over and pull through 2 loops) four times, yarn over and pull through all 5 loops on hook.

Crocheting the Scarf

○ Ch 162. Work Rows 1–5 of Mesh pattern once, then work Rows 2 and 3 once more.

MAKING THE SLIT

○ Next Row: Dc in space formed by ch-2 and tr of previous row, ch 3, skip next sc, sc in next sc, *skip next sc, ch 3, 3 dc in ch-5 space, ch 3, skip next sc, sc in next sc**; repeat from * ten times, ch 16, skip 2 ch-5 spaces, skip next dc, sc in next sc, repeat from * to ** six times, skip next sc, ch 3, 2 dc in ch-6 space, ch 1, turn.

○ Next Row: Sc in second dc, *ch 5, sc in next 3 dc**, repeat from * five times, ch 5, 3 sc in ch-16 sp, ch 5, 3 sc in ch-16 sp; repeat from * to ** eleven times, ch 3, sc in last 2 dc, ch 1, turn.

○ Work Rows 2–5 of Mesh pattern once, then Rows 2 and 3 once more.

○ Finish off.

Crocheting the Two-Layer Rose (make 4)

○ Ch 6, join with slip stitch to first ch to form a ring.

○ Round 1: Ch 3 (counts as dc), work 17 dc into center of ring. Join with slip stitch to top of beginning ch-3. *You now have* 18 dc.

○ Round 2: (Ch 3, skip 2 dc, slipstitch into next dc) six times.

○ Round 3: (Sc, 5 dc, sc) in each ch-3 space around, join with slip stitch to first sc.

○ Round 4: Holding first layer of petals to the front, [ch 4, slipstitch around (in back) of next slip stitch (between petals)] six times.

○ Round 5: (Sc, dc, 4 tr, dc, sc) in each ch-4 space around, join with slip stitch to first sc.

○ Finish off, leaving an 8"/20.5 cm tail for sewing.

Crocheting the Three-Layer Rose (make 2)

○ Ch 4, join with slip stitch to first ch to form a ring.

○ Round 1: Ch 5 (counts as dc and ch 2), (dc in center of ring, ch 2) five times, join with slip stitch to third ch of ch-5.

○ Round 2: (Sc, 4 dc, sc) in each ch-3 space around, join with slip stitch to first sc.

○ Round 3: (Ch 4, slipstitch between last sc of first petal and first sc of next petal) six times.

○ Round 4: (Sc, 5 dc, sc) in each ch-4 space around, join with slip stitch to first sc.

○ Round 5: (Ch 5, slipstitch in slip stitch between petals) six times.

○ Round 6: (Sc, hdc, dc, 4 tr, dc, hdc, sc) in each ch-5 space around.

○ Fasten off, leaving an 8"/20.5 cm tail for sewing.

Crocheting the Leaf
(make 4)

○ Row 1: Ch 4, 4 dc in first ch, turn.

○ Row 2: Ch 3 (counts as dc), dc in first dc, dc in next 3 dc, dc in top of ch-3, turn.

○ Row 3: Ch 3 (counts as dc), dc2tog two times, dc in last st, turn.

○ Row 4: Ch 3, dc4tog beginning with first dc at base of turning chain.

○ Fasten off, leaving an 8"/20.5 cm tail for sewing.

Finishing

○ Arrange roses and leaves on ends of scarf and sew on using tail ends of each motif. Weave in ends.

Pattern Essentials

MESH PATTERN (MULTIPLE OF 8 + 9 STITCHES)

Chain a multiple of 8 plus 10 stitches.

Row 1: Sc in 2nd ch from hook, sc in next ch, *ch 5, skip next 5 ch, sc in next 3 ch; repeat from * to last 7 ch, ch 5, skip next 5 ch, sc in last 2 ch, ch 1, turn.

Row 2: Sc in first sc, *ch 3, skip next sc, 3 dc in ch-5 space, ch 3, skip next sc, sc in next sc; repeat from * across, ch 6, turn.

Row 3: Sc in next 3 dc, *ch 5, sc in next 3 dc; repeat from * across, end ch 2, tr in last sc, ch 3, turn.

Row 4: Dc in space formed by ch 2 and tr of previous row, ch 3, skip next sc, sc in next sc, *skip next sc, ch 3, 3 dc in ch-5 space, ch 3, skip next sc, sc in next sc; repeat from * to last ch-space, skip next sc, ch 3, 2 dc in ch-6 space, ch 1, turn.

Row 5: Sc in 2nd dc, *ch 5, sc in next 3 dc; repeat from * across, ending last repeat, ch 5, sc in last 2 dc, ch 1, turn.

Repeat Rows 2–5 for pattern.

Seattle Bloom Time Scarf

Designed by
Jennifer Chase-Rappaport

This scarf was inspired by the cherry blossom season in Seattle: lovely blossoms on angular branches. The scarf will gain in length when washed, and it can be blocked gently or aggressively, depending on desired length.

Knitting the First Half of Scarf

○ Cast on 51 stitches. Work Seed Stitch until border measures 1"/2.5 cm, ending on a wrong-side row. On last row, place markers after the first 5 stitches and before the last 5 stitches. Continue to work the first and last 5 stitches in Seed Stitch as established and work Chart A between the markers/borders. Work Rows 1–92 of Chart A, then work Rows 81–92 nine more times.

FINISHED MEASUREMENTS	Approximately 9"/23 cm wide and 43"/109 cm long before blocking, 60"/152.5 cm long after blocking
YARN	Hazel Knits Artisan Sock, 90% merino wool/10% nylon, 4.5 oz (125 g)/400 yds (366 m), 50 Rogue (one-of-a-kind color)
NEEDLES	US 5 (3.75 mm) straight needles *or size you need to obtain correct gauge*
GAUGE	24 stitches and 34 rows = 4"/10 cm in stockinette stitch
OTHER SUPPLIES	Stitch markers, tapestry needle

Pattern Essentials

SEED STITCH

Row 1: K1, *P1, K1; repeat from * to end of row.
Repeat Row 1 for pattern.

Knitting the Second Half of Scarf

○ Continuing to work 5-stitch borders in Seed Stitch, work Rows 1–12 of Chart B ten times. Work Rows 13–88 of Chart B. Work 1"/2.5 cm in Seed Stitch for ending border.

Finishing

○ Weave in ends. Wash and block.

CHART A   *Note:* Only right-side rows are charted; purl all wrong-side rows between the borders.

WORK 10 TIMES

41-STITCH PANEL

Symbol key:

☐	knit
⟋	K2tog
⟍	ssk
○	yarn over
⋏	s2kp

CHART B

Note: Only right-side rows are charted; purl all wrong-side rows between the borders.

WORK
10 TIMES

41-STITCH PANEL

	knit
⟋	K2tog
⟍	ssk
○	yarn over
⋏	s2kp

Gambit Unisex Scarf

Designed by
Sarah-Hope Parmeter

This scarf features interlocking chevrons of knit and purl stitches. It begins in the center with a provisional cast on, and it ends in points that echo the chevron pattern. The sample was knit by Chris Polak.

FINISHED MEASUREMENTS	Approximately 7"/18 cm wide and 50"/127 cm long
YARN	Hand Maiden Fine Yarn Casbah, 81% merino wool/9% cashmere/10% nylon, 4 oz (115 g)/355 yds (325 m), Pumpkin
NEEDLES	US 4 (3.5 mm) straight needles *or size you need to obtain correct gauge*
GAUGE	22 stitches and 30 rows = 4"/10 cm in stitch pattern over Chart A
OTHER SUPPLIES	Tapestry needle
ABBREVIATIONS	**LT** left twist **RT** right twist

Pattern Essentials

LEFT TWIST

Knit the second stitch through the back loop and leave it on the needle, then knit the first stitch and slip both stitches off the needle.

RIGHT TWIST

Knit the second stitch and leave it on the needle, then knit the first stitch and slip both stitches off the needle.

Knitting the Scarf

○ Using a provisional method (see page 280), cast on 39 stitches. Work charts as follows. Note that charts begin on a wrong-side row.

○ Work Rows 1–42 of Chart A.

○ Work Rows 1–42 of Chart B.

○ Work Rows 1–50 of Chart C.

○ Work Rows 1–42 of Chart A.

○ Work Rows 1–54 of Chart D.

○ Cut yarn, leaving a 6"/15 cm tail.

○ Undo provisional cast on and place 39 stitches on needle with right side facing.

○ Work Rows 4–42 of Chart A.

○ Work Rows 1–42 of Chart B.

○ Work Rows 1–50 of Chart C.

○ Work Rows 1–42 of Chart A.

○ Work Rows 1–54 of Chart D.

○ Cut yarn, leaving a 6"/15 cm tail.

Finishing

○ Weave in ends. Block lightly.

CHART A

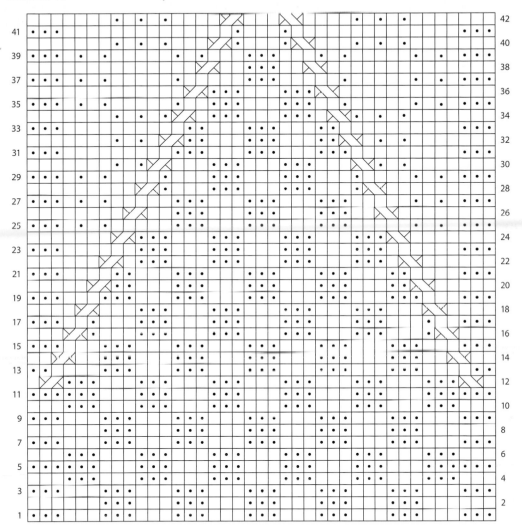

knit on RS rows, purl on WS rows

• purl on RS rows, knit on WS rows

RT

LT

CHART B

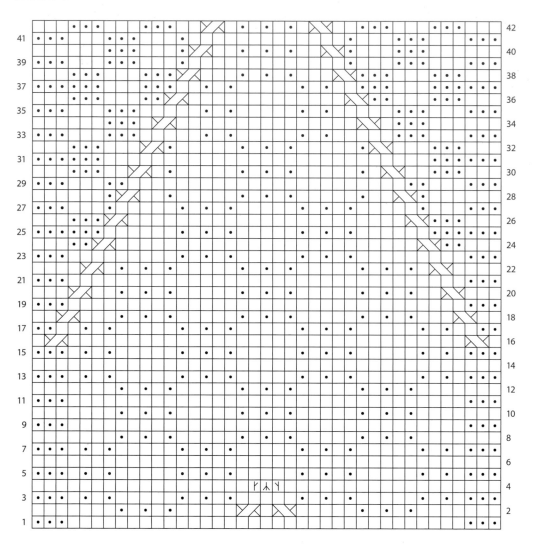

		knit on RS rows, purl on WS rows				left-slanting increase (M1L)
	•	purl on RS rows, knit on WS rows				right-slanting increase (M1R)
	╱	K2tog				2-stitch right cross (RT)
	╲	ssk				2-stitch left cross (LT)
	⋏	s2kp				

CHART C

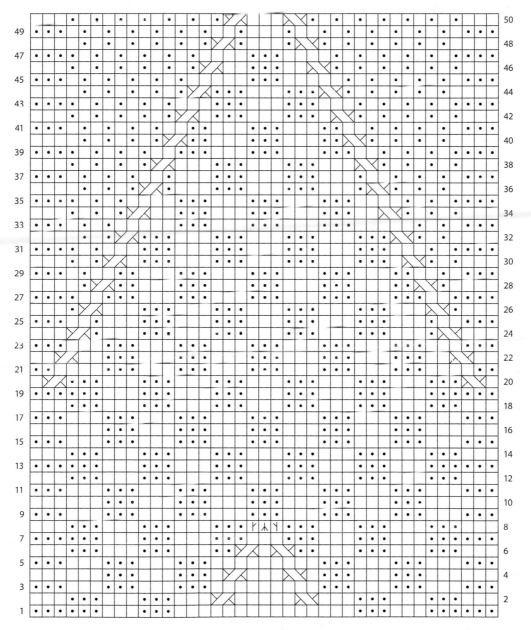

CHART D

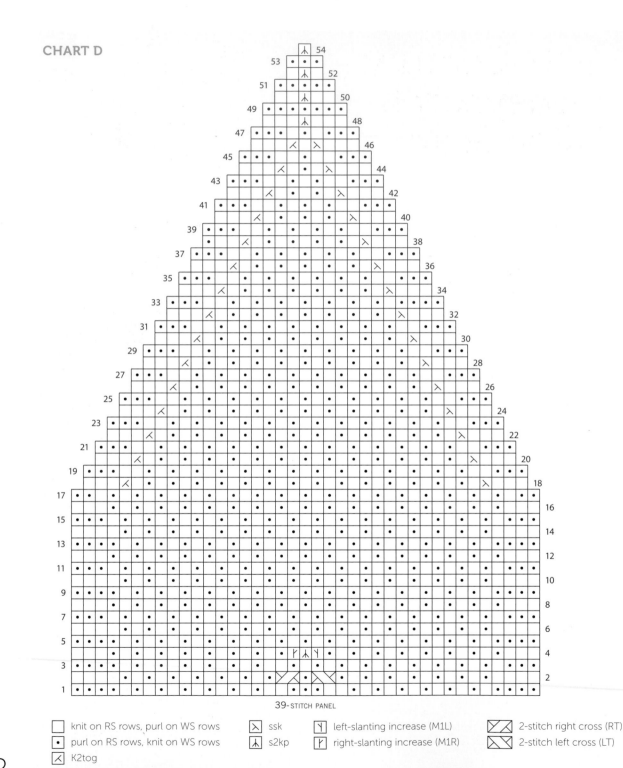

39-STITCH PANEL

	knit on RS rows, purl on WS rows		ssk		left-slanting increase (M1L)		2-stitch right cross (RT)
•	purl on RS rows, knit on WS rows		s2kp		right-slanting increase (M1R)		2-stitch left cross (LT)
	K2tog						

19th-Century Honeycomb Stitch Scarf

Designed by Diana Foster

This scarf was designed for a group called "Old Stone House Knitters" in Vermont to complement their collection of patterns traditional to New England. The stitch pattern comes from *The Workwoman's Guide* by a Lady, 1838.

FINISHED MEASUREMENTS	Approximately 4½"/11.5 cm wide and 55"/140 cm long
YARN	Vermont Organic Fiber Company O-Wool Organic Classic 2-Ply, 100% organic wool, 1.75 oz (50 g)/198 yds (181 m), Color 3104 Sage
NEEDLES	US 7 (4.5 mm) straight needles *or size you need to obtain correct gauge*
GAUGE	18 stitches – 4"/10 cm in garter stitch
OTHER SUPPLIES	Tapestry needle

Knitting the Scarf

○ Loosely cast on 29 stitches.

○ Rows 1–9: Slip 1 purlwise, knit to end of row.

○ Repeat Rows 1 and 2 of Honeycomb stitch for approximately 53"/134.5 cm.

○ Repeat Rows 1–9 for second garter stitch border. Bind off.

Finishing

○ Weave in ends and block.

Pattern Essentials

HONEYCOMB

Row 1: K1, *yo, K2tog; repeat from * to end of row.

Row 2: Knit.

Repeat Rows 1 and 2 for pattern.

Lifted Stitch Scarf

Designed by Carol Scott

With a unique stitch pattern that's pretty on both sides, this scarf is easy to knit and looks fabulous in handpainted sock yarn! The perfect gift for someone special.

FINISHED MEASUREMENTS	Approximately 7"/18 cm wide and 50"/127 cm long
YARN	Misti Alpaca Hand Paint Sock Yarn, 50% alpaca/30% merino wool/10% silk/10% nylon, 3.5 oz (100 g)/437 yds (400 m), Color HS07 Miriam
NEEDLES	US 2 (2.75 mm) straight needles *or size you need to obtain correct gauge*
GAUGE	24 stitches and 48 rows = 4"/10 cm in Lifted Stitch pattern
OTHER SUPPLIES	Tapestry needle

Pattern Essentials

LIFTED STITCH

Row 1 and all odd-numbered rows: Knit.

Row 2: Purl.

Row 4: P3, *P1 in third stitch below the needle (enter the stitch from behind the knitting), drop the stitch from needle as for regular purl, P3; repeat from * to end of row.

Row 6: Purl.

Row 8: P1, *P1 in third stitch below the needle, drop the stitch from needle as for regular purl, P3; repeat from * to last 2 stitches, P1 in third stitch below the needle, drop the next stitch, P1.

Repeat Rows 1–8 for pattern.

RIB

Row 1: *K1, P1; repeat from * to last stitch, K1.

Row 2: *P1, K1; repeat from * to last stitch, P1.

Repeat Rows 1 and 2 for pattern.

Knitting the Scarf

○ Cast on 47 stitches.

○ Work Rows 1–8 of Lifted Stitch pattern for approximately 4"/10 cm, ending with Row 8 of pattern.

○ Work Rows 1 and 2 of Rib pattern three times.

○ Continue in this manner, working 4"/10 cm of Lifted Stitch pattern followed by 6 rows of Rib pattern eight more times.

○ Work Rows 1–8 of Lifted Stitch pattern once more.

○ Bind off loosely.

Finishing

○ Weave in ends. Steam lightly.

Loreli's Gift

Designed by Anne Carroll Gilmour

The lace pattern used here has a "right" and a "wrong" side but is equally attractive on both. The right- and left-hand sides are mirror images, and the scarf is grafted at the center back.

115

FINISHED MEASUREMENTS	Approximately 12"/30.5 cm wide and 60"/152.5 cm long
YARN	Classic Elite Alpaca Sox, 60% alpaca/20% merino wool/20% nylon, 3.5 oz (100 g)/450 yds (411.5 m), Color 1831 Teal
NEEDLES	US 5 (3.75 mm) straight needles *or size you need to obtain correct gauge*
GAUGE	24 stitches = 4"/10 cm in pattern
OTHER SUPPLIES	Scrap yarn for holders, tapestry needle

Knitting the Scarf

○ Using the long-tail method (see page 278), cast on 63 stitches.

○ Knit 1 row. Beginning with Row 1 of chart, work Rows 1–32 of Loreli Lace pattern for four full repeats (128 rows), then work Rows 1–24 once more.

○ Knit 1 row. Place stitches on holder.

○ Knit a second panel as you worked the first, leaving stitches on needle. Use Kitchener stitch (see page 278) to graft the live stitches of the two panels together.

Finishing

○ Weave in ends. Wash and block, pinning out the points.

LORELI LACE

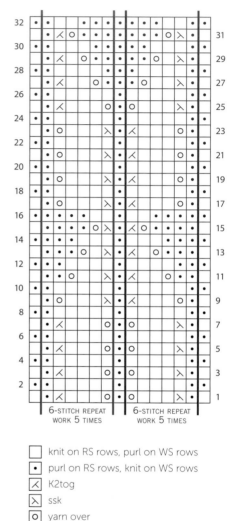

6-STITCH REPEAT WORK 5 TIMES 6-STITCH REPEAT WORK 5 TIMES

	knit on RS rows, purl on WS rows
•	purl on RS rows, knit on WS rows
⟋	K2tog
⟍	ssk
o	yarn over

Lettuce Slide Scarf

Designed by Bobbe Morris

This scarf slides on a thread that runs down its center, allowing you to scrunch it up strategically for extra flair. This one is shown with two flowers, but you may, of course, want more! The scarf is worked back and forth on circular needles to accommodate the large number of stitches.

Knitting the Scarf

○ With larger needle, cast on 213 stitches. Do not join.

○ Work Rows 1 and 2 of Rib pattern.

○ Decrease Row: Continuing in Rib pattern as established, decrease 1 stitch at the beginning and end of the row. *You now have* 211 stitches.

○ Next Row: Work even in pattern as established.

○ Repeat these 2 rows six more times. *You now have* 199 stitches.

○ Change to smaller needle and work 8 rows in garter stitch (knit every row).

FINISHED MEASUREMENTS	Approximately 5½"/14 cm wide and 42"/106.5 cm long before gathering
YARN	Malabrigo Sock, 100% superwash merino wool, 3.5 oz (100 g)/440 yds (402.5 m), Lettuce
NEEDLES	US 9 (5.5 mm) circular needle 24"/60 cm long and US 2 (2.75 mm) circular needle 24" (60 cm) long *or size you need to obtain correct gauge*
GAUGE	20 stitches and 28 rows = 4"/10 cm in pattern on larger needles, slightly stretched
OTHER SUPPLIES	1/B (2.5 mm) crochet hook, tapestry needle
SPECIAL ABBREVIATIONS	**kfbf** knit into front, back, and front of stitch (2 stitches increased)

117

○ Increase Row: Change to larger needle and work Rib pattern, increasing 1 stitch at the beginning and end of the row. *You now have* 201 stitches.

○ Next Row: Work even in pattern as established.

○ Repeat these 2 rows six more times. *You now have* 213 stitches.

○ Bind off loosely. Bring the two corners of the scarf together at each end and sew a short seam, forming the ends into ovals.

Knitting the Ruffle

○ With smaller needle and right side facing, pick up and knit (see page 280) 330 stitches along one side of scarf.

○ Row 1: Increase in every stitch. *You now have* 660 stitches.

○ Row 2: Knit.

○ Row 3: *K1, increase 1; repeat from *. *You now have* 990 stitches.

○ Bind off loosely in K1, P1 rib.

○ Repeat on other side of scarf.

Pattern Essentials

RIB PATTERN

Row 1 (RS): *K3, P2; repeat from * to last 3 stitches, K3.

Row 2: *P3, K2; repeat from * to last 3 stitches, P3.

Repeat Rows 1 and 2 for pattern.

Adding the "Slide"

○ Thread a tapestry needle with approximately 1 yd/91.5 cm of yarn. Fasten the end of the yarn securely to the beginning of one end of the center garter-stitch strip. Weave the yarn in and out of the center of the scarf, going over, then under, 2 stitches, until you reach the other end of the center strip. Fasten the end of the yarn securely to this end of the center strip. You may now manipulate the gathers as you choose — all in the middle, flat in the middle and scrunched at the ends, or evenly distributed.

Knitting the Flowers

○ With smaller needle, cast on 8 stitches.

○ Row 1: Knit.

○ Row 2 (and all even-numbered wrong-side rows): Purl.

○ Row 3: Increase in every stitch. *You now have* 16 stitches.

○ Row 5: Repeat Row 3. *You now have* 32 stitches.

○ Row 7: Kfbf in every stitch. *You now have* 96 stitches.

○ Row 8: Purl.

○ To bind off, slip first stitch to crochet hook, *chain 3, slip next 2 stitches from needle to hook, draw through all 3 stitches on hook; repeat from * until all stitches are bound off. Roll flower up as desired and stitch in place. Repeat for additional flowers.

Horizontal Chevron Petite Fichu

Designed by Betty Balcomb

The long striping pattern of this yarn is the perfect choice for this little neck warmer. The chevron lace pattern creates a wonderful pointy border at the bottom with a soft ripple at the top.

FINISHED MEASUREMENTS	Approximately 7"/18 cm wide and 30"/76 cm long, unbuttoned
YARN	Jojoland Melody, 100% wool, 1.75 oz (50 g)/ 220 yds (200 m), Color MS 26
NEEDLES	US 6 (4 mm) straight needles *or size you need to obtain correct gauge*
GAUGE	18 stitches = 4" (10 cm) in Chevron Lace pattern
OTHER SUPPLIES	Four ⅜"/1 cm buttons, tapestry needle

119

Pattern Essentials

CHEVRON LACE

Row 1 (RS): K6, *yo, K6, s2kp, K6, yo, K3; repeat from * to last 3 stitches, K3.

Row 2: Purl.

Row 3: Repeat Row 1.

Row 4: Knit.

Repeat Rows 1–4 for pattern.

CHEVRON LACE

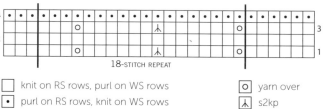

18-STITCH REPEAT

☐ knit on RS rows, purl on WS rows

⊡ purl on RS rows, knit on WS rows

⊙ yarn over

⋏ s2kp

Knitting the Petite Fichu

○ Cast on 171 stitches.

○ Knit 4 rows in garter stitch.

○ Work Rows 1–4 of Chevron Lace 12 times.

○ Knit 3 rows in garter stitch. Bind off loosely.

Finishing

○ Sew two buttons on left side of garter border opposite the first set of double holes in chevron pattern and another two buttons opposite the next set of double holes; the pattern holes on right side of piece are buttonholes. Weave in ends and block.

Traveling Vine Scarf

Designed by Andi Clark

Combining patterns from different sources can yield beautiful projects, such as this vine- and leaf-patterned scarf. The vine pattern is from *Traditional Knitted Lace Shawls* by Martha Waterman, and the leafy edge is found in *Knitting on the Edge* by Nicky Epstein.

FINISHED MEASUREMENTS	Approximately 10"/25.5 cm wide and 60"/152.5 cm long
YARN	Classic Elite Alpaca Sox Kettle Dyes, 60% alpaca/20% merino wool/20% nylon, 3.5 oz (100 g)/450 yds (411.5 m), Color 1870 Watercress
NEEDLES	US 6 (4 mm) straight needles *or size you need to obtain correct gauge*
GAUGE	18 stitches = 4" (10 cm) in Traveling Vine pattern, lightly blocked
OTHER SUPPLIES	Stitch markers, tapestry needle

SCALLOPED LEAVES

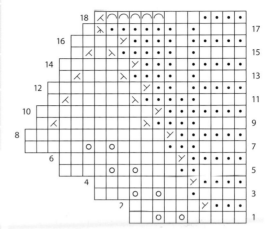

Pattern Essentials
SCALLOPED LEAVES

Cast on 8 stitches.

Row 1 (RS): K5, yo, K1, yo, K2.

Row 2: P6, kfb, K3.

Row 3: K4, P1, K2, yo, K1, yo, K3.

Row 4: P8, kfb, K4.

Row 5: K4, P2, K3, yo, K1, yo, K4.

Row 6: P10, kfb, K5.

Row 7: K4, P3, K4, yo, K1, yo, K5.

Row 8: P12, kfb, K6.

Row 9: K4, P4, ssk, K7, K2tog, K1.

Row 10: P10, kfb, K7.

Row 11: K4, P5, ssk, K5, K2tog, K1.

Row 12: P8, kfb, K2, P1, K5.

Row 13: K4, P1, K1, P4, ssk, K3, K2tog, K1.

Row 14: P6, kfb, K3, P1, K5.

Row 15: K4, P1, K1, P5, ssk, K1, K2tog, K1.

Row 16: P4, kfb, K4, P1, K5.

Row 17: K4, P1, K1, P6, sk2p, K1.

Row 18: P2tog, bind off 5, P3, K4.

Repeat Rows 1–18 for pattern.

TRAVELING VINE

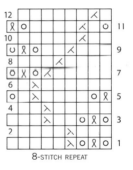

8-STITCH REPEAT

	knit on RS rows, purl on WS rows
•	purl on RS rows, knit on WS rows
⟋	K2tog on RS rows, P2tog on WS rows
⟍	ssk on RS rows, ssp on WS rows
O	yarn over
ℓ	K1 tbl
Y	kfb
⅄	sk2p
⌒	bind off

TRAVELING VINE

Note: Stitch count changes from odd- to even-numbered rows.

Row 1 (RS): *Yo, K1 tbl, yo, ssk, K5; repeat from * to end of row.

Row 2: *P4, ssp, P3; repeat from * to end of row.

Row 3: *Yo, K1 tbl, yo, K2, ssk, K3; repeat from * to end of row.

Row 4: *P2, ssp, P5; repeat from * to end of row.

Row 5: *K1 tbl, yo, K4, ssk, K1, yo; repeat from * to end of row.

Row 6: *P1, ssp, P6; repeat from * to end of row.

Row 7: *K5, K2tog, yo, K1 tbl, yo; repeat from * to end of row.

Row 8: *P3, P2tog, P4; repeat from * to end of row.

Row 9: *K3, K2tog, K2, yo, K1 tbl, yo; repeat from * to end of row.

Row 10: *P5, P2tog, P2; repeat from * to end of row.

Row 11: *Yo, K1, K2tog, K4, yo, K1 tbl; repeat from * to end of row.

Row 12: *P6, P2tog, P1; repeat from * to end of row.

Repeat Rows 1–12 for pattern.

Knitting the Scarf

○ Cast on 8 stitches. Work Rows 1–18 of Scalloped Leaves pattern three times. Bind off. Repeat for second strip of three leaves.

○ With right side of one leaf strip facing, pick up and knit (see page 280) 46 stitches along garter edge.

○ Next Row (WS): K3, place marker, P40, place marker, K3.

○ Next Row (RS): K3, work Row 1 of the Traveling Vine pattern five times across row, K3. Keeping first and last 3 stitches in garter stitch, continue working the Traveling Vine pattern as established until scarf measures 54"/137 cm, ending with Row 12. With right side of second leaf strip facing, pick up and knit 46 stitches along garter edge. Graft scarf and edging together.

Finishing

○ Weave in ends. Block to size.

Athena Scarf

Designed by Tonia Barry

Named for the Greek goddess of heroic endeavor, this lacy scarf has a subtle bobble pattern on either side of the lace panels. It looks equally lovely in green or terra cotta and can be worked in a variety of gauges.

FINISHED MEASUREMENTS	Approximately 10"/25.5 cm wide and 48"/122 cm long; 8½"/21.5 cm wide and 62"/157.5 cm long
YARN	Ivy Brambles Sockscene Sock Yarn, 100% superwash merino wool, 4 oz (113.5 g)/410 yds (375 m), Holly; Madelinetosh Tosh Sock, 100% superwash merino wool, 4 oz (113.5 g)/395 yds (361 m), Terra
NEEDLES	US 8 (5 mm) straight needles *or size you need to obtain correct gauge*
GAUGE	Sockscene: 20 stitches and 25 rounds = 4"/10 cm in pattern, blocked; Tosh Socks: 23 stitches and 29 rounds = 4"/10 cm in pattern, blocked
OTHER SUPPLIES	Tapestry needle
SPECIAL ABBREVIATIONS	**MB (make bobble)** (knit 1, [yarn over, knit 1] twice) in next stitch. With left-hand needle, skip first stitch, slip second stitch over first stitch, slip third stitch over first stitch, slip fourth stitch over first stitch, slip fifth stitch over first stitch.

Pattern Essentials

ATHENA LACE

Row 1 (RS): Slip 1 pwise wyif, K2, (P2, MB, P2, K1, yo, K3tog, yo, K3, yo, sk2p, yo, K4) twice, P2, MB, P2, K3.

Row 2 and all even-numbered WS rows through Row 12: Slip 1 pwise wyif, K4, P1, K2, (P14, K2, P1, K2) twice, K3.

Row 3: Slip 1 wyif, K2, (P2tog, yo, K1, yo, P2tog, yo, K3tog, yo, K5, yo, sk2p, yo, K3) twice, P2tog, yo, K1, yo, P2tog, K3.

Row 5: Slip 1 wyif, K2, (P2, MB, P2, K5, yo, K3tog, yo, K1, yo, sk2p, yo, K2) twice, P2, MB, P2, K3.

Row 7: Slip 1 wyif, K2, (P2tog, yo, K1, yo, P2tog, K4, yo, K3tog, yo, K3, yo, sk2p, yo, K1) twice, P2tog, yo, K1, yo, P2tog, K3.

Row 9: Slip 1 wyif, K2, (P2, MB, P2, K3, yo, K3tog, yo, K5, yo, sk2p, yo) twice, P2, MB, P2, K3.

Row 11: Slip 1 wyif, K2, (P2tog, yo, K1, yo, P2tog, K2, yo, K3tog, yo, K1, yo, sk2p, yo, K5) twice, P2tog, yo, K1, yo, P2tog, K3.

Repeat Rows 1–12 for pattern

ATHENA LACE

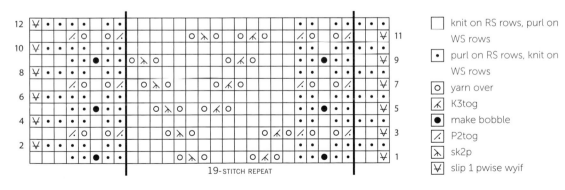

19-STITCH REPEAT

	knit on RS rows, purl on WS rows
•	purl on RS rows, knit on WS rows
O	yarn over
⋏	K3tog
●	make bobble
⁄	P2tog
⋌	sk2p
Ⴡ	slip 1 pwise wyif

Knitting the Scarf

○ Loosely cast on 49 stitches. Knit 4 rows.

○ Following the chart or written instructions, work Rows 1–12 of Athena Lace pattern until piece measures about 48" (62")/122 (157.5) cm.

○ Knit 3 rows.

○ Bind off loosely in pattern.

Finishing

○ Weave in ends. Block scarf to measurements.

Motorcycle Mama's Neck Warmer

Designed by Judith Durant

File this one under "practical," up a few entries before "pretty." This cuff fits snugly around the neck and flares slightly toward the chin and a bit more so toward the sternum. No matter how fast you go, it stays in place with nothing flapping about.

FINISHED MEASUREMENTS	Approximately 9"/23 cm circumference at midneck, unstretched
YARN	Malabrigo Sock, 100% superwash merino wool, 3.5 oz (100 g)/440 yds (402 m), Color 000 Tiziano Red
NEEDLES	Set of five US 1.5 (2.5 mm) double-point needles *or size you need to obtain correct gauge*
GAUGE	60 stitches = 4"/10 cm in K3, P2 rib, unstretched
OTHER SUPPLIES	One US 3 (3.25 mm) straight needle for cast on, tapestry needle

Knitting the Warmer

o Using the straight needle and long-tail method (see page 278), cast on 168 stitches. Divide stitches evenly onto four double-point needles. Join into a round, being careful not to twist the stitches.

KNITTING THE TOP RIBBING

o Work K4, P2 rib for 1½"/4 cm.

KNITTING THE MIDNECK RIBBING

o Next Round: *K1, K2tog, K1, P2; repeat from * to end of round. *You now have 140 stitches.*
o Work K3, P2 rib for 3"/7.5 cm.

KNITTING THE BOTTOM RIBBING

o Next Round: *K1, M1, K1, M1, K1, P2; repeat from * to end of round. *You now have 196 stitches.*
o Work K5, P2 rib for 1½"/4 cm.

Finishing

o To ensure maximum stretch at the bottom, instead of binding off, cut the yarn leaving a 30"/76 cm tail. Thread tail onto tapestry needle and draw through all stitches on needle. Stretch the bottom of the warmer to its maximum, allowing the tail to move through the stitches. Fasten off the tail and weave in the ends.

The Celeste Shawl

Designed by René E. Wells

Flowers bloom in neatly planted rows and then burst into a beaded border in this shawl, worked from the back neck down. Unique construction makes this shawl sit nicely on the shoulders.

FINISHED MEASUREMENTS	Approximately 17"/43 cm deep at center back
YARN	South West Trading Company Tofutsies, 50% superwash wool/25% Soysilk brand fiber/22.5% cotton/2.5% chitin, 3.5 oz (100 g)/465 yds (425 m), Color 733 Magenta
NEEDLES	US 7 (4.5 mm) circular needle 24"/60 cm long *or size you need to obtain correct gauge*
GAUGE	21 stitches = 4" (10 cm) in stockinette stitch, blocked
OTHER SUPPLIES	Scrap yarn and crochet hook for provisional cast on, stitch markers, 552 (50 g) size 6° seed beads, steel crochet hook size 11 (1.1 mm) or smaller for placing beads, tapestry needle
SPECIAL ABBREVIATIONS	**HB (hook bead)** work stitch as indicated, pick up bead onto crochet hook, pick up stitch with hook, slide bead onto stitch, replace stitch on right-hand needle.

Setting Up

○ Using the crochet chain provisional method (see page 281), cast on 5 stitches.

○ Setup Row: K2, P1, K2.

○ Rows 1–22: Slip 1 purlwise wyif, K1, P1, K2.

○ Rotate piece 90° so that the slip-stitched edge is up and stitches are on right-hand needle; there are 11 slipped stitches. *Wyif, insert right-hand needle from back to front under both legs of the next slipped stitch, wrap yarn purlwise and draw up a purl stitch onto right-hand needle; repeat from * 10 more times. Carefully unzip the provisional cast on and place the 5 stitches onto left-hand needle. K2, P1, K2. *You now have* 21 stitches: 5 border stitches, 11 shawl stitches, 5 border stitches.

Knitting the Shawl

KNITTING CHART A

○ Row 1: Slip 1 purlwise wyif, K1, P1, K2, place marker, (work Row 1 of Chart A, place marker, K1, place marker) two times, work Row 1 of Chart A, place marker, K2, P1, K2.

○ Row 2: Slip 1 purlwise wyif, K1, P1, K2, slip marker, purl to last 5 stitches, slip marker, K2, P1, K2.

○ Continue in established border and Chart A pattern, keeping the single stitches between chart repeats in stockinette stitch. Work through Row 24. *You now have 93 stitches.*

KNITTING CHART B

○ Row 1: Work 5-stitch border, slip marker, (work Row 1 of Chart B, slip marker, K1, slip marker) two times, work Row 1 of Chart B, slip marker, work 5-stitch border. Continue in established patterns through Row 32. *You now have 189 stitches.*

KNITTING CHART C

○ Row 1: Work 5-stitch border, slip marker (work Row 1 of Chart C, slip marker, K1, slip marker) two times, work Row 1 of Chart C, slip marker, work 5-stitch border. Continue in established patterns through Row 32. *You now have 285 stitches.*

KNITTING CHART D

○ Row 1: Work 5-stitch border, slip marker, (work Chart D1 to marker, slip marker, K1, HB, slip marker) two times, work Chart D1 to marker, slip marker, work 5-stitch border. Continue in established patterns through Row 8, then work Rows 1–8 of Charts D2 and D3. *You now have 357 stitches.*

KNITTING CHART E

○ Row 1: Work 5-stitch border, slip marker, (work Chart E to marker, slip marker, K1, HB, slip marker) two times, work Chart E to marker, slip marker, work 5-stitch border. Continue in established patterns through Row 5.

○ Bind off on Row 6 as follows: K1, *K1, slip left-hand needle into front of the 2 stitches on right-hand needle and knit them together; repeat from * until all stitches are bound off.

Finishing

○ Weave in ends. Hand wash gently. Lay flat to dry.

CHART B   *Note:* This chart begins on facing page.

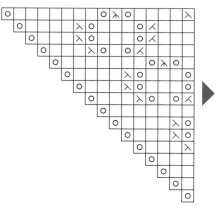

CHART A

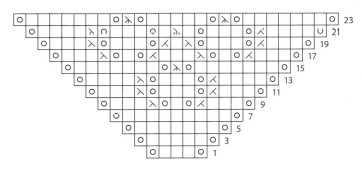

Note: Only right-side rows are charted.
Purl all wrong-side rows.

☐ knit
ↅ K2tog
ↆ ssk
○ yarn over
⅄ slip 2 kwise, k1, p2sso

CHART B (CONTINUED ON FACING PAGE)

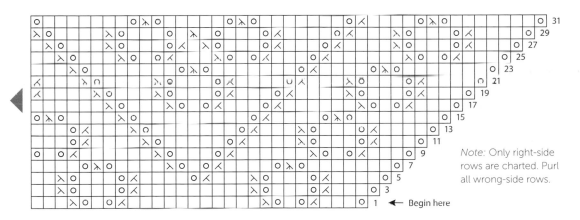

Note: Only right-side
rows are charted. Purl
all wrong-side rows.

← Begin here

CHART C

Note: This chart begins on facing page.

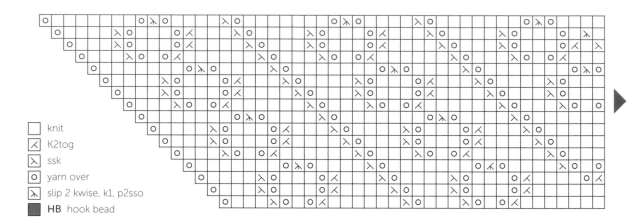

☐ knit

⊿ K2tog

☒ ssk

○ yarn over

⅄ slip 2 kwise, k1, p2sso

■ **HB** hook bead

CHART D1, D2, AND D3

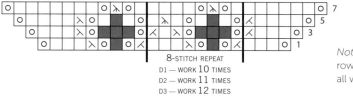

8-STITCH REPEAT
D1 — WORK 10 TIMES
D2 — WORK 11 TIMES
D3 — WORK 12 TIMES

Note: Only right-side rows are charted. Purl all wrong-side rows.

CHART C

(start here and continue on facing page)

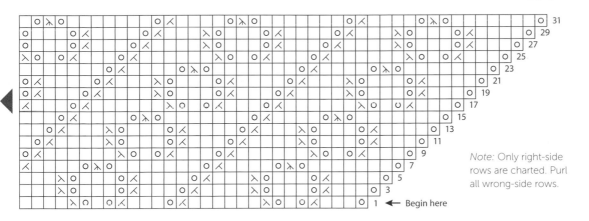

Note: Only right-side rows are charted. Purl all wrong-side rows.

← Begin here

CHART E

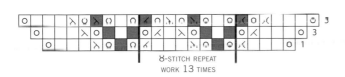

8-STITCH REPEAT
WORK 13 TIMES

Note: Only right-side rows are charted. Purl all wrong-side rows.

Clover Honey Shawlette

Designed by Hannah Six

Beads are all the rage these days, and here they're used to trim a lovely shawlette of shaped garter stitch with a lace insert at the back. This one stays on your shoulders with style.

FINISHED MEASUREMENTS	Approximately 46"/117 cm wide and 16"/41 cm deep
YARN	Shalimar Yarns Zoe Sock, 100% superwash merino wool, 3.5 oz (100 g)/450 yds (411 m), Sno Pea
NEEDLES	US 5 (3.75 mm) circular needle 32"/81 cm long *or size you need to obtain correct gauge*
GAUGE	22 stitches and 40 rows = 4" (10 cm) in garter stitch
OTHER SUPPLIES	Stitch markers, 6"/15 cm dental floss, sewing needle, 48 g size E Czech glass beads, tapestry needle
SPECIAL ABBREVIATIONS	**PB** place bead **RT** right twist

Knitting the Shawl

○ Cast on 41 stitches.

○ Setup Row 1 (WS): Slip 1 purlwise wyif, K1, place marker, K1, place marker, K35, place marker, K1, place marker, K2.

○ Setup Row 2: Slip 1 purlwise wyif, K1, slip marker, yo, K1, yo, slip marker, K2, (yo, ssk, K5, K2tog, yo, K2) three times, slip marker, yo, K1, yo, slip marker, K2.

BEGINNING THE LACE INSERT

○ Next Row (WS): Slip 1 purlwise wyif, K1, slip marker, knit to next marker, slip marker, P35 (Row 2 of Clover Honey Lace), slip marker, knit to next marker, slip marker, K2.

○ Next Row: Slip 1 purlwise wyif, K1, slip marker, yo, knit to next marker, yo, slip marker, work Clover Honey Lace (beginning with Row 3) to next marker, slip marker, yo, knit to next marker, yo, slip marker, K2.

Pattern Essentials

PLACE BEAD

With floss threaded onto sewing needle, bring needle down through a bead, through the stitch to be beaded, and up through the bead. Holding the floss taut, push the bead down onto the stitch, place the stitch back on the left-hand needle, and remove the floss and set aside.

RIGHT TWIST

K2tog but leave stitches on needle, knit the first stitch, slip both stitches from needle.

CLOVER HONEY LACE

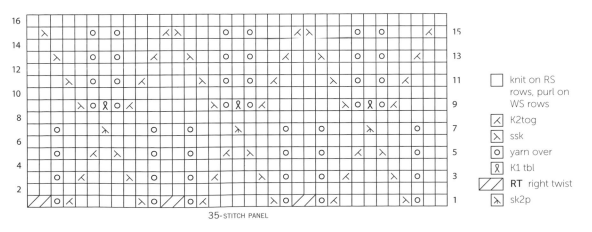

35-STITCH PANEL

☐	knit on RS rows, purl on WS rows
⊠	K2tog
⊠	ssk
⊡	yarn over
⅋	K1 tbl
⧄	**RT** right twist
⊼	sk2p

○ Repeat Rows 1 and 2, working through rows of lace chart as established, until you have 21 stitches on each side of the lace panel, ending with a wrong-side row.

BEGINNING THE SHOULDER SHAPING

○ Row 1 (RS): Slip 1 purlwise wyif, K1, slip marker, yo, K9, M1R, place marker, K1, M1L, K9, yo, slip marker, work lace chart as established, slip marker, yo, K9, M1R, place marker, K1, M1L, K9, yo, slip marker, K2.

○ Row 2: Slip 1 purlwise wyif, knit to lace panel marker, slip marker, work lace chart as established, slip marker, knit to end of row.

○ Row 3: Slip 1 purlwise wyif, K1, slip marker, yo, knit to marker, M1R, slip marker, K1, M1L, knit to marker, yo, slip marker, work lace chart as established, slip marker, yo, knit to marker, M1R, slip marker, K1, M1L, knit to marker, yo, slip marker, K2.

○ Repeat Rows 2 and 3 until piece measures 4"/10 cm from beginning of shoulder shaping. Remove shoulder increase markers only.

CONTINUING WITHOUT SHOULDER SHAPING

○ Row 1 (WS): Slip 1 purlwise wyif, K1, slip marker, knit to marker, slip marker, P35, slip marker, knit to marker, slip marker, K2.

○ Row 2: Slip 1 purlwise wyif, K1, slip marker, yo, knit to marker, yo, slip marker, work lace chart as established, slip marker, yo, knit to marker, yo, slip marker, K2.

○ Continue as established until you have completed the lace chart five times, ending on a wrong-side row.

Binding Off with Beads

○ *Bind off 3 stitches, PB; repeat from * along three lower edges of shawl. Cut yarn but do not weave in ends.

Finishing

○ Wash shawl and pin out on blocking board, being careful not to create "points" along the edges. Allow to dry. Weave in ends.

Wisteria Arbor Shawl

Designed by Carla Kisielnicki

This lovely shawl is fast and easy to knit. And the best part is that the pattern creates deep scalloped edges, so there's no need for a separate border! The 12-row pattern is simple enough for beginners, yet enjoyable for more experienced knitters as well.

FINISHED MEASUREMENTS	Approximately 60"/152.5 cm wide and 25"/63.5 cm deep
YARN	Dream in Color Starry, 98% superfine Australian merino superwash/2% silver fibers, 4 oz (114 g)/450 yds (411 m), Color VF450 Pansy Golightly
NEEDLES	US 9 (5.5 mm) circular needle 32"/81 cm long *or size you need to obtain correct gauge*
GAUGE	One pattern repeat of 13 stitches and 12 rows = 2¾"/7 cm by 2"/5 cm, blocked
OTHER SUPPLIES	Tapestry needle

Knitting the Shawl

○ Using the knitted-on method (see page 278), cast on 15 stitches. Work Rows 1–12 of Foaming Waves Lace pattern.

○ Continuing in pattern, use the knitted-on method to cast on 13 stitches at the beginning of the next 2 rows. *You now have* 41 stitches: 2 edge stitches and three pattern repeats.

○ Work Rows 3–12 of pattern.

○ Continue in this manner, casting on 13 stitches on Rows 1 and 2 of each pattern repeat until you have 223 stitches: 2 edge stitches and 17 pattern repeats.

Pattern Essentials

FOAMING WAVES LACE

Rows 1–4: Knit to last stitch, slip 1 purlwise wyif.

Rows 5, 7, 9, and 11: K1 (edge stitch), *K1, (K2tog) twice, (yo, K1) three times, yo, (K2tog tbl) twice, K1; repeat from * to last stitch, slip 1 purlwise wyif (edge stitch).

Rows 6, 8, 10, and 12: K1 (edge stitch), purl to last stitch, slip 1 purlwise wyif (edge stitch).

Repeat Rows 1–12 for pattern.

RUSSIAN BIND OFF

*K2tog tbl, keeping resulting stitch loose and placing the stitch back on left-hand needle; repeat from * until 1 stitch remains. Pull yarn through last stitch.

○ Work Rows 1–12 of lace pattern two more times without adding stitches, then work Rows 1 and 2 once.

Finishing

○ Bind off loosely using the Russian bind off (see page 135). Weave in ends. Wet the shawl and block, pinning out each point so that it stands out sharply, and pinning the waves created at the top of the shawl.

FOAMING WAVES LACE

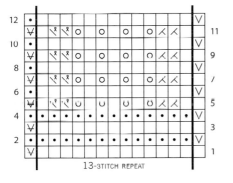

13-STITCH REPEAT

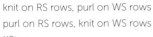

	knit on RS rows, purl on WS rows
•	purl on RS rows, knit on WS rows
⟋	K2tog
○	yarn over
V	slip 1 pwise on WS
⊬	slip 1 pwise on RS
⟍	K2tog tbl

Swan Shawl

Designed by Rebecca Hatcher

The delicate lace in this triangular shawl is at least as graceful as the wings of a swan. The swan is a symbol of love and fidelity, and this shawl would make a lovely wedding gift.

FINISHED MEASUREMENTS	Approximately 58"/147.5 cm at widest point and 24"/61 cm long at center
YARN	Schaefer Yarn Anne, 60% superwash merino wool/25% mohair/15% nylon, 4 oz (113.5 g)/ 560 yds (512 m), Chamomile
NEEDLES	US 6 (4 mm) circular needle 24"/60 cm long *or size you need to obtain correct gauge*
GAUGE	16 stitches and 18 rows = 4" (10 cm) in Chart A lace pattern, blocked
OTHER SUPPLIES	Scrap yarn for cast on, crochet hook (optional), two stitch markers, tapestry needle

Knitting the Shawl

○ Using a provisional method (see page 280), cast on 3 stitches. Knit 50 rows, creating a strip with 25 garter ridges. Pick up and knit (see page 280) 25 stitches along one edge of strip, then remove the provisional cast on and knit these 3 stitches. *You now have 31 stitches.*

○ Setup Row (WS): K3, place marker, P25, place marker, K3.

○ Work lace patterns as follows:

○ Row 1: K3, work Row 1 of Chart A, slip marker, work Row 1 of Chart B, slip marker, work Row 1 of Chart A, K3.

○ Row 2 and all WS rows: K3, purl to last 3 stitches, K3.

○ Row 3: K3, work Row 3 of Chart A, slip marker, work Row 3 of Chart B, slip marker, work Row 3 of Chart A, K3.

o Continue as established, working 3 border stitches, Chart A, Chart B, Chart A, and 3 border stitches as follows:

o Work Rows 1–16 of Chart A once, then work Rows 17–24 seventeen times, repeating the center 8-stitch repeat as required for the number of stitches on needle, then work Rows 25–30 and *at the same time* work Rows 1–14 of Chart B 11 times, then work Rows 15–18. *You now have* 333 stitches.

o Next Row (RS): K3, work Row 31 of Chart A, slip marker, work Row 19 of Chart B, slip marker, work Row 31 of Chart A, K3. Work one wrong-side row as established.

Finishing

o Bind off loosely on right side. Weave in ends and block firmly, pulling yarn overs along bound-off edge into points and creating a scalloped border.

CHART A

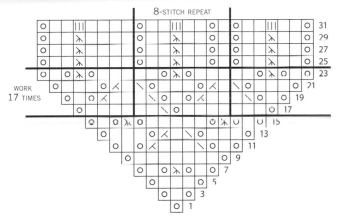

WORK 17 TIMES

8-STITCH REPEAT

CHART B

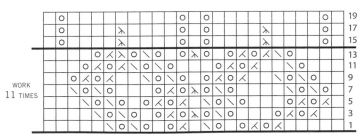

WORK 11 TIMES

25-STITCH PANEL

	knit
⊿	K2tog
O	yarn over
⟍	skp
木	sk2p
木	K3tog
|||	knit 3

Note: Only right-side rows are charted. Purl all wrong-side rows.

Petal Shawlette

Designed by Bonnie Evans

The pattern for this shawl is an old lace tablecloth design by Marianne Kinzel, which appeared in *The First Book of Modern Lace Knitting* (Dover Publications, 1972).

FINISHED MEASUREMENTS	Approximately 50"/127 cm at widest and 24"/61 cm at deepest after blocking
YARN	Fleece Artist Merino 2/6, 100% merino wool, 4 oz (115 g)/355½ yds (325 m), Hercules
NEEDLES	US 4 (3.5 mm) circular needle 24"/60 cm long *or size you need to obtain correct gauge*
GAUGE	20 stitches = 4" (10 cm) in stockinette stitch after blocking
OTHER SUPPLIES	Locking stitch markers, one US 4 (3.5 mm) double-point needle, tapestry needle

Pattern Essentials

LACE LEAF EDGING

Row 1 (RS): K1, P1, K1, (yo, K1) twice, P1.

Row 2: K1, P5, K1, K2tog.

Row 3: K1, P1, M1PL, K2, yo, K1, yo, K2, P1.

Row 4: K1, P7, K2, K2tog.

Row 5: K1, P2, M1PL, K3, yo, K1, yo, K3, P1.

Row 6: K1, P9, K3, K2tog.

Row 7: K1, P3, M1PL, skp, K5, K2tog, P1.

Row 8: K1, P7, K4, K2tog.

Row 9: K1, P2, K1, P1, M1LP, skp, K3, K2tog, P1.

Row 10: K1, P5, K2, P1, K2, K2tog.

Row 11: (K1, P2) twice, M1PL, skp, K1, K2tog, P1.

Row 12: K1, P3, K3, P1, K2, K2tog.

Row 13: K1, P2, K1, P3, M1PL, sk2p, P1.

Row 14: Slip 1, bind off 4 (including slipped stitch), K1, P1, K2, K2tog.

Knitting the Shawl

○ *Note:* Only right-side (odd-numbered) rows are charted; purl all wrong-side rows. A circular needle is used to accommodate the large number of stitches.

○ Using the cable method (see page 276), cast on 5 stitches, placing markers after the first and third stitches.

KNITTING CHART A

○ Beginning with Row 1 of Chart A, work 1 edge stitch, then work stitches between repeat lines twice. The last stitch in each row of the chart represents both the center and the last stitch of each row of the shawl. Continue in established pattern through Row 25, then purl Row 26. *You now have* 69 stitches.

CHART A

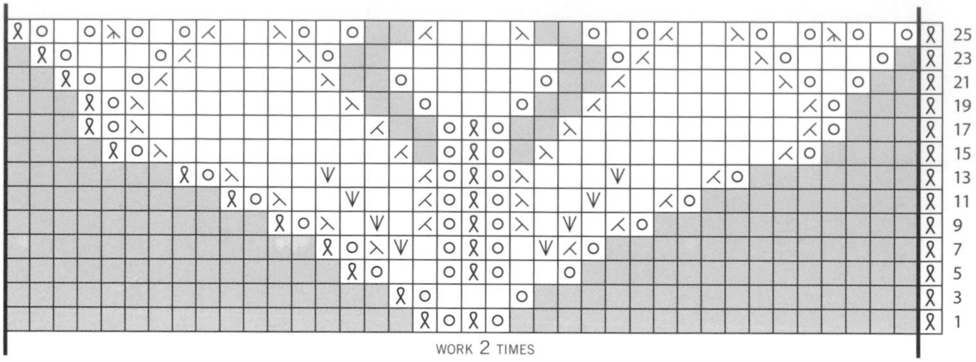
25
23
21
19
17
15
13
11
9
7
5
3
1
WORK 2 TIMES

CHARTS B1 AND B2

Note: This chart begins on facing page.

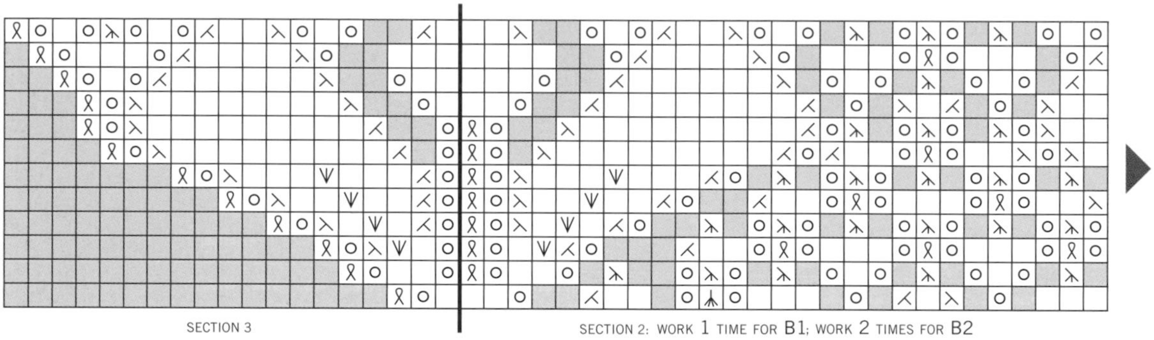
SECTION 3
SECTION 2: WORK 1 TIME FOR B1; WORK 2 TIMES FOR B2

CHART C

Note: This chart begins on facing page.

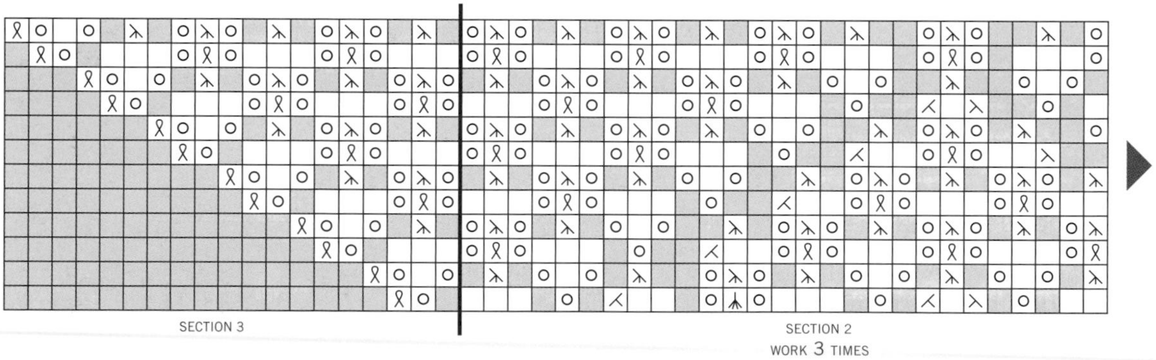
SECTION 3
SECTION 2
WORK 3 TIMES

CHART D

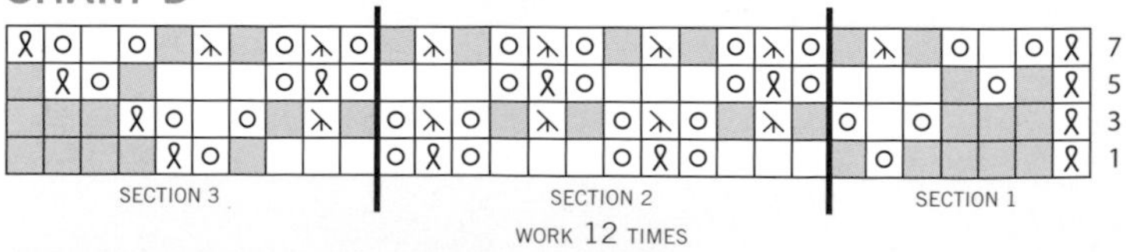
7
5
3
1
SECTION 3
SECTION 2
WORK 12 TIMES
SECTION 1

CHARTS B1 AND B2

(start here and continue on facing page)

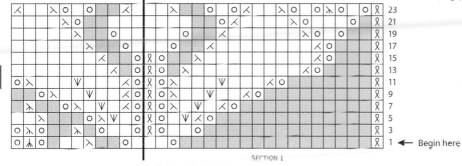

23
21
19
17
15
13
11
9
7
5
3
1 ← Begin here

SECTION 1

CHART C

(start here and continue on facing page)

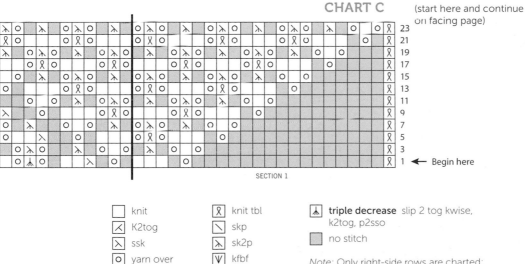

23
21
19
17
15
13
11
9
7
5
3
1 ← Begin here

SECTION 1

	knit		knit tbl		**triple decrease** slip 2 tog kwise, k2tog, p2sso
	K2tog		skp		no stitch
	ssk		sk2p		
	yarn over		kfbf		

Note: Only right-side rows are charted; purl all wrong-side rows.

KNITTING CHART B

○ Keeping the first marker in place, remove remaining markers. Beginning with Row 1 of Chart B1, work 1 edge stitch, slip marker, *work Section 1, place marker, work Section 2 once, place marker, work Section 3, place marker; repeat from * once to complete the row, omitting last place marker. Work in established pattern through Row 23. Purl Row 24. *You now have* 129 stitches.

○ Keeping the first marker in place, remove remaining markers. Beginning with Row 1 of Chart B2, work 1 edge stitch, slip marker, *work Section 1, place marker, (work Section 2, place marker) two times, work Section 3, place marker; repeat from * to complete the row, omitting last place marker. Work in established pattern through Row 23. Purl Row 24. *You now have* 189 stitches.

KNITTING CHART C

○ Keeping the first marker in place, remove remaining markers. Beginning with Row 1 of Chart C, work 1 edge stitch, slip marker, *work Section 1, place marker, (work Section 2, place marker) three times, work Section 3, place marker; repeat from * to complete the row, omitting last place marker. Work in established pattern through Row 23. Purl Row 24. *You now have* 201 stitches.

KNITTING CHART D

○ Keeping the first marker in place, remove remaining markers. Beginning with Row 1 of Chart D, work 1 edge stitch, slip marker, *work Section 1, (work Section 2, place marker) 12 times, place marker, work Section 3, place marker; repeat from * to complete the row, omitting last place marker. Work in established pattern through Row 7. Purl Row 8. *You now have* 217 stitches. Break yarn.

Knitting the Leaf Edging

○ With right side of shawl facing, cast on 6 stitches at left end of circular needle, push them toward the body stitches, turn work. Using the double-point needle, K5, K2tog (the last edging stitch together with the first body stitch). Turn.

○ Begin working Rows 1–14 of Leaf Lace Edging, until you have worked all the way around the outer edge of the shawl and all live stitches from the shawl body have been worked. Bind off. *Note:* At the center back of the shawl, it may be necessary to work a few extra, unattached rows to accommodate the curve or to even out the leaf repeats. Simply work a few extra rows on each side of the center point without attaching them to the shawl body.

Finishing

○ Weave in ends. Block vigorously.

Calypso Shrug/ Shoulder Wrap

Designed by Debbie Haymark

A light and lacy shrug is perfect for those hot summer days when air conditioners run full blast! This one looks great with jeans, black slacks, sundresses, and capris. Unbuttoned, it becomes a small shawl.

Knitting the Shrug

o Cast on 76 stitches.

o Row 1: K3, place marker, (K10, place marker) seven times, K3.

o Row 2: Knit.

o Row 3: Knit.

o Keeping 3 knit stitches at each edge, work Rows 1–8 of Seafoam stitch pattern between the markers 28 times, then work Rows 1–5 once.

o Knit 2 rows. Bind off loosely.

SIZES AND FINISHED MEASUREMENTS	Woman's medium, approximately 17"/43 cm wide and 37"/94 cm long
YARN	Berroco Sox Metallic, 73% superwash wool/ 25% nylon/2% other fiber, 3.5 oz (100 g)/ 380 yds (350 m), Color 1375 Guava
NEEDLES	US 6 (4 mm) circular needle 16"/40 cm long *or size you need to obtain correct gauge*
GAUGE	18 stitches = 4" (10 cm) in pattern, blocked. *Note: Gauge is not critical to this project.*
OTHER SUPPLIES	Stitch markers, size 8 (1.5 mm) steel crochet hook, 400 (approximately 35 g) size 6° seed beads, two ½"/1.3 cm shank buttons
SPECIAL ABBREVIATIONS	**HB (hook bead)** pick up bead onto crochet hook, remove stitch from needle with hook, slide bead onto stitch, replace stitch on left-hand needle and knit it.

Pattern Essentials

SEAFOAM

Row 1: Knit.

Row 2: *K2, HB, K7; repeat from * to end of row.

Row 3: *K5, yo, K1, yo two times, K1, yo three times, K1, yo two times, K1, yo, K1; repeat from * to end of row.

Row 4: Knit, dropping all yarn overs from previous row.

Row 5: Knit.

Row 6: *K7, HB, K2; repeat from * to end of row.

Row 7: *K1, yo, K1, yo two times, K1, yo three times, K1, yo two times, K1, yo, K5; repeat from * to end of row.

Row 8: Repeat Row 4.

Repeat Rows 1–8 for pattern.

Finishing

○ Wet and block, stretching the design to finished measurements. When dry, attach a button to each end, 1"/2.5 cm from short edge of fabric, opposite a yarn over "buttonhole."

Tofutsies Tank Top

Designed by Helen Bingham

Dress it down or dress it up, this top is versatile. Form-fitting yet stretchy, it looks great on its own or over a basic cotton tank paired with blue jeans. It will also look great over a little sundress.

Getting Started

○ With longer needle, cast on 156 stitches and knit 4 rows.

○ Next Row: Bind off 4 stitches, knit to end of row.

○ Repeat this row 11 more times. *You now have 108 stitches.*

○ Work 8 rows in stockinette stitch, ending with a wrong-side row.

○ Next Row: K88, place marker, K20.

○ Join into a round and knit every round until piece measures 14"/ 35.5 cm from cast-on edge.

Knitting the Front

○ Knit to 2 stitches before marker, bind off 4 stitches, K50. Place next 54 stitches on scrap yarn to hold and

SIZES AND FINISHED MEASUREMENTS	Girl's large/Woman's extra small, up to approximately 32"/81 cm chest circumference (piece will measure approximately 24"/61 cm unstretched)
YARN	South West Trading Company Tofutsies, 50% superwash wool/25% Soysilk brand fiber/22.5% cotton/2.5% chitin, 3.5 oz (100 g)/ 465 yds (425 m), Color 727 Tender Foot
NEEDLES	US 9 (5.5 mm) circular needles 16"/40 cm and 24"/60 cm long *or size you need to obtain correct gauge*
GAUGE	17 stitches and 26 rows = 4"/10 cm in stockinette stitch
OTHER SUPPLIES	Stitch marker, scrap yarn for stitch holders, Size I/9 (5.5 mm) crochet hook

work back and forth on remaining 50 stitches for the front as follows:

> ○ Row 1 (WS): Purl.
>
> ○ Row 2: K2, ssk, knit to last 4 stitches, K2tog, K2.

○ Repeat Rows 1 and 2 three more times. *You now have 42 stitches.*

○ Work even in stockinette stitch until armhole measures 3"/7.5 cm, ending with a wrong-side row.

SHAPING THE FRONT NECK

○ Knit 25, place the last 8 stitches worked on a holder, knit to end of row.

○ Work 17 right shoulder stitches as follows:

> ○ Row 1 (WS): Purl.
>
> ○ Row 2: K2, ssk, knit to end of row.

○ Repeat Rows 1 and 2 three more times. *You now have 13 stitches.*

○ Work even until armhole measures 6"/15 cm from beginning of armhole shaping. Place stitches on holder.

○ With wrong side facing, attach yarn to 17 left shoulder stitches and work as follows:

> ○ Row 1: Purl.
>
> ○ Row 2: Knit to last 4 stitches, K2tog, K2.

○ Repeat Rows 1 and 2 three more times. *You now have 13 stitches.* Work even until armhole measures 6"/15 cm. Place stitches on holder.

Knitting the Back

○ Place 54 held stitches onto needle. With right side facing, attach yarn, bind off 4 stitches, knit to end of row.

○ Row 1: Purl.

○ Row 2: K2, ssk, knit to last 4 stitches, K2tog, K2.

○ Repeat Rows 1 and 2 three more times. *You now have 42 stitches.*

○ Work even in stockinette stitch until piece measures same as front. Place first and last 13 stitches on hold for shoulders, place remaining 16 stitches on holder for back neck.

Finishing

○ With right sides together, join shoulders with three-needle bind off (see page 282). Work 3 rounds of single crochet (see page 281) around each armhole and around edges of keyhole waist opening.

KNITTING THE NECK EDGING

○ With shorter circular needle, knit 16 held back neck stitches, pick up and knit (see page 280) 16 stitches along left front neck, knit 8 held front neck stitches, pick up and knit 16 stitches along right front neck. *You now have 56 stitches.* Join into a round and knit 3 rounds.

○ Move first stitch to crochet hook and *chain 3 (see page 277), insert hook through next 2 stitches, yarn over and pull yarn through both stitches, yarn over and pull yarn through 2 stitches on hook. Repeat from * until 1 stitch remains. Join with slip stitch (see page 281) to first crochet chain. Fasten off. Weave in ends. Steam lightly.

Knits for Kids

Small Wonders

Clothes for Dolls

Tri-Corner Baby Hat

Designed by Patricia McGregor

Your baby will bring a smile to the lips of the most jaded passerby when wearing this jaunty hat. The hat is knitted in the round, then joined into points with a three-needle bind off.

Knitting the Hat

○ Using circular needle, cast on 120 stitches. Place marker and join into a round, being careful not to twist the stitches. Work K2, P2 ribbing for 1"/2.5 cm. Work stockinette stitch (knit every round) until piece measures 5½"/14 cm from cast-on edge.

○ Place the last 20 stitches worked onto a double-point needle. Place the next 20 stitches onto a second double-point needle. The working yarn is between the two needles. Using a third needle, join the two sets of stitches with the three-needle bind off (see page 282). Place the remaining stitch on hold, cutting a tail about 6"/15 cm long.

SIZES AND FINISHED MEASUREMENTS	To fit a toddler, approximately 17"/43 cm circumference
YARN	Claudia Hand Painted Yarns Fingering Weight, 100% merino wool, 1.75 oz (50 g)/ 175 yds (160 m), Watermelon
NEEDLES	US 3 (3.25 mm) circular needle 16"/40 cm long and set of four US 3 (3.25 mm) double-point needles *or size you need to obtain correct gauge*
GAUGE	28 stitches and 36 rounds = 4"/10 cm in stockinette stitch
OTHER SUPPLIES	Stitch marker, scrap yarn for holders, tapestry needle

○ Place the next 20 stitches onto a double-point needle. Place the following 20 stitches onto a second double-point needle. Join yarn between the two needles. Using a third needle, join the two sets of stitches with the three-needle bind off. Place the remaining stitch on hold, cutting a tail about 6"/15 cm long.

○ Place the next 20 stitches onto a double-point needle. Place the last 20 stitches onto a second double-point needle. Join yarn between the two needles. Using a third needle, join the two sets of stitches with the three-needle bind off. Leave the last stitch on the needle (do not cut the yarn) and place the two held stitches onto same needle. Following the instructions on page 277, make a 3-stitch I-cord about 2"/5 cm long. Cut the yarn, leaving a 6"/15 cm tail. Thread yarn onto tapestry needle and draw through the 3 stitches. Fasten off and weave end into cord. Knot the I-cord near the top of the hat. Weave in remaining ends, closing any small gaps that may appear at the top of the hat.

Making the Tassels

○ Following the instructions on page 281, make three tassels about 2"/ 5 cm long. To make the tassels swing, braid the strands at the top of the tassels for about ½"/1.3 cm before attaching. Attach one tassel to each point of the hat. Weave in all ends.

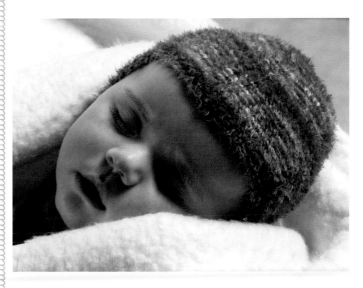

Baby Helmet

Designed by Brigitte Lang

This "novelty" sock yarn is particularly well suited for a baby's hat. Soft and fuzzy, it looks and feels just right for baby.

SIZES AND FINISHED MEASUREMENTS	To fit an infant, approximately 13"/33 cm circumference
YARN	Regia Softy Color, 39% superwash wool/ 61% polyamide, 1.75 oz (50 g)/136.5 yds (125 m), Color 00480
NEEDLES	US 5 (3.75 mm) circular needle 16"/40 cm long and set of four US 5 (3.75 mm) double-point needles *or size you need to obtain correct gauge*
GAUGE	24 stitches and 32 rounds = 4"/10 cm in stockinette stitch
OTHER SUPPLIES	Stitch marker, tapestry needle

Knitting the Helmet

○ Using circular needle, cast on 78 stitches. Work 4 rows back and forth in garter stitch. Place marker and join into a round, being careful not to twist the stitches.

○ Round 5: Knit.

○ Round 6: K2, M1, K1, M1, K10, ssk, K1, K2tog, *K10, M1, K1, M1, K10, ssk, K1, K2tog; repeat from * to last 8 stitches, K8. Remove marker, K1, replace marker.

○ Repeat Rounds 5 and 6 thirteen more times, being sure to move the marker 1 stitch to the left at the end of Round 6 each time.

○ Knit 1 round even.

DECREASING FOR THE CROWN

○ *Note:* Marker remains in the same place throughout crown shaping. Change to double-point needles when there are too few stitches for the circular needle.

○ Round 1: K13, ssk, K1, K2tog, *K21, ssk, K1, K2tog; repeat from * to last 8 stitches, K8. *You now have 72 stitches.*

○ Round 2 and all even-numbered rounds through Round 12: Knit.

○ Round 3: K12, ssk, K1, K2tog, *K19, ssk, K1, K2tog; repeat from * to last 7 stitches, K7. *You now have 66 stitches.*

○ Round 5: K11, ssk, K1, K2tog, *K17, ssk, K1, K2tog; repeat from * to last 6 stitches, K6. *You now have 60 stitches.*

○ Round 7: K10, ssk, K1, K2tog, *K15, ssk, K1, K2tog; repeat from * to last 5 stitches, K5. *You now have 54 stitches.*

○ Round 9: K9, ssk, K1, K2tog, *K13, ssk, K1, K2tog; repeat from * to last 4 stitches, K4. *You now have 48 stitches.*

○ Round 11: K8, ssk, K1, K2tog, *K11, ssk, K1, K2tog; repeat from * to last 3 stitches, K3. *You now have 42 stitches.*

○ Round 13: *Ssk, K1, K2tog, K2; repeat from * to end of round. *You now have 30 stitches.*

○ Round 14: Knit to last stitch, move marker 1 stitch to the right. The last stitch of Round 14 becomes the first stitch of Round 15.

○ Round 15: *Ssk, K1, K2tog; repeat from * to end of round. *You now have 18 stitches.*

○ Round 16: *K2tog; repeat from * to end of round. *You now have 9 stitches.*

Finishing

○ Cut yarn leaving a 6"/15 cm tail. Thread tail onto tapestry needle and draw through remaining stitches. Pull up snug and fasten off on the inside. Weave in ends, sewing a small seam in the garter-stitch border. Following the instructions on page 282, make two twisted cords about 8"/20.5 cm long. Fasten to hat with slipknot on the pattern points to the right and left of the border seam. *Note:* Be sure to tie the cords securely around baby's chin so there's no chance of their becoming untied and tangled.

Baby Hoodie

Designed by Diana Foster

This adorable hoodie uses a Broken Garter Stitch pattern, which is featured in Margaret Radcliffe's book *The Essential Guide to Color Knitting Techniques*. The stitch works great for variegated yarns. The hoodie is worked in one long piece and seamed up the back.

SIZES AND FINISHED MEASUREMENTS	To fit an infant, approximately 5½"/14 cm by 7½"/19 cm
YARN	Knit Picks Imagination, 50% superwash merino wool, 25% superfine alpaca, 25% nylon, 1.75 oz (50 g)/219 yds (200 m), Looking Glass
NEEDLES	US 2 (2.75 mm) and US 3 (3.25 mm) straight needles *or size you need to obtain correct gauge*
GAUGE	24 stitches and 48 rows = 4"/10 cm in Broken Garter Stitch pattern on larger needles
OTHER SUPPLIES	Tapestry needle, one ⅜"/1 cm button

Pattern Essentials

BROKEN GARTER

Row 1 (RS): *K3, P3; repeat from * to end of row.

Row 2: *P3, K3; repeat from * to end of row.

Repeat Rows 1 and 2 for pattern.

Knitting the Hoodie

○ With larger needles, cast on 42 stitches. Work Broken Garter stitch pattern for ¾"/2 cm, ending with a wrong-side row.

○ Next Row: K1, ssk (this is the front edge), continue in pattern to end of row.

○ Next Row: Work even in pattern.

○ Repeat the last 2 rows until 36 stitches remain.

153

KNITTING THE RIB AND MAKING THE BUTTONHOLE

○ Change to smaller needles and work K2, P2 rib for ¼"/0.5 cm, ending on a wrong-side row. Following the instructions on page 277, make a K2, P2 buttonhole, work to end. Continue in rib for a total rib of ¾"/2 cm.

CONTINUING THE HOODIE

○ Change to larger needles and work in Broken Garter stitch pattern for 11"/28 cm, ending on a wrong-side row.

○ Change to smaller needles and work K2, P2 rib for ¾"/2 cm, ending on a wrong-side row.

○ Next Row (RS): Working new stitches into pattern, work 1, M1, work in pattern to end of row.

○ Next Row: Work even in pattern.

○ Repeat the last 2 rows until you have 42 stitches. Work even in pattern for ¾"/2 cm. Bind off.

Finishing

○ Fold the hoodie in half with short edges together and seam along center back. Sew button on ribbing opposite buttonhole. Following the instructions on page 281, make a 2½"/6.5 cm tassel. Following the instructions on page 282, make a two-strand twisted cord 4"/10 cm long. Attach one end of the cord to the tassel and pull the other end through the top of the back seam. Adjust length and fasten off the cord on the inside. Weave in all ends.

Knotted Openwork Baby Hat

Designed by Mary McGurn

The knotted openwork pattern in this hat really exploits the variegated yarn — it almost looks as though each "knot" is knitted from a different skein of yarn! The hat is knit back and forth and seamed up the back, and you could easily get two hats from one skein of the yarn shown.

SIZES AND FINISHED MEASUREMENTS	To fit 6–24 months, 18½"/47 cm circumference
YARN	Misti Alpaca Hand Paint Sock Yarn, 50% superfine alpaca/30% merino wool/10% silk/10% nylon, 3.5 oz (100 g)/437 yds (400 m), Birds in Paradise
NEEDLES	US 3 (3.25 mm) straight needles *or size you need to obtain correct gauge*
GAUGE	24 stitches = 4"/10 cm in Knotted Openwork pattern
OTHER SUPPLIES	Tapestry needle

Pattern Essentials

KNOTTED OPENWORK

Row 1 (RS): K2, *yo, K3, pass the first of 3 stitches just knitted over last 2 stitches knitted; repeat from * to last stitch, K1.

Row 2: Purl.

Row 3: K1, *K3, pass the first of 3 stitches just knitted over last 2 stitches knitted, yo; repeat from * to last 2 stitches, K2.

Row 4: Purl.

PICOT CAST ON

*Cast on 5 stitches using the cable method (see page 276). Bind off 2 stitches. Slip the last stitch on the right-hand needle to the left-hand needle. Repeat from * until you have the required number of stitches.

Knitting the Hat

○ Using the Picot Cast On (see box above), cast on 108 stitches, then cast on 3 more stitches using the cable method (see page 276). *You now have 111 stitches.*

○ Work Knotted Openwork pattern until piece measures 6"/15 cm, ending with Row 1 of pattern stitch.

SHAPING THE CROWN

○ Row 1 (WS): Purl, decreasing 15 stitches evenly spaced. *You now have 96 stitches.*

○ Row 2: *K2, K2tog; repeat from * to end of row. *You now have 72 stitches.*

○ Row 3: Purl.

○ Row 4: *K1, K2tog; repeat from * to end of row. *You now have 48 stitches.*

○ Row 5: Purl.

○ Row 6: *K2tog; repeat from * to end of row. *You now have 24 stitches.*

○ Row 7: *P2tog; repeat from * to end of row. *You now have 12 stitches.*

○ Row 8: Repeat Row 6. *You now have 6 stitches.*

Finishing

○ Cut yarn leaving a 15"/38 cm tail. Thread tail onto tapestry needle and draw through remaining stitches. Pull up snug, then use tail to sew the center back seam. Weave in ends.

Meghan's and Mia's Matching Caps

Designed by Diana Foster

These hats are a great example of how variegated yarn changes its look depending on the width of the knitted piece. Although the two caps are knitted from the same skein of yarn, the color patterns are not identical.

Pattern Essentials

TWISTED RIBBING

Round 1: *K1 tbl, P1; repeat from * to end of round.

Repeat Row 1 for pattern.

CABLE

Round 1: *K4, P4; repeat from * to end of round.

Round 2: *C4F, P4; repeat from * to end of round.

Rounds 3 and 4: Repeat Round 1.

Repeat Rounds 1–4 for pattern.

CORKSCREW

Row 1: *Kfb; repeat from * to end of row.

Row 2: Bind off.

SIZES AND FINISHED MEASUREMENTS	To fit 18"/45.5 cm doll, approximately 10½"/26.5 cm circumference, and Child's medium, approximately 18¾"/47.5 cm circumference
YARN	Kangaroo Dyer Franklin Sock Yarn, 75% wool/25% nylon, 4 oz (113.5 g)/450 yds (411.5 m), Miami Vice
NEEDLES	US 3 (3.25 mm) circular needle 16"/40 cm long, set of five US 3 (3.25 mm) double-point needles, and two US 1 (2.25 mm) double-point needles for doll-cap corkscrews *or size you need to obtain correct gauge*
GAUGE	34 stitches and 40 rounds = 4"/10 cm in cable pattern on larger needle
OTHER SUPPLIES	Stitch marker, cable needle, tapestry needle
SPECIAL ABBREVIATIONS	**C4F** slip 2 stitches onto cable needle and hold in front, knit 2, knit 2 from cable needle

KNITTING THE DOLL'S CAP

○ Cast on 88 stitches and divide evenly onto four double-point needles. Place marker and join into a round, being careful not to twist the stitches.

○ Work Twisted Ribbing for ½"/1.3 cm.

○ Work Cable pattern for 3"/7.5 cm.

Decreasing for the Crown

○ *Note:* "Work 4" means to continue in Cable pattern as established.

○ Round 1: *Work 4, P2, P2tog; repeat from * to end of round. *You now have 77 stitches.*

○ Round 2: *Work 4, P1, P2tog; repeat from * to end of round. *You now have 66 stitches.*

○ Round 3: *Work 4, P2tog; repeat from * to end of round.

○ Round 4: *(K2tog) twice, P1; repeat from * to end of round.

○ Round 5: *K2tog, P1; repeat from * to end of round.

○ Round 6: *K2tog; repeat from * to end of round.

○ Round 7: K1, *K2tog; repeat from * to end of round. *You now have 6 stitches.*

Finishing

○ Cut yarn leaving a 6"/15 cm tail. Thread tail onto tapestry needle and draw through remaining stitches. Pull up snug and fasten off.

○ Using smaller needles, make three corkscrews leaving 6"/15 cm tails as follows:

○ Corkscrew 1: Cast on 20 stitches and follow Corkscrew pattern.

○ Corkscrew 2: Cast on 15 stitches and follow Corkscrew pattern.

○ Corkscrew 3: Cast on 10 stitches and follow Corkscrew pattern.

○ Thread all three tails onto tapestry needle and thread through top of cap from outside to inside. Fasten off tails and weave in ends.

KNITTING THE CHILD'S CAP

○ Cast on 160 stitches onto circular needle. Place marker and join into a round, being careful not to twist the stitches.

○ Work Twisted Ribbing for 1"/2.5 cm.

○ Work Cable pattern for 6"/15 cm.

Decreasing for the Crown

○ Work Rounds 1–6 as for Doll's Cap, changing to double-point needles when there are too few stitches for the circular needle.

○ Rounds 7 and 8: *K2tog; repeat from * to end of round. You have 5 stitches at the end of Round 8.

Finishing

○ Work as for Doll's Cap, but make the corkscrews on larger double-point needles with 30, 25, and 20 stitches.

157

SIZES AND FINISHED MEASUREMENTS	To fit a newborn, bootees approximately 3"/7.5 cm circumference, bonnet approximately 11"/28 cm around face
YARN	Schaefer Yarns Anne, 60% merino wool superwash/25% mohair/15% nylon, 4 oz (113.5 g)/560 yds (512 m), Elizabeth Zimmerman
NEEDLES	US 2 (2.75 mm) straight needles *or size you need to obtain correct gauge*
GAUGE	30 stitches and 48 rows = 4"/10 cm in Cross-Stitch pattern
OTHER SUPPLIES	Tapestry needle, US E/4 (3.5 mm) crochet hook
SPECIAL ABBREVIATIONS	**cross 4** Slip next 4 stitches to right-hand needle, dropping extra loops. Slip 4 elongated stitches back to left-hand needle. Cross fourth stitch over other 3 stitches and knit it. Cross third stitch over remaining 2 long stitches and knit it. Knit next 2 long stitches

G. W.'s Bonnet and Bootees

Designed by Melissa Morgan-Oakes

Based on a single bootee found in her grandmother's knitting things, Melissa has created these patterned bootees and matching classic baby bonnet for a newborn. Her grandmother, known to the family as G. W., would surely be proud.

KNITTING THE BONNET

Knitting the Brim

○ Cast on 80 stitches. Knit 4 rows (2 garter ridges).

○ Eyelet Row: K2, *K2tog, yo; repeat from * to last 2 stitches, K2.

○ Next Row: *K1, P1; repeat from * to end of row.

○ Repeat this row nine more times.

○ Knit 4 rows (2 garter ridges), increasing 1 stitch on last row. *You now have 81 stitches.*

o Work Rows 1–4 of pattern seven times (brim should measure approximately 3½"/9 cm from cast-on edge), then work Row 1 once more.

Shaping the Back

o Row 1 (RS): Work Row 2 of established pattern on 50 stitches, ssk, turn.

o Row 2: Slip 1, work Row 3 of established pattern on 19 stitches, P2tog, turn.

o Row 3: Slip 1, work 19 stitches in pattern, ssk, turn.

o Row 4: Slip 1, work 19 stitches in pattern, P2tog, turn.

o Repeat Rows 3 and 4 until all stitches on sides of bonnet have been attached to back. Bind off back bonnet stitches.

Pattern Essentials

CROSS STITCH

Row 1 (WS): Knit.

Row 2: Knit.

Row 3: P1, *(P1 wrapping yarn twice around needle) four times, p1; repeat from * to end of row.

Row 4: K1, cross 4, *k1 into stitch 2 rows below, cross 4; repeat from * to last stitch, k1.

Repeat Rows 1–4 for pattern.

o With right side facing and beginning at left front corner of bonnet side, pick up and knit (see page 280) 36 stitches across left side, 18 stitches across back, and 36 stitches across right side. *You now have* 90 stitches.

○ Next Row (WS): K3, *K2tog, K7; repeat from * to last 6 stitches, K2tog, K4. *You now have* 80 stitches.

○ Knit 6 rows (3 garter ridges). Bind off.

Finishing

○ Weave in ends. Wash and block.

○ For the bonnet tie, make a crochet chain (see page 277) 24"/61 cm long. Slip-stitch crochet (see page 281) back along chain to create thickness. Weave tie through eyelets. Note that the tie goes around baby's face, not neck.

KNITTING THE BOOTEES

Knitting the Leg

○ Cast on 36 stitches. Knit 6 rows (3 garter ridges).

○ Work Rows 1–4 of Cross Stitch pattern three times total (12 rows worked), then work Row 1 once more.

○ Next Row: *K1, P1; repeat from * to end of row.

○ Repeat this row nine more times.

○ Eyelet Row (RS): K2, *K2tog, yo; repeat from * to last 2 stitches, K2.

○ Knit 2 rows.

Knitting the Instep

○ Row 1 (WS): K24, turn, leaving remaining stitches on hold.

○ Row 2: Slip 1, K11, turn.

○ Repeat Row 2 twenty more times. *You now have* 11 garter ridges.

○ Next Row (RS): Pick up and knit 11 stitches down left side of instep then knit next 12 held foot stitches. Turn.

○ Knit 35 to end of instep stitches, pick up and knit (see page 280) 11 stitches down right side of instep (being careful here to pick up only the outside of each slipped stitch made while creating the instep). Knit 12 to end of foot.

○ Working back and forth on these 58 stitches, knit 12 more rows (6 ridges).

Working the Sole Decreases

○ Next Row: *K1, K2tog, K23, K2tog, K1; repeat from * once more.

○ Knit 1 row. Bind off. Make second bootee.

Finishing

○ Seam back of bootees. Weave in ends. Wash and block.

○ For the bootee ties, make two crochet chains each 12"/30.5 cm long. Slip-stitch crochet back along chain to create thickness. Weave tie through bootee's eyelets.

CROSS STITCH

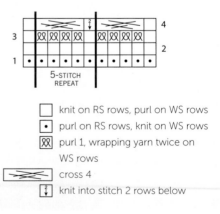

3
4
2
1

5-STITCH REPEAT

☐ knit on RS rows, purl on WS rows

• purl on RS rows, knit on WS rows

⧓ purl 1, wrapping yarn twice on WS rows

⤬ cross 4

⇕ knit into stitch 2 rows below

Shibui Baby Hat and Socks

Designed by Helen Bingham

This delightful ensemble will bring your newborn home in style. Ribbing helps keep the hat on and the socks up!

SIZES	To fit a newborn, hat approximately 13"/33 cm circumference, socks approximately 4½"/ 11.5 cm circumference
YARN	ShibuiKnits Sock, 100% superwash merino wool, 1.75 oz (50 g)/191 yds (175 m), Color 51301 Spectrum
NEEDLES	Set of four US 1 (2.25 mm) double-point needles for socks, US 3 (3.25 mm) circular needle 16"/40 cm long, and set of four US 3 (3.25 mm) double-point needles for hat *or sizes you need to obtain correct gauges*
GAUGE	30 stitches and 40 rounds = 4"/10 cm in stockinette stitch for hat; 32 stitches and 52 rounds = 4"/10 cm in stockinette stitch for socks
OTHER SUPPLIES	Stitch marker, tapestry needle

KNITTING THE HAT

o With circular needle, cast on 100 stitches. Place marker and join into a round, being careful not to twist the stitches.

o Rounds 1–13. Work K2, P2 rib.

o Round 14: Knit.

o Repeat Round 14 until piece measures 3½"/9 cm from cast on edge.

DECREASING FOR THE CROWN

o Round 1: *K8, K2tog; repeat from * to end of round. *You now have 90 stitches.*

o Round 2 and all even-numbered rounds through Round 14: Knit.

o Round 3: *K7, K2tog; repeat from * to end of round. *You now have 80 stitches.*

o Round 5: *K6, K2tog; repeat from * to end of round. *You now have 70 stitches.*

161

○ Continue in this manner, decreasing every other round, knitting 1 fewer stitch between the decreases on each decrease round, and changing to larger double-point needles when necessary, until you have 30 stitches, ending with a knit round.

○ Round 15: *K2tog; repeat from * to end of round. *You now have* 15 stitches.

○ Round 16: K1, *K2tog; repeat from * to end of round. *You now have* 8 stitches.

○ Round 17: *K2tog; repeat from * to end of round. *You now have* 4 stitches.

○ Round 18: K1, K2tog. *You now have* 3 stitches.

Finishing

○ Following the instructions on page 277, work 3-stitch I-cord for 2"/5 cm. Bind off and weave in all ends. Tie a knot in the I-cord. Steam lightly.

KNITTING THE SOCKS

○ With smaller double-point needles, cast on 40 stitches and divide onto three double-point needles so there are 10 stitches each on Needles 1 and 3 and 20 stitches on Needle 2. Join into a round, being careful not to twist the stitches.

Knitting the Cuff

○ Work K2, P2 rib until piece measures 2"/5 cm from cast-on edge.

Knitting the Heel Flap

○ Knit the 10 stitches on Needle 1. Work the flap back and forth on the 20 stitches on Needle 2 and hold remaining stitches on Needles 1 and 3 for instep.

○ Row 1: K1, *K1, slip 1; repeat from * to last stitch, K1.

○ Row 2: Slip 1, purl to end of row.

○ Row 3: Slip 1, *K1, slip 1; repeat from * to last stitch, K1.

○ Repeat Rows 2 and 3 seven more times.

Turning the Heel

○ Continuing back and forth on the same 20 stitches, turn the heel as follows.

○ Row 1: Slip 1, P10, P2tog, P1, turn.

○ Row 2: Slip 1, K3, K2tog, K1, turn.

○ Row 3: Slip 1, purl to 1 stitch before the gap, P2tog, P1, turn.

○ Row 4: Slip 1, knit to 1 stitch before the gap, K2tog, K1, turn.

○ Repeat Rows 3 and 4 until all stitches have been worked. *You now have* 12 stitches.

Knitting the Gusset

○ With right side facing and using an empty needle (Needle 1), pick up and knit (see page 280) 8 stitches along side of heel. With Needle 2, knit the 20 held instep stitches. With Needle 3, pick up and knit 8 stitches along other side of heel and K6 from heel-turning needle. Slip remaining 6 stitches from heel-turning needle onto Needle 1. *You now have* 48 stitches, with 14 stitches each on Needles 1 and 3 and 20 stitches on Needle 2.

○ Round 1: Knit to last 3 stitches on Needle 1, K2tog, K1; on Needle 2, K20; on Needle 3, K1, ssk, knit to end of round.

○ Round 2: Knit.

o Repeat Rounds 1 and 2 until 36 stitches remain.

Knitting the Foot

o Rounds 1–8: Knit. Redistribute the stitches so there are 9 stitches each on Needles 1 and 2 and 18 stitches on Needle 3.

Shaping the Toe

o Round 1: On Needle 1, knit to last 3 stitches, K2tog, K1; on Needle 2, K1, ssk, knit to last 3 stitches, K2tog, K1; on Needle 3, K1, ssk, knit to end of round.

o Round 2: Knit.

o Repeat Rounds 1 and 2 until 12 stitches remain. Knit the 3 remaining stitches from Needle 1 to Needle 3. *You now have* 6 stitches on each of two needles.

Finishing

o Following the instructions on page 278, use Kitchener stitch to join the toe stitches. Weave in ends.

Hannah's Special Slippers

Designed by Lise A. Gill

These slippers are designed to stay securely on baby's feet. And because the yarn has elastic, they stretch enough to fit for a longer-than-usual number of months. To produce the contrasting white yarn for embroidery, use a little bleach to remove the color.

SIZES AND FINISHED MEASUREMENTS	To fit 6–24 months, approximately 3¾"/ 9.5 cm long
YARN	Cascade Fixation, 98.3% cotton/1.7% elastic, 1.75 oz (50 g)/100 yds (91 m), Color 3077 Pink
NEEDLES	US 6 (4 mm) straight or circular needle 16"/40 cm long or size you need to obtain correct gauge
GAUGE	24 stitches and 32 rows = 4"/10 cm in stockinette stitch
OTHER SUPPLIES	Two stitch markers, stitch holder, tapestry needle, bleach

Knitting the Sole

○ Cast on 8 stitches.

○ Row 1: Knit.

○ Row 2: Purl.

○ Row 3: K2, kfb, K2, kfb, K2. *You now have* 10 stitches.

○ Rows 4–12: Work even in stockinette stitch.

○ Row 13: K2, kfb, K4, kfb, K2. *You now have* 12 stitches.

○ Rows 14–30: Work even in stockinette stitch.

○ Row 31: K2, ssk, K4, ssk, K2. *You now have* 10 stitches.

○ Rows 32–34: Work even in stockinette stitch.

○ Row 35: K2, ssk, K2, ssk, K2. *You now have* 8 stitches.

○ Row 36: Purl.

○ Place stitches on holder.

Knitting the Back

○ Count down 20 rows from held stitches and place a marker at each edge of sole. With right side facing, beginning at marker pick up and knit (see page 280) 13 stitches along side of sole to held stitches, knit 8 held stitches, pick up and knit 13 stitches along side of sole to marker. *You now have* 34 stitches.

○ Work back and forth in stockinette stitch for 11 rows, beginning and ending with a wrong-side (purl) row.

○ Next Row: *K1, P1; repeat from * to end of row.

○ Repeat this row two more times.

○ Bind off. Weave in all ends at this point.

Knitting the Toe

○ Row 1. With right side facing, pick up and knit 5 stitches along toe of sole.

○ Row 2: Purl.

○ Row 3: Pick up and knit 1 stitch in sole, K5, pick up and knit 1 stitch in sole.

○ Row 4: Purl.

○ Row 5: Pick up and knit 1 stitch in sole, K7, pick up and knit 1 stitch in sole.

○ Row 6: Purl.

○ Continue in this manner, picking up 1 stitch in sole at beginning and end of right-side rows until you have 15 stitches.

○ Row 13: Pick up and knit 1 stitch in sole, K2, ssk, K7, K2tog, K2, pick up and knit 1 stitch in sole.

○ Row 14 and all even-numbered rows through Row 22: Purl.

○ Row 15 and all odd-numbered rows through Row 23: Repeat Row 13.

○ Rows 24–29: Work even in Seed Stitch.

○ Bind off. Sew edges of Seed Stitch border to sole. Weave in ends.

Finishing

○ Bring front corners of back piece together, laying one over the other, and secure them on wrong side to center of Seed Stitch border.

Making the Daisy

○ Place a few yards of yarn in a 50/50 mixture of water and bleach and soak for a few minutes until color is removed. Rinse in cold water and allow to dry.

○ To embroider daisy, bring needle from back to front at center of flower (A). Form a loop and hold it in place while bringing needle from front to back through the same spot (A). Bring needle from back to front at outer edge of loop (B), then back down at same spot (B), overlapping the loop to fasten it in place.

○ Repeat for five more petals.

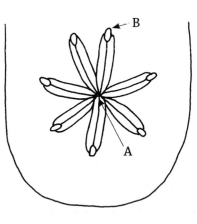

Baby Brights Tights

Designed by Lion Brand Design Team

Here's a unique use of a large ball of self-striping sock yarn. The wool keeps baby warm, the nylon makes the fabric durable. These are fitted with an elastic waist for easy changing.

SIZES AND FINISHED MEASUREMENTS	To fit 6 (12) months, approximately 20 (21)"/51 (53.5) cm waist and 14¼ (16¼)"/36 (41.5) cm length
YARN	Lion Brand Sock-Ease, 75% superwash wool/25% nylon, 3.5 oz (100 g)/438 yds (400 m), Color 205 Cotton Candy
NEEDLES	US 2 (2.75 mm) and US 3 (3.25 mm) needles *or size you need to obtain correct gauge*
GAUGE	28 stitches and 37 rows = 4"/10 cm in stockinette stitch
OTHER SUPPLIES	Tapestry needle, 1 yd/91.5 cm of ¾"/2 cm elastic

Knitting the Legs (make 2)

○ With smaller needles, cast on 46 (55) stitches.

○ Knit 16 rows.

○ Next Row (RS): Knit, increasing 6 stitches evenly spaced. *You now have* 52 (61) stitches.

○ Change to larger needles and stockinette stitch, increasing 1 stitch at each edge every right-side row two (three) times, then increase 1 stitch at each edge every other right-side row 16 (17) times. *You now have* 88 (101) stitches.

○ Work even until piece measures 7½" (9)"/19 (23) cm, ending with a wrong-side row.

Shaping the Crotch

○ Bind off 4 (6) stitches at the beginning of the next 2 rows. *You now have* 80 (89) stitches.

○ Decrease 1 stitch at each edge every right-side row four (six) times. *You now have* 72 (77) stitches.

○ Work even until piece measures 5¾" (6¼)"/14.5 (16) cm from beginning of crotch shaping, ending with a wrong-side row.

○ Next Row: Knit, decreasing 6 (3) stitches evenly spaced. *You now have* 66 (74) stitches.

○ Change to smaller needles and knit 1 row.

Knitting the Waistband

○ Row 1: K3, *P4, K4; repeat from * to last 7 stitches, P4, K3.

○ Row 2: P3, *K4, P4; repeat from * to last 7 stitches, K4, P3.

○ Repeat Rows 1 and 2 for 1"/2.5 cm, ending with a right-side row.

○ Turning Row (WS): Knit.

○ Repeat Rows 1 and 2 for 1"/2.5 cm. Bind off loosely.

Finishing

○ Sew crotch seam. Sew leg seams. Fold waistband to inside along turning row for casing and sew in place on inside, leaving an opening for the elastic. Cut elastic to desired length, thread through casing, and sew ends together. Sew casing closed. Weave in ends. Block.

Patches Baby Sweater

Designed by Christiane Burkhard

This adorable cardigan is knitted in strips, which are in turn knitted together. The self-patterning sock yarn works up in a unique patchwork design.

SIZES AND FINISHED MEASUREMENTS	To fit 6 months, approximately 19"/48 cm chest circumference
YARN	Opal Hundertwasser, 75% superwash wool/ 25% polyamid, 3.5 oz (100 g)/465 yds (425 m), Color 1437
NEEDLES	US 1 (2.25 mm) straight needles *or size you need to obtain correct gauge*
GAUGE	28 stitches and 40 rows = 4"/10 cm in stockinette stitch
OTHER SUPPLIES	Tapestry needle, three ½"/1.3 cm buttons

Pattern Essentials

KNITTING THE STRIPS TOGETHER

On the right side of the first row of the strip to be joined, slip the last stitch knitwise.

Pick up and knit (see page 280) the corresponding stitch from the already knitted strip.

Pass the slipped stitch over this stitch.

Turn work, slip the first stitch purlwise with yarn in front, purl to end of row.

Continue joining the last stitch of the new strip with the corresponding stitch of the knitted strip.

Knitting the Back

o Cast on 17 stitches. Work garter stitch for 6 rows.

o Change to stockinette stitch and work until piece measures 9"/23 cm from cast-on edge. Bind off loosely.

o Cast on 17 stitches. Work as for first strip, joining the last stitch of each right-side row to the corresponding stitch of the first strip.

o Add two more strips the same way.

Knitting the Right Front

o Cast on 17 stitches. Work garter stitch for 6 rows.

o Change to stockinette stitch and work until piece measures 9"/23 cm from cast-on edge. Bind off loosely.

o Work the second strip as for the back until this strip measures 6"/15 cm from cast-on edge.

SHAPING THE NECK

o Continuing to join the right side of the strip as established; on the next 12 right-side rows slip 1 purlwise, ssk, knit to end of row. *You now have* 5 stitches.

o Work even until piece 9"/23 cm. Bind off loosely.

Knitting the Left Front

o Cast on 17 stitches. Work garter stitch for 6 rows.

o Change to stockinette stitch and work until piece measures 6"/15 cm from cast-on edge.

SHAPING THE NECK

o On the next 12 right-side rows, knit to last 3 stitches, K2tog, K1. *You now have* 5 stitches.

o Work even until piece measures 9"/23 cm. Bind off loosely.

o Work second strip as for back, joining to first strip, until piece measures 9"/23 cm from cast-on edge. Bind off loosely.

Knitting the Sleeves

o Cast on 17 stitches. Work 6 rows in garter stitch. Change to stockinette stitch and work 2 rows.

o Increase Row (RS): Knit to last stitch, M1, K1.

o Continuing in stockinette stitch, work the Increase Row every other right-side row 14 times. *You now have* 32 stitches.

o Work even until piece measures 6½"/16.5 cm. Bind off loosely.

o Work second strip the same as the first, joining to first strip on straight edge and working the increase row as follows.

o Increase Row: K1, M1, knit to end of row.

Joining the Pieces

o Sew shoulder seams together.

o To form a decorative ridge along sleeve and side seams, hold the pieces to be seamed next to each other with wrong sides together. Join with a running stitch under and inside the 2 edge stitches, allowing these edge stitches to curl up and form a ridge (see page 170). Be careful to keep the tension even and not too tight.

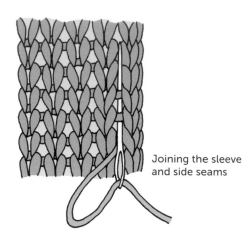

Joining the sleeve and side seams

Knitting the Neck and Button Band

○ With right sides facing and beginning at lower right front, pick up and knit (see page 280) 32 stitches along right front edge, 19 stitches along right neck, 24 stitches along back neck, and 19 stitches along left neck, and 32 stitches along left front edge. *You now have 126 stitches.*

○ Row 1 (WS): Knit.

○ Row 2: K4, bind off 2, (K10, bind off 2) twice, (K1, M1) twice, K62, M1, K1, M1, K31.

○ Row 3: K100, (cast on 2, K10) twice, cast on 2, K4.

○ Row 4: K32, M1, K1, M1, K64, M1, K1, M1, K32.

○ Row 5: Knit.

○ Row 6: K33, M1, K1, M1, K66, M1, K1, M1, K33.

○ Bind off loosely.

Finishing

○ Weave in ends. Sew buttons opposite buttonholes. Block.

"Sock" It to Me (for Girls)

Designed by Vicki K. Byram

Simple increases, decreases, and yarn overs combine for this patterned and plain cardigan for girls. The sweater is knitted from the top down.

SIZES AND FINISHED MEASUREMENTS	To fit 6 months, approximately 21"/53.5 cm finished chest, 11"/28 cm length
YARN	Ellen's ½ Pint Farm Sock Yarn, 60% merino wool/30% bamboo/10% nylon, 4 oz (113.5 g)/ 475 yds (435 m), Deep Ocean Waters
NEEDLES	US 5 (3.75 mm) circular needle 16"/40 cm long *or size you need to obtain correct gauge*
GAUGE	24 stitches and 32 rows = 4"/10 cm in stockinette stitch
OTHER SUPPLIES	Stitch markers, scrap yarn for holders, three ⅜"/1 cm buttons

Knitting the Upper Body

○ *Note:* Sweater is knitted back and forth on a circular needle to accommodate the number of stitches in the body.

○ Cast on 62 stitches.

○ Rows 1 and 2: Knit.

○ Row 3: Knit to last 3 stitches, yo, K2tog, K1.

○ Rows 4 and 5: Knit.

○ Row 6: K13, place marker, K6, place marker, K24, place marker, K6, place marker, K13.

○ *Note:* You begin knitting the yoke on the next row.

○ Row 7: *Knit to 1 stitch before marker, kfb, slip marker, kfb; repeat from * three more times, knit to end of row.

○ Row 8: K5, purl to last 5 stitches, K5.

○ Rows 9–20: Repeat Rows 7 and 8. *You now have* 118 stitches at the end of Row 20.

○ Row 21: *Knit to 1 stitch before marker, kfb, slip marker, kfb; repeat from * three more times, knit to last 3 stitches, yo, K2tog, K1.

○ Row 22: Repeat Row 8.

○ Rows 23–38: Repeat Rows 7 and 8. *You now have* 190 stitches at the end of Row 38.

○ Row 39: Repeat Row 21.

○ Row 40 (Dividing Row): K5, P25, place these 30 stitches on holder, P40, place remaining 128 stitches on holder.

Knitting the Sleeves

○ Row 1 (RS): Cast on 3 stitches, K40.

○ Row 2: Cast on 3 stitches, P43. *You now have* 46 stitches.

○ Rows 3–12: Work even in stockinette stitch.

○ Row 13: Knit, decreasing 1 stitch at the beginning and end of the row.

○ Continue in stockinette stitch, decreasing 1 stitch at the beginning and end of every sixth row until 38 stitches remain.

171

○ Work even in stockinette stitch until sleeve measures 6½"/16.5 cm from underarm. Decrease 8 stitches evenly on next row. Work 6 rows in garter stitch. Bind off loosely.

○ Place 128 held stitches on needle. With wrong side facing, join yarn at underarm, purl 58 back stitches and place them on holder, P40 for second sleeve, place remaining 30 stitches on holder. Work second sleeve as for first.

Knitting the Lower Body

○ With wrong side facing, place 30 left front stitches on needle, join yarn, and P25, K5.

○ Joining Row (RS): K13, M1, K9, M1, K8, pick up and knit (see page 280) 6 underarm cast-on stitches, place 58 held back stitches on needle, (K9, M1, K10, M1) twice, K10, M1, K10, pick up and knit 6 underarm cast-on stitches, place 30 held right front stitches on needle, K8, M1, K9, M1, K13. *You now have* 139 stitches.

○ Next Row: K5, purl to last 5 stitches, K5.

○ Work Rows 1–16 of Lacy Garter stitch three times, then work Rows 1–8 once more. Work 7 rows in garter stitch. Bind off.

Finishing

○ Sew sleeve seams. Weave in ends. Sew three buttons to band opposite buttonholes.

Pattern Essentials
LACY GARTER

Rows 1, 3, 5, and 7 (RS): K5, *(ssk, yo) four times, K8; repeat from * to last 6 stitches, K6.

Rows 2, 4, 6, and 8 (WS): K5, *K9, P7; repeat from * to last 6 stitches, K6.

Rows 9, 11, 13, and 15: K6, *K8, (yo, K2tog) four times; repeat from * to last 5 stitches, K5.

Rows 10, 12, 14, and 16: K6, *P7, K9; repeat from * to last 5 stitches, K5.

Repeat Rows 1–16 for pattern.

LACY GARTER

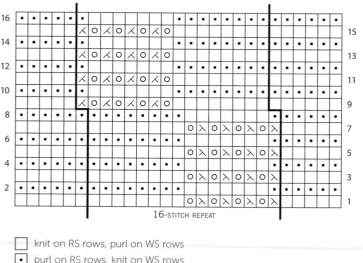

16-STITCH REPEAT

☐ knit on RS rows, purl on WS rows

• purl on RS rows, knit on WS rows

⟋ K2tog

⟍ ssk

○ yarn over

Heritage Baby Sweater

Designed by Liz Nields

This heirloom-quality baby sweater is knit side to side in two pieces from sleeve to center, seamed at the sides, and joined with Kitchener stitch at the center back. A single pearly button holds it together at the neck.

SIZES AND FINISHED MEASUREMENTS	To fit 0–3 months, approximately 17"/43 cm chest circumference
YARN	Cascade Heritage, 75% superwash merino/25% nylon, 3.5 oz (100 g)/437 yds (400 m), Color 5618 Cream
NEEDLES	US 1 (2.25 mm) straight needles *or size you need to obtain correct gauge*
GAUGE	34 stitches and 50 rows = 4"/10 cm in Heritage Lace pattern
OTHER SUPPLIES	Stitch markers, tapestry needle, size B/1 (2.25 mm) crochet hook, one ½"/1.3 cm button

Knitting the Left Section

o Cast on 43 stitches.

o Row 1 (WS): *P1, K1; repeat from * to last stitch, P1.

o Row 2 (RS): *K1, P1; repeat from * to last stitch, K1.

o Repeat Rows 1 and 2 once more.

o Purl 1 row.

o Next Row: K1, P3, place marker, work Row 1 of Heritage Lace chart five times, place marker, P3, K1.

o Next Row: P1, K3, slip marker, work Row 2 of Heritage Lace chart five times, slip marker, K3, P1.

o Work in pattern as established until chart rows 1–4 are complete.

o Next Row: Continue working from the chart on stitches between the markers, and increase 1 stitch at each end of needle, 1 stitch in from the edge, working extra stitches in reverse stockinette stitch, until you have 45 stitches.

o Continue to increase every sixth row, working extra stitches in reverse stockinette stitch, until you have 51 stitches. End having completed Row 24.

o Row 25: Placing new markers as given and removing old markers as you come to them, K1, place marker, work Row 25 of chart seven times, place marker, K1.

o Continue to increase each end of needle every sixth row until second repeat of pattern Row 18 is complete. *You now have 63 stitches.*

o Using one 24"/61 cm length of yarn and long-tail cast on (see page 278), add 57 stitches to end of Row 18. Turn.

o Pattern Row 19 (RS): K1, work chart on 118 stitches, K1. Use another length of yarn and long-tail cast on to add 57 stitches to end of Row 19. *You now have* 177 stitches. Turn. Markers can be removed on next row.

o Pattern Row 20: P1, work chart over 175 stitches, P1.

o Work in pattern as established until piece measures approximately 3"/7.5 cm from body cast on; end having completed Row 14.

DIVIDING FOR FRONT AND BACK

○ Pattern Row 15 (RS): K1, work in pattern for 87 stitches, place remaining stitches on holder for front. Turn.

KNITTING THE BACK

○ Pattern Row 16: Bind off 1 stitch, work in pattern to end of row.

○ Bind off 1 stitch at beginning of next wrong-side row. *You now have* 86 stitches.

○ Work even until neck measures approximately 1½"/4 cm; end having completed a wrong-side row. Make a note of ending pattern row number. Place stitches on holder.

KNITTING THE FRONT

○ With right side facing, return held front stitches to needle and rejoin yarn.

○ Pattern Row 15 (RS): Bind off 7 stitches, work in pattern to end of row.

○ Pattern Rows 16, 18, and 20 (WS): Work in pattern.

○ Rows 17, 19, and 21: Bind off 1 stitch, work in pattern to end of row.

○ Continue in pattern on remaining 79 stitches, keeping 1 edge stitch each end in stockinette stitch, until front neck measures same as back neck, ending with the same row number as back.

○ Bind off all stitches.

Knitting the Right Section

o Work sleeve body as for left section until ready to divide.

DIVIDING FOR FRONT AND BACK

o Work in pattern over 89 stitches, place stitches just worked on holder for front.

KNITTING THE BACK

o Row 15 (RS): Bind off 1 stitch, work to end of row.

o Row 16: Work in pattern.

o Bind off 1 stitch at beginning of next right-side. *You now have* 86 stitches.

o Work even until neck measures approximately 1½"/4 cm, ending on same row number as left back. Place stitches on holder.

KNITTING THE FRONT

o Row 16: With wrong side facing, return held stitches to needle and rejoin yarn. Bind off 7 stitches, work in pattern to end of row. Continue to work in pattern, bind off 1 stitch at beginning of wrong-side rows three times. *You now have* 79 stitches. Continue in pattern on remaining 79 stitches, keeping 1 edge stitch at each end in stockinette stitch, until front neck measures same as back, ending with the same row number as back.

o Bind off all stitches.

Finishing

o Use Kitchener stitch (see page 278) to graft right and left sections of back together. Sew all seams. With right side facing and beginning at bottom left corner, pick up and knit (see page 280) 153 stitches across bottom of all sections. Work 2 rows of P1, K1 rib. Bind off in rib.

o With crochet hook, work 1 row single crochet (see page 281) along fronts and neck, making loop for button at top of left front. Weave in all ends. Sew button opposite button loop. Block.

HERITAGE LACE

☐	knit on RS rows, purl on WS rows
•	purl on RS rows, knit on WS rows
⋌	K2tog
⋋	ssk
○	yarn over

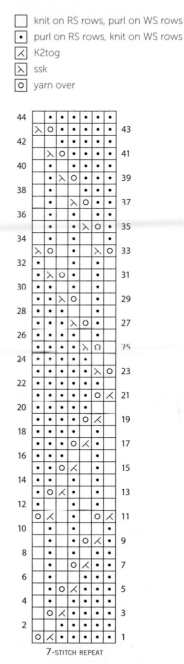

7-STITCH REPEAT

Little Hanten

Designed by Cheryl Oberle

The alternating triangle–patterned front panels of this darling kimono are created with increases and decreases. The back is plain garter stitch. Sleeves are knitted along the armhole edge, and the sides and under-arms are joined in one seam on each side.

SIZES AND FINISHED MEASUREMENTS	To fit 12–18 months, approximately 22"/ 56 cm chest circumference
YARN	Weaving Southwest Hand-dyed Superwash Sport, 100% superwash merino wool, 4 oz (113 g)/375 yds (342 m), Magenta Mix
NEEDLES	US 5 (3.75 mm) straight needles *or size you need to obtain correct gauge*
GAUGE	22 stitches and 44 rows = 4"/10 cm in garter stitch
OTHER SUPPLIES	Safety pins for markers, scrap yarn for holders, tapestry needle, size G/6 (4 mm) crochet hook, sewing needle and coordinating thread, two 1"/2.5 cm buttons

Knitting the Front Panels

○ Cast on 2 stitches.

○ Row 1: Kfb, K1. *You now have* 3 stitches.

○ Row 2: Kfb, knit to end of row. *You now have* 4 stitches.

○ Repeat Row 2 twenty-six more times. *You now have* 30 stitches.

○ Turn the work and place a safety pin in the middle of the triangle on the side facing you. The pins will be your guide to constructing the kimono.

SHAPING WITH INCREASES AND DECREASES

○ *Row 1: Kfb, K2tog, turn.

○ Row 2 and all even-numbered rows: Knit.

○ Row 3: Kfb, K1, K2tog, turn.

○ Row 5: Kfb, K2, K2tog, turn.

○ Row 7: Kfb, K3, K2tog, turn.

○ Continue in this manner, working 1 more stitch before the decrease on every odd-numbered row until all stitches have been worked. The last row will be kfb, K27, K2tog, turn. Do not work a knit row after this last pattern row.**

○ Repeat from * to ** once more.

SHAPING THE SHOULDERS

○ Next Row: K2tog, knit to end of row.

○ Repeat this row until 2 stitches remain. K2tog and pull yarn through last loop. Panel measures approximately 10½"/26.5 cm.

○ Make a second front panel the same as the first.

Knitting the Back

○ Cast on 60 stitches. Work even in garter stitch until piece measures 1"/2.5 cm less than front panels (approximately 9½"/24 cm).

SHAPING THE NECK

○ Place the center 20 stitches on holder. Working the right and left back separately, work even for 1"/2.5 cm.

Joining the Shoulders

○ *Note:* The right front has a safety pin on the right side, and the left front has a safety pin on the wrong side.

○ With right sides together, sew fronts to back at shoulders.

Knitting the Sleeves

○ Place markers for the underarm 4"/10 cm from shoulder seam on fronts and back at side seam. With right side facing and beginning at underarm, pick up and knit (see page 280) 22 stitches up to shoulder seam and 22 stitches from shoulder seam to other marker. Work even in garter stitch until sleeve measures 3"/7.5 cm. Bind off. Repeat for second sleeve.

○ Sew fronts and back together along the side and underarm seams.

Knitting the Front Band

○ With right side facing and beginning at bottom right front, pick up and knit 45 stitches to shoulder seam and 4 stitches from shoulder seam to back neck, K20 from holder, pick up and knit 4 stitches to shoulder seam and 45 stitches from shoulder seam to bottom left front. *You now have 118 stitches.*

○ Work even in garter stitch for 2"/5 cm, ending with a right-side row. Bind off loosely in knit.

177

Finishing

○ *Note:* The buttons are decorative and are used to anchor the ties to the fronts.

○ With doubled yarn and crochet hook, make two crochet chains (see page 277) 6"/15 cm long. Lay one chain horizontally on each front panel, about 3"/7.5 cm up from the bottom edge and with the end about 1"/2.5 cm in from the edge. Stitch in place with sewing needle and thread. Use project yarn if possible to sew buttons over the sewn chains. Tie a knot in the end of each chain. Weave in all ends. Steam lightly.

I-Point Baby Jacket

Designed by Janice Bye

This is a fine example of a textured stitch softening the stripes in a self-patterning yarn. I-cord decoration adds a bit of whimsy!

SIZES AND FINISHED MEASUREMENTS	To fit 6–24 months, approximately 21"/53.5 cm chest circumference
YARN	Plymouth Italian Collection Sockotta, 45% cotton/40% superwash wool/15% nylon, 3.5 oz (100 g)/414 yds (379 m), Color 6511
NEEDLES	US 2 (2.75 mm) straight needles and two US 2 (2.75 mm) double-point needles for I-cord *or size you need to obtain correct gauge*
GAUGE	28 stitches = 4"/10 cm in Sand Stitch pattern
OTHER SUPPLIES	Stitch markers, scrap yarn for holders, tapestry needle
SPECIAL ABBREVIATIONS	**kfbf** knit in front, back, and front of same stitch (2 stitches increased)

Knitting the Back

o With straight needles, cast on 73 stitches.

o Rows 1–3: P1, *K1, P1; repeat from * to end of row.

o Row 4 (RS): Knit.

o Next Rows: Begin Sand Stitch pattern (see page 180) and work Rows 1–4 until piece measures 7"/18 cm, ending with Row 3 of pattern.

WORKING THE NECK AND SHOULDERS

o Row 1: K21, place marker, K1, (P1, K1) 15 times, place marker, knit to end of row.

o Working established ribbing between markers and Sand Stitch pattern outside markers, work 3 more rows even.

o Next row (RS): K25, bind off 23, knit to end of row.

o Place the 25 right shoulder and 25 left shoulder stitches on hold.

Knitting the Right Front

KNITTING THE POINT

o Following the instructions on page 277, work 3-stitch I-cord for 4½"/11.5 cm.

o Change to straight needles and kfb, K1, kfb. *You now have* 5 stitches.

o Row 1 (WS): P1, *K1, P1; repeat from * to end of row.

o Row 2: Kfb, knit to last stitch, kfb.

o Repeat Rows 1 and 2 until you have 29 stitches, ending with a right-side row.

o Cast on 6 stitches. *You now have* 35 stitches. *Note:* This is the row that will line up with the bottom of the sweater back.

KNITTING THE BODY

o Row 1 (WS): Work in established Sand Stitch pattern to last 3 stitches, place marker, K3.

o Keeping 3 stitches at front edge in garter stitch, work even until piece measures 3"/7.5 cm from tip of point, ending with a right-side row. Place a stitch marker at this row to indicate I-cord placement.

DECREASING THE NECKLINE

o Row 1 (WS): Work in established Sand Stitch pattern to 2 stitches before marker, K2tog, slip marker, K3.

o Row 2: Knit.

o Repeat Rows 1 and 2 until 25 stitches remain. Work even in pattern until piece measures same as back, ending with a wrong-side row.

o With wrong sides together, use the three-needle bind off (see page 282) to join right front and back shoulders together. Do not cut yarn. Kfbf in remaining stitch and knit 3-stitch I-cord for 4½"/11.5 cm. Cut yarn and weave in end.

Knitting the Left Front

KNITTING THE POINT

○ Work as for right front point, until you have 29 stitches, ending with a right-side row.

○ Next Row (WS): Work in established Sand Stitch pattern to end of row. Cast on 6 stitches. *You now have* 35 stitches.

○ Next Row: Knit.

KNITTING THE BODY

○ Row 1 (WS): K3, place marker, work in established Sand Stitch pattern to end of row.

○ Row 2: Knit.

○ Keeping 3 stitches at front edge in garter stitch, work even until piece measures 3"/7.5 cm from tip of point, ending with a right-side row. Place a stitch marker at this row to indicate I-cord placement.

DECREASING THE NECKLINE

○ Row 1 (WS): K3, slip marker, ssk, work in established Sand Stitch pattern to end of row.

○ Row 2: Knit.

○ Repeat Rows 1 and 2 until 25 stitches remain. Work even in pattern until piece measures same as back, ending with a right-side row.

○ With wrong sides together, use the three-needle bind off (see page 282) to join left front and back shoulders together. Do not cut yarn. Kfbf in remaining stitch and knit 3-stitch I-cord for 4½"/11.5 cm. Cut yarn and weave in end.

Knitting the Sleeves

○ Cast on 43 stitches.

○ Row 1 (WS): P1, *K1, P1; repeat from * to end of row.

○ Row 2: K1, *P1, K1; repeat from * to end of row.

○ Repeat Rows 1 and 2 once more.

○ Beginning with Row 3 of Sand Stitch pattern, work 5 rows.

Pattern Essentials

SAND STITCH

Row 1 (WS): K1, *P1, K1; repeat from * to end of row.

Row 2: Knit.

Row 3: P1, *K1, P1; repeat from * to end of row.

Row 4: Knit.

Repeat Rows 1–4 for pattern.

○ Increase Row: Kfb, knit to last stitch, kfb.

○ Bringing new stitches into pattern, increase 1 stitch each side every 6 rows seven more times. *You now have* 59 stitches.

○ Work even in pattern until piece measures 7½"/19 cm. Bind off.

○ Repeat for second sleeve.

Finishing

○ Measure down 4¼"/11 cm from shoulders and place markers on front and back edges. Sew sleeve to body between these markers. Sew sleeve and side seams.

○ Knit two 3-stitch I-cords 6"/15 cm long. Sew one I-cord on each front edge at marker for closing ties. Tie knots near ends of I-cords. Weave in all ends.

SAND STITCH

☐ knit on RS rows, purl on WS rows

▪ purl on RS rows, knit on WS rows

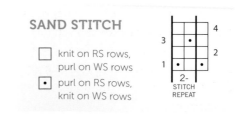

Windowpane Cardigan

Designed by Bonnie Evans

This sweet baby sweater features modular knitting for the fronts, Moss Stitch for the back, stockinette stitch for the sleeves, and garter stitch as an accent throughout.

SIZES AND FINISHED MEASUREMENTS	To fit 3 months, approximately 16"/40.5 cm chest circumference
YARN	Online Supersocke 100 Summer Color, 45% cotton/40% superwash wool/15% nylon, 3.5 oz (100 g)/416 yds (380 m), Color 793
NEEDLES	US 4 (3.5 mm) straight and set of four US 4 (3.5 mm) double-point needles *or size you need to obtain correct gauge*
GAUGE	24 stitches and 36 rows = 4"/10 cm in stockinette stitch; each mitered square measures about 2"/5 cm
OTHER SUPPLIES	Tapestry needle, five ½"/1.3 cm buttons
SPECIAL ABBREVIATIONS	**sk2p** slip 1, knit 2 together, pass slipped stitch over knit together stitches **sp2p** slip 1, purl 2 together, pass slipped stitch over purl together stitches

Knitting the Right Front

○ Using two double-point needles, cast on 25 stitches and make a Mitered Square (see page 183). With last stitch still on needle and right side facing, pick up and knit (see page 280) 12 stitches along top of completed square, then cast on 12 stitches with the backward-loop method (see page 276) (Fig. 1). *You now have 25 stitches.*

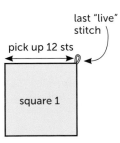

Fig. 1

○ Turn work and knit another mitered square, beginning with Row 1.

○ Repeat two more times so you have a column of four squares. Cut yarn and pull through last stitch.

KNITTING THE SECOND COLUMN

○ *Note:* Depending on yarn patterning, you may want to pull out a length of yarn and set aside or begin from the opposite end of the ball to keep the colors from repeating in adjacent squares.

○ Cast on 12 stitches, pick up 1 stitch in lower right corner of square 1 (A), then pick up 12 stitches along the right side of the same square (Fig. 2). *You now have 25 stitches.*

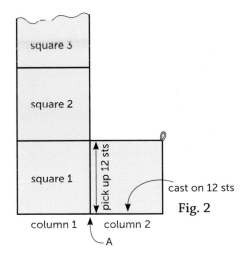

Fig. 2

○ Turn work and knit another mitered square.

○ For the next square, pick up and knit 12 stitches along the top of the last square knitted, then pick up and knit 12 stitches along the right side of the second square (Fig. 3).

○ Turn work and knit another mitered square.

○ Repeat two more times so you have two columns with four squares each. Cut yarn and pull through last stitch. Set piece aside.

Fig. 3

square 3

square 2

pick up 12 sts

pick up 12 sts

square 1

last "live" stitch

column 1

column 2

Knitting the Left Front

○ Work as for right front.

Knitting the Back

○ With straight needles, cast on 52 stitches. Knit 2 rows. Work even in Moss Stitch until piece measures same as fronts. Bind off.

Joining the Fronts and Back

○ Lightly block all pieces. Join fronts to back along outer square of shoulders with mattress stitch (see page 280), leaving the inner squares open for the neck. Join fronts to back along bottom two side squares, leaving the upper two squares open for the armholes.

. . . .

Pattern Essentials

MITERED SQUARE

Cast on 25 stitches.

Row 1 (WS): K11, sk2p, K11.

Row 2 and all even-numbered rows through Row 20: Knit or purl (see Note below).

Row 3: P10, sp2p, P10.

Row 5: P9, sp2p, P9.

Row 7: P8, sp2p, P8.

Continue in this manner, working 1 fewer stitch before and after the decrease on odd-numbered rows and knitting even-numbered rows until 3 stitches remain.

Row 22: Sk2p. Do not cut yarn.

Note: For added interest, make a random row or two in garter stitch; try the second row after a color change in the yarn.

MOSS STITCH

Row 1: K1, *P2, K2; repeat from * to last 3 stitches, P2, K1.

Row 2: P1, *K2, P2; repeat from * to last 3 stitches, K2, P1.

Row 3: Repeat Row 2.

Row 4: Repeat Row 1.

Repeat Rows 1–4 for pattern.

. . . .

Knitting the Sleeves

○ Using three double-point needles, pick up and knit 54 stitches around armhole. Divide stitches evenly and join into a round.

○ Knit 7 rounds.

○ Decrease Round: K1, K2tog tbl, knit to last 3 stitches, K2tog, K1.

○ Continue in stockinette stitch and work the decrease round every sixth round until 42 stitches remain.

○ Purl 1 round. Bind off in purl.

○ Repeat for second sleeve, being sure to start at the same place in the color pattern if you want the sleeves to match.

Knitting the Front Bands

○ With right side of right front facing, begin at bottom and pick up and knit 48 stitches along front edge.

○ Knit 3 rows.

○ Buttonhole Row: K4, yo, K2tog, *K8, yo, K2tog; repeat from * to last 2 stitches, K2.

○ Knit 2 rows.

○ Bind off.

○ With right side of left front facing, begin at top and pick up and knit 48 stitches along front edge.

○ Knit 6 rows.

○ Bind off.

Knitting the Collar

○ With right side facing, begin at top of buttonhole band and pick up and knit 16 stitches along right front neck edge, 24 stitches along back neck, and 16 stitches along left front edge. *You now have 56 stitches.*

○ Knit 11 rows.

○ Bind off loosely.

Finishing

○ Weave in ends. Sew buttons to button band, opposite buttonholes.

Baby Boy Vest and Bow Tie

Designed by Patti Ghezzi

Cute isn't just for little girls! This smart ensemble is great for special occasions and for keeping baby warm on cool days. The vest is designed for a loose fit, and the bow tie can be pinned right to baby's Onesie. Worked in heavy sock yarn, this is a quickie.

KNITTING THE VEST

Knitting the Ribbing

○ With circular needle, cast on 92 stitches. Place marker and join into a round, being careful not to twist the stitches.

○ Rounds 1–4: *K2, P2; repeat from * to end of round.

○ Round 5: (K2tog, K5) two times, K2tog, K2, P2, K6, P2, K2tog, (K5, K2tog) eight times, K6. *You now have 80 stitches.*

SIZES AND FINISHED MEASUREMENTS	To fit 6 months, approximately 20"/51 cm chest circumference
YARN	Briggs & Little Tuffy Canadian Sock Yarn, 80% wool/20% nylon, 4 oz (113 g)/215 yds (197 m), Color 95 Red Mix
NEEDLES	US 8 (5 mm) circular needle 16"/40 cm long, set of four US 8 (5 mm) double-point needles, and US 5 (3.75 mm) straight needles *or size you need to obtain correct gauge*
GAUGE	15 stitches and 22 rows = 4"/10 cm in stockinette stitch
OTHER SUPPLIES	Stitch markers, cable needle, scrap yarn for holders, tapestry needle, 1½"/4 cm safety pin
SPECIAL ABBREVIATIONS	**C6B** slip 3 stitches to cable needle and hold in back, knit 3 from left-hand needle, knit 3 from cable needle **C6F** slip 3 stitches to cable needle and hold in front, knit 3 from left-hand needle, knit 3 from cable needle

Knitting the Body

○ Next Round: K15, place marker, work Round 1 of Cable chart, place marker, K15, place marker for right underarm, K40.

○ Working Cable chart on the 10 center front stitches and stockinette stitch on all other stitches, work even in pattern until piece measures 4½"/11.5 cm from cast-on edge.

Knitting the Front

○ Row 1: Remove marker, bind off 2 stitches, work in established pattern to right underarm marker. Place remaining 40 stitches on holder for the back. Turn.

○ Row 2: Bind off 2, work in established pattern to end of row.

○ Row 3: Bind off 1, work in established pattern to end of row.

○ Row 4: Bind off 1, work in established pattern to end of row. *You now have* 34 stitches.

○ Row 5: Slip 1, ssk, work in established pattern to last 3 stitches, K2tog, K1 *You now have* 32 stitches.

○ Row 6: Slip 1, work in established pattern to end of row.

○ Repeat Rows 5 and 6 three more times. *You now have* 26 stitches. Work even in established pattern until piece measures 7½"/19 cm from cast-on edge.

SHAPING THE FRONT NECK

○ Row 1: Slip 1, work in established pattern over 10 stitches, K2tog. Place remaining 13 stitches on holder for right side.

○ Rows 2, 4, and 6: P2tog, work in established pattern to end of row.

○ Rows 3, 5, 7, and 9: Slip 1, work in established pattern to last 2 stitches, K2tog.

○ Rows 8 and 10: Purl.

○ You have 5 stitches at the end of Row 10.

○ Work even, slipping the first stitch purlwise on right-side rows, until piece measures 10"/25.5 cm from cast-on edge. Bind off.

○ Place held 13 stitches on needles for right front and work as above, reversing the shaping.

Knitting the Back

○ Place 40 held back stitches on needle and attach yarn with right side facing.

○ Row 1 (RS): Bind off 2, knit to end of row.

○ Row 2: Bind off 2, purl to end of row.

○ Row 3: Bind off 1, knit to end of row.

○ Row 4: Bind off 1, purl to end of row. *You now have* 34 stitches.

○ Row 5: Slip 1, ssk, knit to last 3 stitches, K2tog, K1.

○ Row 6: Slip 1, purl to end of row.

○ Repeat Rows 5 and 6 three more times. *You now have* 26 stitches.

○ Work even, slipping the first stitch of every row, until piece measures 9"/23 cm from cast-on edge, ending with a wrong-side row.

SHAPING THE BACK NECK

○ Next Row (RS): Slip 1, K3, ssk, place next 14 stitches on holder, place last 6 stitches on separate holder.

○ Work 3 rows in stockinette stitch, slipping the first stitch of each row at armhole edge. Bind off.

○ Place 6 held shoulder stitches on needle. With right side facing and beginning at neck edge, attach yarn and K2tog, knit to end of row. *You now have* 5 stitches.

○ Work 3 rows in stockinette stitch, slipping the first stitch of each row at armhole edge. Bind off.

○ Sew front and back together at shoulder seams.

Knitting the Armhole Edges

○ With double-point needles and right side facing, pick up and knit (see page 280) 36 stitches around armhole.

○ Join into a round and work 3 rounds of K2, P2 rib. Bind off.

○ Repeat for second armhole.

Knitting the Neck Edge

○ Place 14 held back stitches on one double-point needle. With right side facing, pick up and knit 38 stitches around neck onto two double-point needles. *You now have* 52 stitches. Join into a round and work 3 rounds of K2, P2 rib. Bind off.

Finishing

○ Weave in ends. Block.

KNITTING THE BOW TIE

○ With smaller needle, cast on 5 stitches. Work stockinette stitch for 7"/18 cm. Bind off.

○ With wrong sides together, fold cast-on and bound-off edges to center and sew to join. Sew side openings closed. Thread needle with 12"/30.5 cm of yarn and secure at center back of tie. Wrap the yarn around the center of the tie, pulling firmly to shape. Sew safety pin to back. Weave in ends.

CABLE

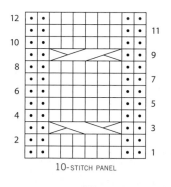

10-STITCH PANEL

☐ knit on RS rows, purl on WS rows

⊡ purl on RS rows, knit on WS rows

C6B

C6F

Fiesta Frock

Designed by Elizabeth (Beth) Hood

A combination of Feather and Fan pattern, stockinette, and Seed Stitch make this frock a simple joy to knit. And baby will be ready for any party when donning matching bootees! (Use your favorite bootee pattern.)

SIZES AND FINISHED MEASUREMENTS	To fit 0–3 months, approximately 17"/43 cm chest circumference
YARN	Noro Silk Garden Sock Yarn, 40% lamb's wool/25% silk/25% nylon/10% kid mohair, 3.5 oz (100 g)/328 yds (300 m), Color S87
NEEDLES	US 4 (3.5 mm) circular needle 24"/60 cm long and set of four US 4 (3.5 mm) double-point needles *or size you need to obtain correct gauge*
GAUGE	28 stitches = 4"/10 cm in stockinette stitch
OTHER SUPPLIES	Stitch marker, scrap yarn for holders, two straight pins, three ½"/1.3 cm buttons, tapestry needle

Knitting the Skirt

○ With circular needle, cast on 204 stitches. Place marker and join into a round, being careful not to twist the stitches.

○ Rounds 1 and 2: Knit.

○ Round 3: *Yo, K2tog; repeat from * to end of round.

○ Rounds 4–6: Knit.

○ Round 7: Turn hem to inside along picot folding (yarn over) row. Knit first stitch from needle together with first cast-on stitch. Continue until the hem is complete.

○ Round 8: Knit.

○ Work Rows 1–4 of Fiesta Feather and Fan pattern three times.

Pattern Essentials

FIESTA FEATHER AND FAN

Round 1: Knit.

Round 2: K2tog twice, *(yo, K1) four times, K2tog four times; repeat from * to last 8 stitches, (yo, K1) four times, K2tog twice.

Round 3: Knit.

Round 4: Purl.

Repeat Rounds 1–4 for pattern.

SEED STITCH

Row 1: *K1, P1; repeat from * to last stitch, K1.

Repeat Row 1 for pattern.

○ Work stockinette stitch until piece measures 5"/12.5 cm from picot edge.

DECREASING FOR THE BODICE

○ Round 1: *K2tog; repeat from * to end of round. *You now have* 102 stitches.

○ Round 2: *P2tog; repeat from * to end of round. *You now have* 51 stitches. *Note:* Stitches will be stretched on needles; allow them to remain so.

○ Round 3: *K1, M1; repeat from * to end of round. *You now have* 102 stitches.

○ Repeat Rounds 2 and 3 once more.

Knitting the Bodice

○ Knit 51 stitches for the front and place remaining 51 stitches on hold for the back.

○ Work back and forth in Seed Stitch until bodice measures 2¼"/5.5 cm.

○ Continuing in Seed Stitch pattern, work 21 stitches, attach second strand of yarn, bind off 9 stitches, work 21 stitches in pattern. Working both sides at the same time, continue in pattern and bind off 1 stitch at each neck edge every other row six times. *You now have 15 stitches for each shoulder.* At the same time, when bodice measures 4"/10 cm, work buttonholes on left front shoulder as follows.

○ Buttonhole Row: Continuing in pattern, work 1, yo, K2tog, work 2, yo, K2tog, work 2, yo, K2tog, work to end of row.

○ Work even until bodice measures 4½"/11.5 cm. Bind off left shoulder, place right shoulder stitches on hold.

KNITTING THE BACK BODICE

○ With right sides facing, place 51 held stitches onto circular needle.

○ Work even until piece measures same as front, ending with a wrong side row. With right side facing, place 51 held stitches onto circular needle.

○ Next Row (RS): Work 15 stitches and place on hold for right shoulder; bind off 21 stitches; work remaining 15 stitches in pattern for 1"/2.5 cm more. Bind off.

○ Join right shoulders together with three-needle bind off (see page 282). Pin front shoulder flap over back shoulder flap.

Knitting the Sleeves

○ With double-point needles, right side facing, and beginning at underarm, pick up and knit (see page 280) 20 stitches to shoulder and 20 stitches from shoulder back to underarm, picking up through two layers at the shoulder. Place marker and join into a round.

○ Round 1: K2, *(yo, K1) four times, K2tog four times; repeat from * to last 2 stitches, K2.

○ Round 2: Knit.

○ Round 3: Purl.

○ Round 4: Knit.

○ Repeat Rounds 1–4 three times or to desired length. Bind off.

Finishing

○ Sew three buttons to left back shoulder, opposite buttonholes.

○ With circular needle and right side facing, pick up and knit 50 stitches along neck edge. Working back and forth, work stockinette stitch for ¾"/2 cm. Bind off. Weave in ends.

FIESTA FEATHER AND FAN

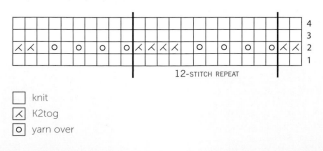

12-STITCH REPEAT

☐ knit

☒ K2tog

☉ yarn over

Garden Trellis Dress

Designed by Susan Boye

Three stitch patterns combine with stockinette stitch to make this lively baby jumper. Because it's knitted in the round, finishing is minimal — just join two 10-stitch shoulder seams and you're done!

SIZES AND FINISHED MEASUREMENTS	To fit 0–3 months, approximately 17"/43 cm circumference
YARN	SRK Kertzer On Your Toes Bamboo, 75% bamboo/25% nylon, 3.5 oz (100 g)/328 yds (300 m), Rainforest Dew
NEEDLES	US 6 (4 mm) circular needle 24"/60 cm long *or size you need to obtain correct gauge*
GAUGE	23 stitches and 34 rounds = 4"/10 cm in stockinette stitch
OTHER SUPPLIES	Stitch markers, scrap yarn for holders, tapestry needle

Knitting the Skirt

○ Cast on 144 stitches. Place marker and join into a round, being careful not to twist the stitches.

○ Work Rounds 1–4 of Feather and Fan chart three times.

○ Round 13: K72, place marker, knit to end of round.

○ Round 14: Knit.

○ Rounds 15–24: *K33, work Diamond Eyelet chart over 6 stitches, knit to marker; repeat from * to end of round.

○ Rounds 25–34: *K13, work Diamond Eyelet chart over 6 stitches, K34, work Diamond Eyelet chart over 6 stitches, knit to marker; repeat from * to end of round.

○ Rounds 35–54: Repeat Rounds 15–34.

○ Rounds 55–64: Repeat Rounds 15–24.

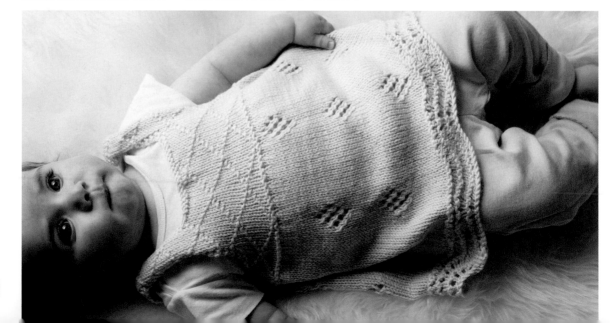

○ Round 65: *K1, K2tog; repeat from * to end of round. *You now have 96 stitches.*

Setting Up for the Yokes

○ Purl 1 round.

○ Work Rounds 1–11 of Diamond Trellis chart, ending 3 stitches before end of last round.

○ Next Round: Bind off 6 stitches (removing marker), work established Diamond Trellis chart to 3 stitches before marker, place 42 stitches just worked on holder for back yoke, bind off 6 stitches (removing marker), work established Diamond Trellis chart to end of round. Yoke is now worked back and forth.

Knitting the Front Yoke

○ Row 1 (WS): K2, work Diamond Trellis chart as established to last 2 stitches, K2.

○ Row 2: K2, ssk, work chart as established to last 4 stitches, K2tog, K2. *You now have* 40 stitches.

○ Row 3: Repeat Row 1.

○ Row 4: Repeat Row 2. *You now have* 38 stitches.

○ Rows 5–15: Keeping the first and last 2 stitches in garter stitch, work chart as established on center 34 stitches.

FEATHER AND FAN

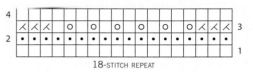

18-STITCH REPEAT

DIAMOND EYELET

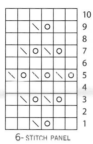

6-STITCH PANEL

DIAMOND TRELLIS

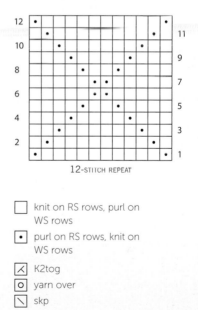

12-STITCH REPEAT

☐ knit on RS rows, purl on WS rows

☐ purl on RS rows, knit on WS rows

☐ K2tog

☐ yarn over

☐ skp

○ Row 16: K2, work the chart as established on the next 8 stitches, P18, work chart as established to the last 2 stitches, K2.

○ Row 17: K2, work chart as established on next 6 stitches, K2; place these 10 stitches on holder for right shoulder strap, bind off 18 pwise, K2, work chart as established on next 6 stitches, K2. Work left shoulder strap on remaining 10 stitches as follows.

KNITTING THE LEFT SHOULDER STRAP

○ Keeping the first and last 2 stitches in garter stitch, work in chart as established for 20 rows more, ending on a wrong-side row. Place 10 stitches on holder.

KNITTING THE RIGHT SHOULDER STRAP

○ Place 10 held right shoulder stitches on needle with right side facing. Join yarn and work as for left shoulder strap. Place stitches on holder.

Knitting the Back Yoke

○ With wrong side facing, place 42 held back stitches on needle. Work as for front yoke.

Finishing

○ Join shoulders with three-needle bind off (see page 282). Weave in ends. Block.

Crazy Wavy Toddler Dress

Designed by Kimberly Conterio

This dress is worth the effort required to "rearrange" the self-patterning yarn to create a dramatically striped skirt and smooth transitional top. Be prepared to pull out sections to make things pretty!

SIZES AND FINISHED MEASUREMENTS	To fit toddler, approximately 19"/48 cm chest circumference
YARN	Schoppel Wolle Zauberball, 75% wool/ 25% nylon, 3.5 oz (100 g)/462 yds (420 m), Fuchsienbeet
NEEDLES	US 3, 4, and 5 (3.25, 3.5, and 3.75 mm) circular needles 24"/60 cm long, and set of four US 3 (3.25 mm) double-point needles *or size you need to obtain correct gauge*
GAUGE	26 stitches and 34 rows = 4"/10 cm in stockinette stitch on medium-size needle
OTHER SUPPLIES	Scrap yarn for holders, tapestry needle, five ½"/1.3 cm buttons
SPECIAL ABBREVIATIONS	**WT** wrap and turn (see page 282)

Knitting the Waistband

○ With medium-size needle, cast on 13 stitches.

○ Row 1 (RS): *K1, P1; repeat from * to last stitch, K1.

○ Row 2: *P1, K1; repeat from * to last stitch, P1.

○ Repeat Rows 1 and 2 until piece measures 20½"/52 cm, ending with a wrong-side row. Bind off, leaving last stitch on needle.

Knitting the Top

○ Pick up and knit (see page 280) 127 stitches along long edge of band. *You now have* 128 stitches.

○ Row 1 (WS): Purl.

○ Row 2: Knit.

○ Repeat Rows 1 and 2 two more times, then work Row 1 once.

○ Next Row (RS): K26, bind off 10, K56, bind off 10, K26.

KNITTING THE RIGHT BACK

○ Next (WS): Purl 26. Place remaining stitches on holders.

○ Armhole Decrease Row: K2, ssk, knit to end of row.

○ Next Rows: Continue in stockinette stitch, working Armhole Decrease Row on right-side rows three more times. *You now have* 22 stitches.

○ Next Rows: Work even in stockinette stitch until armhole measures 3½"/9 cm, ending with a right-side row.

○ Next Row (WS): Bind off 9, purl to end of row.

○ Neck Decrease Row: Knit to last 4 stitches, K2tog, K2.

○ Next Rows: Continue in stockinette stitch, working Neck Decrease Row on right-side rows three more times. *You now have* 9 stitches.

○ Next Row: Work 1 more wrong-side row. Bind off.

- -

Pattern Essentials

CRAZY WAVY

Note: Do NOT pick up and knit wraps; leave wraps at base of wrapped stitches throughout.

Rounds 1–3: Knit.

Round 4: K11, *WT, P8, WT, K7, WT, P6, WT, K5, WT, P4, WT, K20; repeat from * to end of round, ending last repeat with a K9.

Rounds 5–9: Knit.

Note: The first set of short rows on Round 10 is worked across the marker; slip the marker each time you come to it.

Round 10: K4, *WT, P8, WT, K7, WT, P6, WT, K5, WT, P4, WT, K20, repeat from * to end of round, ending last repeat with a K16.

Rounds 11–12: Knit.

Repeat Rounds 1–12 for pattern.

- -

KNITTING THE LEFT BACK

○ With right side facing, place 26 held left-back stitches on needle and attach yarn.

○ Armhole Decrease Row: Knit to last 4 stitches, K2tog, K2.

○ Continue in stockinette stitch, working Armhole Decrease Row on right-side rows three more times. *You now have* 22 stitches. Work even in stockinette stitch until armhole measures 3½"/9 cm, ending with a wrong-side row.

○ Next Row (RS): Bind off 9, knit to end of row.

○ Next Row: Purl 1 row.

○ Neck Decrease Row: K2, ssk, knit to end of row.

○ Continue in stockinette stitch, working Neck Decrease Row on right-side rows three more times. *You now have* 9 stitches. Bind off.

KNITTING THE FRONT

○ With right side facing, place 56 held front stitches on needle and attach yarn.

○ Decrease Row: K2, ssk, knit to last 4 stitches, K2tog, K2.

○ Continue in stockinette stitch, working Decrease Row on right-side rows three more times. *You now have* 48 stitches. Work even in stockinette stitch until armhole measures 2¾"/7 cm, ending with a wrong-side row.

○ Next Row: K19 and place on holder, bind off 10, K19.

○ Purl 1 row.

○ Continue in stockinette stitch and bind off 2 stitches at the beginning of next 3 right-side rows.

○ Purl 1 row.

○ Decrease Row: K2, ssk, knit to end of row.

○ Continue in stockinette stitch, working Decrease Row on right-side rows three more times. *You now have* 9 stitches. Bind off.

○ With right side facing, place held 19 stitches on needle and attach yarn.

○ Knit 1 row.

○ Continue in stockinette stitch and bind off 2 stitches at the beginning of next 3 wrong-side rows.

○ Decrease Row: Knit to last 4 stitches, K2tog, K2.

○ Continue in stockinette stitch, working Decrease Row on right-side rows three more times. *You now have* 9 stitches. Bind off.

Finishing the Top

○ Sew shoulder seams together.

KNITTING THE BUTTON BAND

○ With right side facing, using smallest needle, and beginning at top of right back, pick up and knit (see page 280) 36 stitches to base of right back. Knit 4 rows. Bind off.

KNITTING THE BUTTONHOLE BAND

○ With right side facing, using smallest needle, and beginning at base of left back, pick up and knit 36 stitches to top of left back. Knit 3 rows.

○ Next Row: K5, *yo, K2tog, K7; repeat from * two times, yo, K2tog, K2.

○ Knit 1 row. Bind off.

KNITTING THE NECK EDGE

○ With right side facing, using smallest needle, and beginning at top of buttonhole band, pick up and knit 75 stitches along neck edge to end of button band. Knit 4 rows. Bind off.

KNITTING THE ARMHOLE EDGES

○ With right side facing, using double-point needles and beginning at underarm, pick up and knit 66 stitches. Join into a round. Purl 1 round, knit 1 round, purl 1 round, knit 1 round. Bind off.

Knitting the Skirt

○ *Note:* The skirt is worked from both the inside and outside of the ball of yarn. If necessary, rewind into a center-pull ball.

○ With yarn from outside of ball, using smallest needle, and beginning with the stitch just past the button band, pick up and knit 168 stitches along edge of waistband, ending at edge of buttonhole band. *Note:* The button band will be sewn to the inside.

○ Work Rounds 1–6 of Crazy Wavy stitch pattern using yarn from outside of ball.

○ Work Rounds 7–12 of Crazy Wavy stitch pattern using yarn from inside of ball.

○ Repeat Rounds 1–6 using yarn from outside of ball.

○ Change to medium-size needle.

○ Repeat Rounds 7–12 using inside of ball.

○ Repeat Rounds 1–12, changing colors as indicated above.

○ Change to larger needle.

○ Work Rounds 1–12 twice more, changing colors as indicated above.

KNITTING THE SKIRT BORDER

○ Round 1: Knit with yarn from outside of ball.

○ Round 2: Purl with yarn from outside of ball.

○ Round 3: Knit with yarn from inside of ball.

○ Round 4: Purl with yarn from inside of ball.

○ Repeat Rounds 1–4 twice more, then work Rounds 1 and 2 once more. Bind off loosely.

○ *Note:* Your style of knitting will determine yarn usage. Based on this, your border may be longer or it may have to be shorter.

Finishing

○ Sew button band to inside of waistband. Sew buttons opposite buttonholes. Weave in ends. Block.

Play-with-Your-Sock-Yarn Blocks

Designed by Linda Burt

Here's a way to control the look of your self-patterning yarn. Simply start each square at the same place on the color repeat. One ball of Encore will make four blocks.

FINISHED MEASUREMENTS	Approximately 3½"/9 cm square
YARN	Plymouth Encore Sock Yarn, 75% acrylic/25% wool, 3.5 oz (100 g)/300 yds (274 m), Color 7511
NEEDLES	Two US 3 (3.25 mm) circular needles 24"/60 cm long and set of five US 3 (3.25 mm) double-point needles *or size you need to obtain correct gauge*
GAUGE	24 stitches and 36 rounds = 4"/10 cm in stockinette stitch
OTHER SUPPLIES	Tapestry needle, four 3½"/9 cm foam blocks

Knitting the First Square

○ For illustration of assembly, see page 198.

○ Cast on 12 stitches and divide them evenly onto four double-point needles. Join into a round, being careful not to twist the stitches.

○ Round 1 and all odd-numbered rounds: Knit.

○ Round 2: *K1, yo, K1, yo, K1; repeat from * to end of round. *You now have* 20 stitches.

○ Round 4: *K2, yo, K1, yo, K2; repeat from * to end of round. *You now have* 28 stitches.

○ Round 6: *K3, yo, K1, yo, K3; repeat from * to end of round. *You now have* 36 stitches.

○ Round 8: *K4, yo, K1, yo, K4; repeat from * to end of round. *You now have* 44 stitches.

○ Round 10: *K5, yo, K1, yo, K5; repeat from * to end of round. *You now have* 52 stitches.

○ Round 12: *K6, yo, K1, yo, K6; repeat from * to end of round. *You now have* 60 stitches.

○ Round 14: *K7, yo, K1, yo, K7; repeat from * to end of round. *You now have* 68 stitches.

○ Round 15: Knit.

○ Cut yarn. Thread tail from cast on onto tapestry needle and draw through the stitches in Round 1. Pull up snug and fasten off on inside.

○ Transfer 68 stitches to a circular needle, allowing stitches to rest on the cable.

Knitting the Second Square

○ Make another square like the first but leave stitches on double-point needles and *do not cut the yarn.*

○ *Slip the last 9 stitches worked onto an empty double-point needle. Knit 8 stitches from next needle onto this one. *You now have* 17 stitches on the needle. Slip the remaining 51 stitches onto two double-point needles.** Set aside.

○ Pick up Square #1 on circular needle with right side facing. Slip 9 stitches from right-hand side of needle onto an empty double-point needle. Slip 8 stitches from left-hand side of needle onto the same double-point needle. *You now have* 17 stitches on the double-point needle.

○ With wrong side together, use three-needle bind off (see page 282) to join the two sets of 17 stitches on double-point needles. Cut the yarn and pull through the last stitch. Place the live stitches from the two squares, now joined, onto the circular needle, allowing stitches to rest on the cable.

Knitting the Third Square

○ Make a third square like the second, including instructions between * and ** and *do not cut the yarn.* Pick up the circular needle with two attached squares and slip the 17 Square #2 stitches opposite the seamed edge onto an empty double-point needle, leaving an equal number of stitches on each side of the circular needle.

○ With wrong sides together, use the three-needle bind off (see page 282) to join the two sets of 17 stitches from Squares #2 and #3 (see Fig. 1 on page 198). Cut the yarn and pull through the last stitch. Place the live stitches from this square onto the same circular needle.

Knitting the Fourth Square

○ Make another square as before and join it to Square #3. *You now have four joined squares.* Place 17 stitches opposite the last seamed edge onto one double-point needle. Slip the stitches from one side of Squares #4, 3, 2, and 1 onto a spare circular needle, then slip 17 stitches opposite the first bound-off edge onto one double-point needle (see Fig. 2 below). Join 17 stitches of Square #4 (B) to 17 stitches of Square #1 (A).

Knitting the Fifth Square

○ Slip the last 9 stitches onto an empty double-point needle. Knit the next 8 stitches onto same needle. This square will form the bottom of the block. Reposition the stitches on the four needles so there are 17 stitches on each needle.

○ With wrong sides together, line up one edge of Square #5 with one edge of Square #1. Use the three-needle bind off to join all four edges of

Square #5 with existing squares. Cut yarn and weave in all ends.

Knitting the Sixth Square

○ Make a final square and attach two edges for the top as for the bottom. Insert foam block and adjust until all sides are even. Continue with three-needle bind off on last two edges. Weave in end.

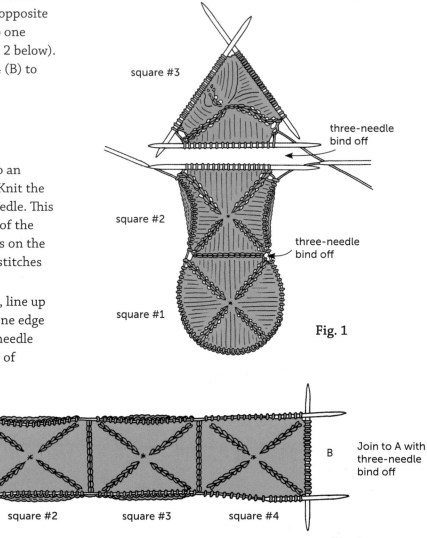

square #3

three-needle bind off

square #2

three-needle bind off

square #1

Fig. 1

A

square #1 square #2 square #3 square #4

B

Join to A with three-needle bind off

Fig. 2

Doll's Pinafore, Cap, and Shawl

Designed by Naomi Herzfeld

This adorable ensemble uses most of the sock yarn for the dress and cap. The shawl is knitted from the reinforcement spool that's tucked inside the yarn skein for the look of a cobweb shawl.

SIZE	To fit an 18"/45.5 cm doll
YARN	Lang Jawoll Bambus, 50% superwash wool/35% bamboo/15% nylon, 3.5 oz (100 g)/460 yds (420 m), Color 136.002
NEEDLES	US 2 (2.25 mm), US 3 (3.25 mm), and US 4 (3.5 mm) circular needles 16"/40 cm long and set of four US 2 (2.25 mm) double-point needles *or size you need to obtain correct gauge*
GAUGE	28 stitches and 36 rounds = 4"/10 cm in stockinette stitch on smallest needle
OTHER SUPPLIES	Scrap yarn for holders, stitch marker, tapestry needle
SPECIAL ABBREVIATIONS	**kfb** knit into the front and back of stitch (1 stitch increased) **kfbf** knit into the front, back, and front of stitch (2 stitches increased)

KNITTING THE PINAFORE

Knitting the Bib

○ Using two double-point needles for working back and forth, cast on 35 stitches.

○ Work flat Raised Rib pattern for 3"/7.5 cm, ending with Row 2.

Pattern Essentials

RAISED RIB (WORKED FLAT)

Row 1: K3, *slip 1 wyif, K3; repeat from * to end of row.

Row 2: K1, *slip 1 wyif, K3; repeat from * to last 2 stitches, slip 1 wyif, K1.

Repeat Rows 1 and 2 for pattern.

RAISED RIB (WORKED CIRCULARLY)

Round 1: *K3, slip 1 wyif; repeat from * to end of round.

Round 2: *P1, slip 1 wyib, P2; repeat from * to end of round.

DIVIDING FOR THE SHOULDER STRAPS

○ K3, (slip 1 wyif, K3) twice and place these 11 stitches on holder, bind off 13 stitches, K3, (slip 1 wyif, K3) twice. Work flat Raised Rib pattern on remaining 11 stitches until shoulder strap measures 4"/10 cm, ending with Row 2. Break yarn and place stitches on holder. With wrong side facing, place held 11 stitches on needle, join yarn, and work until strap matches the first one.

JOINING THE STRAPS

○ Place all 22 stitches on double-point needle. With right side facing, K3, (slip 1 wyif, K3) twice, kfb, K2 (slip 1 wyif, K3) twice. *You now have 23 stitches.*

○ Beginning with Row 2, work flat Raised Rib pattern for 1"/2.5 cm, ending with Row 2.

SETTING UP FOR THE SKIRT

○ With four double-point needles and right side facing, K23, cast on 7 stitches, pick up and knit (see page 280) 35 stitches from bib cast-on row, cast on 7 stitches. *You now have 72 stitches.* Place marker and join into a round, being careful not to twist the stitches. Purl 4 rounds.

Knitting the Skirt

○ Next Round: *Kfb, kfbf; repeat from * to end of round. *You now have 180 stitches.*

○ Change to smallest circular needle and work stockinette stitch for 3"/ 7.5 cm.

○ Change to medium-size circular needle and work stockinette stitch for 2½"/6.5 cm.

○ Change to largest circular needle and work stockinette stitch for 1½"/ 4 cm.

KNITTING THE HEM BAND

○ Continue on largest circular needle.

○ Round 1: Purl.

○ Round 2: Knit.

○ Round 3: Purl.

○ Rounds 4 and 5: Knit.

○ Repeat Rounds 1–5 two more times.

○ Bind off loosely in purl. Weave in all ends.

KNITTING THE CAP

○ Using double-point needles, cast on 76 stitches and divide evenly over three needles. Place marker and join into a round, being careful not to twist the stitches. Work circular Raised Rib pattern for ½"/1.3 cm.

○ Next Round: K2, *kfb; repeat from * to end of round. *You now have 150 stitches.*

○ Change to medium circular needle and knit 4 rounds.

○ Change to largest circular needle and work stockinette stitch for 1"/ 2.5 cm.

DECREASING FOR THE CROWN

○ Round 1: *K13, K2tog; repeat from * to end of round. *You now have* 140 stitches.

○ Rounds 2 and all even-numbered rounds through Round 18: Knit.

○ Round 3: *K12, K2tog; repeat from * to end of round. *You now have* 130 stitches.

○ Round 5: *K11, K2tog; repeat from * to end of round. *You now have* 120 stitches.

○ Continue in this manner, decreasing every other round, working 1 fewer stitch between the decreases, and changing to double-point needles when necessary, through Round 19. *You now have* 50 stitches.

○ Round 20: *K3, K2tog; repeat from * to end of round. *You now have* 40 stitches.

○ Round 21: *K2, K2tog; repeat from * to end of round. *You now have* 30 stitches.

○ Round 22: *K1, K2tog; repeat from * to end of round. *You now have* 20 stitches

○ Round 23: *K2tog; repeat from * to end of round. *You now have* 10 stitches.

○ Round 24: Repeat Round 23. *You now have* 5 stitches.

○ Cut yarn, leaving a 6"/15 cm tail. Thread tail onto tapestry needle and draw through remaining stitches. Pull up snug and fasten off on inside. Weave in all ends.

KNITTING THE SHAWL

○ With reinforcing yarn and the smallest circular needle for knitting back and forth, cast on 5 stitches.

○ Rows 1–6: Knit.

○ Row 7: Cast on 5 stitches, knit to end of row. *You now have* 10 stitches.

○ Row 8: Cast on 5 stitches, knit to end of row. *You now have* 15 stitches.

○ Rows 9–14: Knit.

○ Repeat Rows 7–14 until there are 105 stitches. Bind off loosely. Weave in all ends.

Summer Party Frock

Designed by Jean Austin

This adorable frock is sized for an 18"/45.5 cm doll and is sure to brighten up any girl's party. It is knitted in the round from the bottom to the armholes, then divided and finished back and forth.

SIZES	To fit an 18"/45.5 cm doll
YARN	South West Trading Company Tofutsies, 50% superwash wool/25% Soysilk fibers/22.5% cotton/2.5% chitin, 3.5 oz (100 g)/465 yds (425 m), Color 725 Foot in the Door
NEEDLES	US 2 (2.75 mm) circular needle 16"/40 cm long and set of four US 2 (2.75 mm) double-point needles *or size you need to obtain correct gauge*
GAUGE	32 stitches and 40 rounds = 4" (10 cm) in stockinette stitch
OTHER SUPPLIES	Stitch markers, scrap yarn for holders, one ½"/1.3 cm button, 20"/51 cm length of ¾"/2 cm ribbon

Knitting the Skirt

○ *Note:* Change to double-point needles when there are too few stitches for circular needle.

○ With circular needle, cast on 250 stitches. Place marker and join into a round, being careful not to twist the stitches.

○ Round 1: Knit.

○ Round 2: Purl.

○ Repeat Rounds 1 and 2 one more time.

○ Knit 10 rounds. Skirt is approximately 1¼"/3 cm from cast-on edge.

○ Next Round: *K23, K2tog; repeat from * to end of round. *You now have 240 stitches.*

○ Knit 10 rounds.

o Next Round: *K22, K2tog; repeat from * to end of round. *You now have 230 stitches.*

o Knit 10 rounds.

o Next Round: *K21, K2tog; repeat from * to end of round. *You now have 220 stitches.*

o Knit 5 rounds.

o Next Round: *K2tog; repeat from * to end of round. *You now have 110 stitches.*

o Next Round: *K4, K2tog, K3, K2tog; repeat from *. *You now have 90 stitches.*

Knitting the Waist

o Work K1, P1 rib for 8 rounds.

Knitting the Top

o K45, place marker, knit to end of round.

o Knit 13 rounds.

Knitting the Back

o Row 1: Bind off 3 stitches and knit to first marker. Turn.

o Row 2: Bind off 3 stitches purlwise, purl to end of row. Work back and forth on these 39 stitches for the back.

o Row 3: K1, ssk, knit to last 3 stitches, K2tog, K1.

o Row 4: Purl.

o Repeat Rows 3 and 4 once. *You now have 35 stitches.*

o Work stockinette stitch until top measures 3¼"/8.5 cm above ribbing, ending on a wrong-side row.

SHAPING THE NECK

o K13 and place on hold, bind off center 9 stitches, K13.

o Left back: Work 5 rows in stockinette stitch, decreasing 1 stitch at neck edge on every row. *You now have 8 stitches.*

o Knit 6 rows (garter stitch). Bind off knitwise on wrong side.

o Right back: Place 13 held stitches on needle. With wrong side facing, join yarn at neck edge. P2tog, purl to end of row. Work 4 more rows in stockinette stitch, decreasing 1 stitch at neck edge every row. *You now have 8 stitches.*

o Work 2 more rows, bind off knitwise.

Knitting the Front

o Join yarn with right side facing.

o Row 1: Bind off 3 stitches, knit to end of row.

o Row 2: Bind off 3 stitches, purl to end of row.

o Row 3: K1, ssk, knit to last 3 stitches, K2tog, K1.

o Row 4: Purl.

o Repeat Rows 3 and 4 once. *You now have 35 stitches.*

o Work stockinette stitch until top measures 2¾"/7 cm above ribbing, ending on a wrong-side row.

SHAPING THE NECK

o K15 and place on hold, bind off center 5 stitches, K15.

o Right front: Work 7 rows in stockinette stitch, decreasing 1 stitch at neck edge every row. *You now have 8 stitches.*

o Bind off knitwise on right side.

o Left front: Place 15 held stitches on needle. With wrong side facing, join yarn at neck. P2tog, purl to end of row. Work 6 more rows in stockinette stitch, decreasing 1 stitch at neck edge every row. *You now have 8 stitches.* Knit 2 rows.

o Buttonhole Row: K3, bind off 2 stitches, K3.

o Next row: K3, cast on 2 stitches, K3.

o Knit 2 rows. Bind off.

Knitting the Collar

○ Join right shoulder seam.

○ With wrong side facing, pick up and knit (see page 280) 44 stitches along entire neck edge. Knit 2 rows.

○ Row 1: K2, *M1, K4; repeat from * to last 2 stitches, M1, K2. *You now have* 55 stitches.

○ Row 2 and all even rows: Knit.

○ Row 3: K2, *M1, K4; repeat from * to last stitch, M1, K1. *You now have* 69 stitches.

○ Row 5: K2, *M1, K4; repeat from * to last 3 stitches, M1, K3. *You now have* 86 stitches.

○ Row 7: K2, *M1, K4; repeat from * to end of row. *You now have* 107 stitches.

○ Bind off.

Working the Armholes

○ With double-point needles and beginning at underarm, pick up and knit 36 stitches around armhole. Purl 1 row. Bind off.

Finishing

○ Weave in all ends. Block, using spray starch if desired. Sew button to left back shoulder. Add ribbon at waist, attaching belt loops of single yarn on both sides of the waist.

Sassy in Stripes

Designed by Carol J. Sorsdahl

This sassy doll sweater has raglan styling and is knitted from the top down. It features a rolled-edge collar and ribbing on the cuffs and bottom.

SIZES AND FINISHED MEASUREMENTS	To fit 18"/45.5 cm doll, approximately 13½"/34.5 cm chest circumference
YARN	Coats & Clark Moda Dea Sassy Stripes, 100% acrylic, 1.75 oz (50 g)/250 yds (228 m), Color 6980 Rave
NEEDLES	US 5 and US 6 (3.75 and 4 mm) circular needles 16"/40 cm long and sets of five US 5 (3.75 mm) and US 6 (5 mm) double-point needles *or size you need to obtain correct gauge*
GAUGE	20 stitches and 28 rounds = 4"/10 cm in stockinette stitch on larger needles
OTHER SUPPLIES	Eight stitch markers, scrap yarn for holders, tapestry needle

Knitting the Neck

○ With smaller double-point needles, cast on 48 stitches. Divide stitches so you have 15 stitches each on Needles 1 and 3 and 9 stitches each on Needles 2 and 4. Join into a round, being careful not to twist the stitches. Knit 6 rounds.

Shaping the Body

○ Change to larger double-point needles.

○ Round 1: Knit.

○ Round 2: Continuing in stockinette stitch, on Needle 1, *M1, place marker, K1, place marker, M1, knit to end of needle; repeat from * on Needles 2, 3, and 4. *You now have* 56 stitches.

○ Repeat Rounds 1 and 2 six more times. *You now have* 104 stitches.

○ Work even until piece measures 3"/7.5 cm, changing to larger circular needle when able.

○ Slip stitches in sections onto separate pieces of scrap yarn as follows:

> ○ Section 1: seam stitch, 28 front stitches, seam stitch;
>
> ○ Section 2: 22 sleeve stitches;
>
> ○ Section 3: seam stitch, 28 back stitches, seam stitch;
>
> ○ Section 4: 22 sleeve stitches.

Knitting the Body

○ With larger circular needle, cast on 2 stitches, knit front stitches, cast on 2 stitches, place marker, cast on 2 stitches, knit back stitches, cast on 2 stitches, place marker. *You now have 68 stitches.* Join into a round and work stockinette stitch until piece measures 2½"/6.5 cm from underarm.

○ Decrease Round: K6, (K2tog, K5, K2tog, K6) two times, (K2tog, K6) four times. *You now have 60 stitches.*

○ Change to smaller circular needle.

○ Next Round: *K1, P1; repeat from * to end of round.

○ Repeat last round five times. Bind off loosely in pattern.

205

Knitting the Sleeves

○ With larger double-point needle, cast on 2 stitches, K22 sleeve stitches from section 2, cast on 2 stitches. *You now have* 26 stitches. Place marker and join into a round, being careful not to twist the stitches.

○ Knit 1 round.

○ Working in stockinette stitch, decrease 1 stitch on each side of the marker on this round and then on the tenth round. *You now have* 22 stitches.

○ Work even until sleeve measures 3"/7.5 cm.

○ Change to smaller double-point needles.

○ Decrease Round: (K6, K2tog), two times, K6. *You now have* 20 stitches.

○ Next Round: *K1, P1; repeat from * to end of round.

○ Repeat last round five times. Bind off loosely in pattern.

○ Repeat for second sleeve.

Finishing

○ Sew underarm seams. Weave in ends.

Pretty in Picots

Designed by Terry Liann Morris

Sock yarn is just the right gauge for realistic doll clothing. This design features picot edgings on the bottom hem and cuffs of the sweater and along the edges of the headband.

SIZES	To fit 18"/45.5cm doll, approximately 13½"/34.5 cm chest circumference
YARN	Schoeller Esslinger Fortissima Cottou Colori, 75% cotton/25% nylon, 1.75 oz (50 g)/229 yds (210 m), Color 0004
NEEDLES	Set of five US 2.5 (3 mm) double-point needles *or size you need to obtain correct gauge*
GAUGE	30 stitches and 40 rounds = 4" (10 cm) in stockinette stitch
OTHER SUPPLIES	Scrap yarn, tapestry needle, one hook and eye set, sewing needle and coordinating thread

KNITTING THE SWEATER

○ Cast on 100 stitches and distribute evenly onto four double-point needles. Join into a round, being careful not to twist the stitches.

Knitting the Lower Edging

○ Rounds 1–5: Knit.

○ Round 6 (Eyelet Round): *K2tog, yo; repeat from * to end of round.

○ Rounds 7–11: Knit.

○ With wrong sides together, fold along the Eyelet Round so the cast-on edge meets the needles. Pick up 1 stitch from the cast-on edge and knit it together with the first stitch on the needle. Continue to knit 1 cast-on stitch together with 1 live stitch until all stitches are joined.

Knitting the Body

○ Continue in stockinette stitch until piece measures 2¼"/6 cm from picot points, ending 2 stitches before end of last round.

Dividing for Front and Back

○ Next Round: Bind off 4 stitches, K46 and place these stitches on another needle for the back, bind off 4 stitches, K46 for front. Turn.

KNITTING THE FRONT

○ Working back and forth on front stitches only, continue in stockinette stitch until piece measures 4¾"/12 cm from picot points, ending with a wrong-side row.

○ Next Row: K16 and place on holder, bind off 14, knit to end.

Knitting the Right Shoulder

○ Rows 1, 3, 5, and 7: Purl.

○ Rows 2, 4, and 6: Bind off 2, knit to end of row.

○ Bind off remaining 10 stitches knitwise.

Knitting the Left Shoulder

○ Place held 16 stitches on needle with right side facing.

○ Rows 1, 3, 5, and 7 (RS): Knit.

○ Rows 2, 4, and 6 (WS): Bind off 2, purl to end of row.

○ Bind off purlwise.

KNITTING THE BACK

○ With wrong side facing, attach yarn and purl 46 back stitches. Continue in stockinette stitch for 8 more rows, ending with a wrong-side row.

Dividing for Center Back Opening

○ Next Row (RS): K23, turn.

○ Continue in stockinette stitch on these 23 stitches for right back until piece measures the same as the front to shoulder. Bind off.

○ With right side facing, attach yarn at center back and work the left back as for right back.

Joining the Shoulders

○ With right sides together, sew shoulder seams.

Knitting the Sleeves

○ Beginning at center of underarm, pick up and knit (see page 280) 40 stitches around armhole, distributing them evenly onto three needles. Join to knit in the round and work stockinette stitch until sleeve measures 1¾"/4.5 cm.

○ Decrease Round: K1, ssk, knit to last 3 stitches, K2tog, K1. *You now have* 38 stitches.

○ Knit 4 rounds even.

○ Repeat Decrease Round. *You now have* 36 stitches.

○ Work even in stockinette stitch until sleeve measures 3½"/9 cm.

KNITTING THE CUFFS

○ Next Round (Eyelet Round): *K2tog, yo; repeat from * to end of round.

○ Knit 5 rounds.

○ Bind off, leaving a 12"/30.5 cm tail. Thread tail onto tapestry needle, fold along Eyelet Round with wrong sides together, and sew bound-off edge to inside of sleeve.

FINISHING THE NECK

○ With right sides facing and beginning at back left center opening, attach yarn and pick up and knit 12 stitches along back neck edge, 30 stitches along front neck edge, and 12 stitches along right back neck edge. *You now have* 54 stitches.

○ Row 1: Knit.

○ Row 2: K12, K2tog, *K5, K2tog; repeat from * three more times, K12. *You now have* 49 stitches.

○ Bind off loosely knitwise.

○ With right sides facing and beginning at right back neck edge, attach yarn and pick up and knit 14 stitches along edge of back opening, 1 stitch at the bottom of opening, and 14 stitches along other edge of back opening. *You now have* 29 stitches. Turn and bind off knitwise.

Finishing

○ Weave in all ends. Sew hook and eye to top of center back opening with sewing needle and thread. Block, emphasizing picot points.

KNITTING THE HEADBAND

○ Cast on 90 stitches and distribute evenly onto four double-point needles. Join into a round, being careful not to twist the stitches. Knit 5 rounds.

○ Next Round (Eyelet Round): *K2tog, yo; repeat from * to end of round.

○ Knit 10 rounds even.

○ Repeat Eyelet Round.

○ Knit 4 rounds. Bind off, leaving a 20"/51 cm tail.

Finishing

○ Thread tail onto tapestry needle. Fold both edges along Eyelet Round with wrong sides together and sew cast-on edge to bound-off edge. Weave in all ends. Block, emphasizing picot points.

Bag It and More

Bags and Purses

Decorative Wearables

(Not) Just for the Home

Crocheted Market Bag

Designed by Patricia Colloton-Walsh

Here's a fast, fun, and useful bag that is also very handsome! The yarn is used doubled throughout, making a bag strong enough to hold lots of groceries.

FINISHED MEASUREMENTS	Approximately 12"/30.5 cm wide and 12"/30.5 cm tall
YARN	Noro Kureyon Sock Yarn, 70% wool/30% nylon, 3.5 oz (100 g)/459 yds (420 m), Color 164
CROCHET HOOKS	Sizes H/8 (5 mm) and K/10.5 (6.5 mm) *or sizes you need to obtain correct gauge*
GAUGE	14 single crochet = 4"/10 cm; 8 double crochet post plus 1 chain = 4"/10 cm with larger hook and using yarn doubled
OTHER SUPPLIES	Stitch marker, tapestry needle
SPECIAL ABBREVIATIONS	**FPdc** front post double crochet (see page 212)

Crocheting the Bag

○ *Note:* Yarn is used doubled throughout. Bag is worked with wrong side facing, then turned right side out before completing strap. All FPdc's are worked loosely.

○ Using smaller crochet hook, ch 2 loosely.

○ Round 1: Sc 6 in first chain to create a circle. Slipstitch to first stitch to close circle. Place marker on the first stitch of the round, moving it up each round.

○ Round 2: 2 sc in each stitch around. *You now have 12 stitches.*

○ Round 3: *Sc in next stitch, 2 sc in next stitch [inc made]; repeat from * to end of round. *You now have 18 stitches.*

○ Round 4: *Sc in next 2 sc, inc in next stitch; repeat from * to end of round. *You now have 24 stitches.*

○ Round 5: *Sc in next 3 sc, inc in next stitch; repeat from * to end of round. *You now have 30 stitches.*

○ Round 6: *Sc in next 4 sc, inc in next stitch; repeat from * to end of round. *You now have 36 stitches.*

○ Continue to increase in this manner until you have 60 stitches and Round 10 is complete.

○ Round 11: *Sc in next sc, inc in next stitch; repeat from * to end of round. *You now have 90 stitches.*

○ Round 12: Ch 3 (counts as dc), dc to end of round. Join with slip stitch to top of ch-3.

○ Round 13: Ch 4 (counts as dc and ch-1), skip 1 stitch, *FPdc around next stitch, ch 1, skip 1 stitch; repeat from * to end of round. Join with slip stitch to third ch of beginning ch-4. *You now have 45 posts.*

○ Rounds 14–23: Using larger crochet hook, ch 4 (counts as dc and ch-1), skip 1 chain, *FPdc around next dc, ch 1, skip 1 ch; repeat from * to end of round. Join with slip stitch to third ch of beginning ch-4.

○ Round 24: Ch 3 (counts as hdc), hdc in each stitch and ch-space around. Join with slip stitch to second ch of beginning ch-3. *You now have 90 stitches.*

○ Round 25: Using smaller crochet hook, sc in each stitch to end of round. Mark beginning of round.

○ Rounds 26–28: Sc around.

○ Turn the bag inside out. This is the right side of the bag. Do not cut yarn.

Crocheting the Straps

○ Row 1: With yarn still attached, ch 2, hdc in next 12 stitches. Turn.

○ Working back and forth on these 12 stitches only, continue in hdc for 5 more rows.

○ Decrease Row 1: Ch 2, hdc in next 3 stitches, yarn over, insert hook into next stitch and pull up a loop, yarn over and pull through all 4 loops on hook [dec made], hdc in next 2 stitches, dec, hdc in next 3 stitches. Turn. *You now have* 10 stitches.

○ Next 5 Rows: Continue in hdc.

○ Decrease Row 2: Ch 2, hdc 2, dec, hdc in next 2 stitches, dec, hdc in next 2 stitches. Turn. *You now have* 8 stitches.

○ Continue in hdc on these 8 stitches for 6"/15 cm.

○ Increase Row 1: Ch 2, hdc in next stitch, 2 hdc in next stitch [inc made], hdc in next 2 stitches, 2 hdc in next stitch, hdc in next 3 stitches. Turn. *You now have* 10 stitches.

○ Next 5 Rows: Ch 2, hdc 10. Turn.

○ Increase Row 2: Ch 2 (counts as hdc), hdc in next 2 stitches, inc in next stitch, hdc in next 2 stitches, inc in next stitch, hdc in next 4 stitches. Turn. *You now have* 12 stitches.

○ Continue in hdc for 5 more rows.

○ Attach strap to middle of opposite side of bag with slip stitch. Fasten off. Weave in ends.

○ ○ ○ ○ ○ ○ ○ ○ ○ ○ ○ ○ ○ ○ ○ ○

Pattern Essentials

FRONT POST DOUBLE CROCHET

Yarn over, insert hook from front to back to front around vertical post from the previous round and pull up a loop, (yarn over and pull through 2 loops on hook) two times.

○ ○ ○ ○ ○ ○ ○ ○ ○ ○ ○ ○ ○ ○ ○ ○

FINISHED MEASUREMENTS	Approximately 11½"/29 cm wide and 8"/20.5 cm tall
YARN	Schoppel Wolle Zauberball, 75% wool/25% nylon, 3.5 oz (100 g)/459 yds (420 m), Color 1564 Tropical Fish
CROCHET HOOK	Size C/2 (2.75 mm) *or size you need to obtain correct gauge*
GAUGE	8 double crochet = 1"/2.5 cm; each completed square = 3¾"/9.5 cm square
OTHER SUPPLIES	Coilless safety pins, tapestry needle, four ¾"/2 cm buttons

Zaubertote

Designed by Erin Elkins

One Zauberball and a little crochet know-how is all it takes to make this simple stunner! The color repeats in this yarn make it perfect for working in squares — you can simply let the yarn do the work.

Crocheting the Squares (make 12)

○ Begin with loose slipknot on hook. Work Round 1 stitches into beginning slipknot, then tighten knot when Round 1 is complete.

○ Round 1: Ch 3 (counts as dc), 2 dc, (ch 3, 3 dc) three times, ch 1, hdc in third ch of starting chain.

○ Round 2: Ch 3 (counts as dc), dc in space made by hdc join, *dc in next 3 dc, in corner sp make 2 dc, ch 3, and 2 dc. Repeat from * around, ending with 2 dc in sp. Join with ch 1, half dc in third ch of starting chain.

○ Round 3: Ch 3, dc in sp, *dc in each dc to corner, in corner make 2 dc, ch 3 and 2 dc. Repeat from * around, ending last repeat with 2 dc in corner (eliminate ch 3 and 2 dc). Join with ch 1, half dc in third ch of starting chain.

○ Rounds 4–7: Repeat Round 3. Fasten off.

213

Assembling the Front and Back

○ Arrange the squares as desired with six squares for the front and six squares for the back. To join the squares, place wrong sides together and use safety pins to hold them in place. Single crochet the edges together, first assembling three pieces of two squares each, and then joining those three pieces together.

Crocheting the Gusset

○ With right side facing, join yarn at one corner of back piece, ch 3, dc in each stitch down short edge, across long edge, then up other short edge. Turn. Work 3 more rows in dc.

Assembling the Bag

○ With right sides together, single crochet gusset and front piece together along three sides of bag. Turn bag right side out.

Finishing

○ With right side facing, join yarn at top of gusset, *ch 1, sc through back loop only in all stitches along top edge of bag. Join with slip stitch to first sc. Repeat from * once more. Fasten off.

Making the Bag Handles

○ Ch 63. Dc into third stitch from hook and in each dc across. *Turn. Ch 3 (counts as dc), dc in each dc across. Repeat from * once more. Fasten off. Sew ends of handles securely to right side of bag front and back as shown in photo on page 213. Sew buttons to conceal join. Weave in ends.

Beady Little Bags

Designed by Marji LaFreniere

Here's a great way to use up smaller bits of leftover sock yarn. One bag uses about 1 yard (approximately 1 meter) of yarn. Several yarns are used in the knitted samples.

Knitting the Top of the Bag

○ Thread yarn onto big eye beading needle and string 162 beads. Using the long-tail method (see page 278), cast on 72 stitches as follows: *Cast on 2 stitches, push up three beads; repeat from *. The beads will form a little loop between the stitches. Be careful not to let the beads slip through a stitch. Divide the stitches evenly onto three double-point needles. Join into a round, being careful not to twist the stitches.

○ Round 1: Knit. *Note:* This first round may be awkward to knit, but it will get easier on subsequent rounds.

○ Rounds 2–5: *K3, P3; repeat from * to end of round.

○ Round 6: *K2tog; repeat from * to end of round. *You now have 36 stitches.*

FINISHED MEASUREMENTS	Approximately 2½"/6.5 cm wide and 3½"/9 cm tall
YARN	Regia 4-fädig Mosaik Color, 75% wool/25% nylon, 1.75 oz (50 g)/ 230 yds (210 m), Color 5560 Mosaik; Regia Design Line, 75% wool/25% nylon, 1.75 oz (50 g)/230 yds (210 m), Color 4354 Kaffe Fassett; Colinette Jitterbug, 100% superwash wool, 3.8 oz (110 g)/318 yds (291 m), Color 159 Morello Mash
NEEDLES	Set of four US 2 (2.75 mm) double-point needles *or size you need to obtain correct gauge*
GAUGE	28 stitches and 36 rounds = 4" (10 cm) in stockinette stitch
OTHER SUPPLIES	Big eye beading needle, 200 (approximately 17 g) size 6° seed beads, tapestry needle
SPECIAL ABBREVIATIONS	**SS1B** (slipstitch 1 bead) *Working on the right side:* With yarn in front, slide 1 bead up to needle, slip 1 stitch purlwise, bring the yarn to the back, leaving a bead on the right side of the work.

○ Round 7: Knit.

○ Round 8 (Eyelet Round): *K2tog, yo; repeat from * to end of round.

○ Rounds 9 and 10: Knit.

○ Round 11: *K4, M1; repeat from * to end of round. *You now have* 45 stitches.

○ Rounds 12–14: Knit.

Knitting the Beaded Body

○ Round 1: *SS1B, K4; repeat from * to end of round.

○ Rounds 2–4: Knit.

○ Round 5: K1, *SS1B, K4; repeat from * to last 4 stitches, SS1B, K3.

○ Rounds 6–8: Knit.

○ Round 9: K2, *SS1B, K4; repeat from * to last 3 stitches, SS1B, K2.

○ Rounds 10–12: Knit.

○ Round 13: K3, *SS1B, K4; repeat from * to last 2 stitches, SS1B, K1.

○ Rounds 14–16: Knit.

○ Round 17: K4, *SS1B, K4; repeat from * to last stitch, SS1B.

○ Rounds 18–20: Knit.

○ Repeat Rounds 1–4.

DECREASING FOR THE BOTTOM

○ Round 1: *K7, K2tog; repeat from * to end of round. *You now have* 40 stitches.

○ Round 2: *K6, K2tog; repeat from * to end of round. *You now have* 35 stitches.

○ Round 3: *K5, K2tog; repeat from * to end of round. *You now have* 30 stitches.

○ Continue in this manner, working one fewer stitch between the decreases, until 10 stitches remain.

Finishing

○ Cut the yarn, leaving a 6"/15 cm tail. Thread the tail onto a tapestry needle and draw through remaining stitches. Fasten off on the inside. Weave in ends.

○ Following the instructions on page 277, make a 2-stitch I-cord (or follow the instructions on page 282 and make a twisted cord) about 15"–18"/38–45.5 cm long. Thread the cord through the eyelets, and sew a cluster of beads to the cord ends.

Steppin' Out Wristlet

Designed by Linda Burt

Glitzy yarn too flashy for your feet? Double it up for a quick knit evening purse. With its rhinestone zipper, this one will work for any special occasion. This zipper was purchased online at www.zipperstop.com.

FINISHED MEASUREMENTS	Approximately 9"/23 cm wide and 6"/15 cm tall
YARN	Kraemer Sterling Silk & Silver Sock, 63% superwash merino wool/20% silk/15% nylon/2% silver, 3.5 oz (100 g)/420 yds (384 m), Tuxedo
NEEDLES	US 8 (5 mm) straight needles and set of two US 8 (5 mm) double-point needles *or size you need to obtain correct gauge*
GAUGE	21 stitches = 4"/10 cm in Steppin' Out Cable pattern
OTHER SUPPLIES	Cable needle, tapestry needle, sewing needle and thread, 8"/20.5 cm closed-bottom rhinestone zipper
SPECIAL ABBREVIATIONS	**C4B** slip 2 stitches to cable needle and hold in back, knit 2 from left needle, knit 2 from cable needle **C4F** slip 2 stitches to cable needle and hold in front, knit 2 from left needle, knit 2 from cable needle

Pattern Essentials

STEPPIN' OUT CABLE

Row 1: Knit.

Row 2 and all even-numbered rows through Row 8: Purl.

Row 3: K3, *C4B, K2; repeat from * to last 5 stitches, C4B, K1.

Row 5: Knit.

Row 7: K1, *C4F, K2; repeat from * to last stitch, K1.

Repeat Rows 1–8 for pattern.

STEPPIN' OUT CABLE

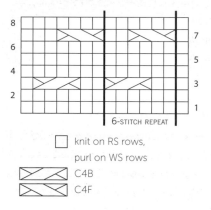

6-STITCH REPEAT

☐ knit on RS rows, purl on WS rows

⬛ C4B

⬛ C4F

Preparing the Yarn

○ Yarn is used doubled throughout. You can either wind it into a center-pull ball and knit from the inside and outside of the ball at the same time, or wind two balls of equal length and knit with one strand from each ball.

Knitting the Purse Front

○ With doubled yarn and straight needles, use long-tail method (see page 278) to cast on 44 stitches. Work Rows 1–8 of Steppin' Out Cable pattern four times, then work Rows 1–3 once. The piece measures approximately 5¾"/14.5 cm.

Knitting the Folding Ridge

○ Row 1 (WS): Knit.

○ Rows 2 and 3: Purl.

Knitting the Purse Back

○ Work Rows 7 and 8 of Steppin' Out Cable pattern once, work Rows 1–8 of cable pattern four times, then work Row 1.

○ Bind off purlwise.

Knitting the Strap

○ With doubled yarn and double-point needles, cast on 3 stitches, leaving a 6"/15 cm tail. Following the instructions on page 277, knit a 3-stitch I-cord 14"/35.5 cm long. Cut yarn, leaving a 6"/15 cm tail. Thread tail through remaining stitches, pull up snug, and fasten off.

Finishing

○ Fold the bag in half along folding ridge and sew side seams. With sewing needle and thread, sew zipper to top opening. Fold I-cord strap in half and attach to top edge of bag at zipper stop. Weave in all ends.

Beaded Party Bag

Designed by Doreen L. Marquart

Dotted with colorful beads, this party bag can be carried by any girl — big or little! With plenty of room for your essentials, the bag stays in shape with some plastic canvas in the base.

FINISHED MEASUREMENTS	Approximately 6"/15 cm tall with 4"×4"/10×10 cm base
YARN	Claudia Hand Painted Fingering, 100% merino wool, 1.75 oz (50 g)/175 yds (160 m), Limeade
NEEDLES	Two sets of five US 2 (2.75 mm) double-point needles *or size you need to obtain correct gauge* (Note: One US 2 [2.75 mm] circular needle 16"/40 cm long may be used in place of one set of double-point needles)
GAUGE	28 stitches and 36 rounds = 4" (10 cm) in stockinette stitch
OTHER SUPPLIES	Scrap yarn for cast on, big eye beading needle, 504 (approximately 42 g) size 6° seed beads, 4"/10 cm square of plastic needlepoint canvas, stitch marker, tapestry needle
SPECIAL ABBREVIATIONS	**SS1B** (slip stitch 1 bead) *Working on the right side:* With yarn in front, slide 1 bead up to needle, slip 1 stitch purlwise, bring the yarn to the back, leaving a bead on the right side of the work.

Stringing the Beads

o With yarn threaded in big eye beading needle, string all beads.

o *Note:* You may opt to knit and join the bases before stringing the beads. Although this lessens the need to push the beads along the yarn, it does require cutting the yarn after making the bases in order to string the beads before starting the body of the bag.

Knitting the Bases (make 2)

o Using a provisional method (see page 280), cast on 28 stitches onto one double-point needle. Working back and forth, knit in garter stitch (knit every row) for 56 rows (28 ridges), ending with a wrong-side row.

o Next Row: Knit 28 onto Needle 1, pick up and knit (see page 280) 28 stitches along side of square onto Needle 2, remove provisional cast on and knit 28 stitches onto Needle 3, pick up and knit 28 stitches along second side of square onto Needle 4. *You now have* 112 stitches. Cut yarn and make second square but do not cut the yarn.

Joining the Bases

o Hold base squares together with right sides out. Knit the stitches of three sides together. Insert the square of plastic canvas and knit the stitches of the last side together. Place a marker for end of round.

Knitting the Bag

o *Note:* After working approximately 1"/2.5 cm you may change to circular needle.

o Rounds 1 and 2: Knit.

o Round 3: *K3, SS1B; repeat from * to end of round.

o Rounds 4 and 5: Knit.

o Round 6: K1, *SS1B, K3; repeat from * to last 3 stitches, SS1B, K2.

○ Repeat Rounds 1–6 eight more times (18 rounds of beads).

KNITTING THE TOP OF THE BAG

○ Rounds 1–3: Knit.

○ Round 4: *K4, bind off 3 stitches; repeat from * to end of round.

○ Round 5: *K4, cast on 3 stitches; repeat from * to end of round.

○ Round 6: Knit.

○ Bind off knitwise.

Finishing

○ Following the instructions on page 277, make a 4-stitch I-cord 24"/61 cm long. Beginning at the center of one side, thread the cord through the buttonholes. After tying the ends of the cord together, locate the center of the cord and tie there also. Weave in ends.

Big Bang Market Bag

Designed by Naomi Herzfeld

This is called the "big bang" because it just keeps expanding. With this bag you can tote enough groceries for one meal or several days. Gauge doesn't matter here because the fabric is so stretchy.

FINISHED MEASUREMENTS	Approximately 24"/61 cm circumference and 13"/33 cm deep, before expanding
YARN	Zitron Trekking XXL, 75% superwash wool/25% nylon, 3.5 oz (100 g)/459 yds (420 m), Color 1002 Avocado Stripe
NEEDLES	US 5 (3.75 mm) circular needle 24"/60 cm long and set of four US 5 (3.75 mm) double-point needles
GAUGE	20 stitches and 22 rounds = 4" (10 cm) in Bella Mesh pattern, unstretched
OTHER SUPPLIES	Tapestry needle, four safety pins or locking stitch markers

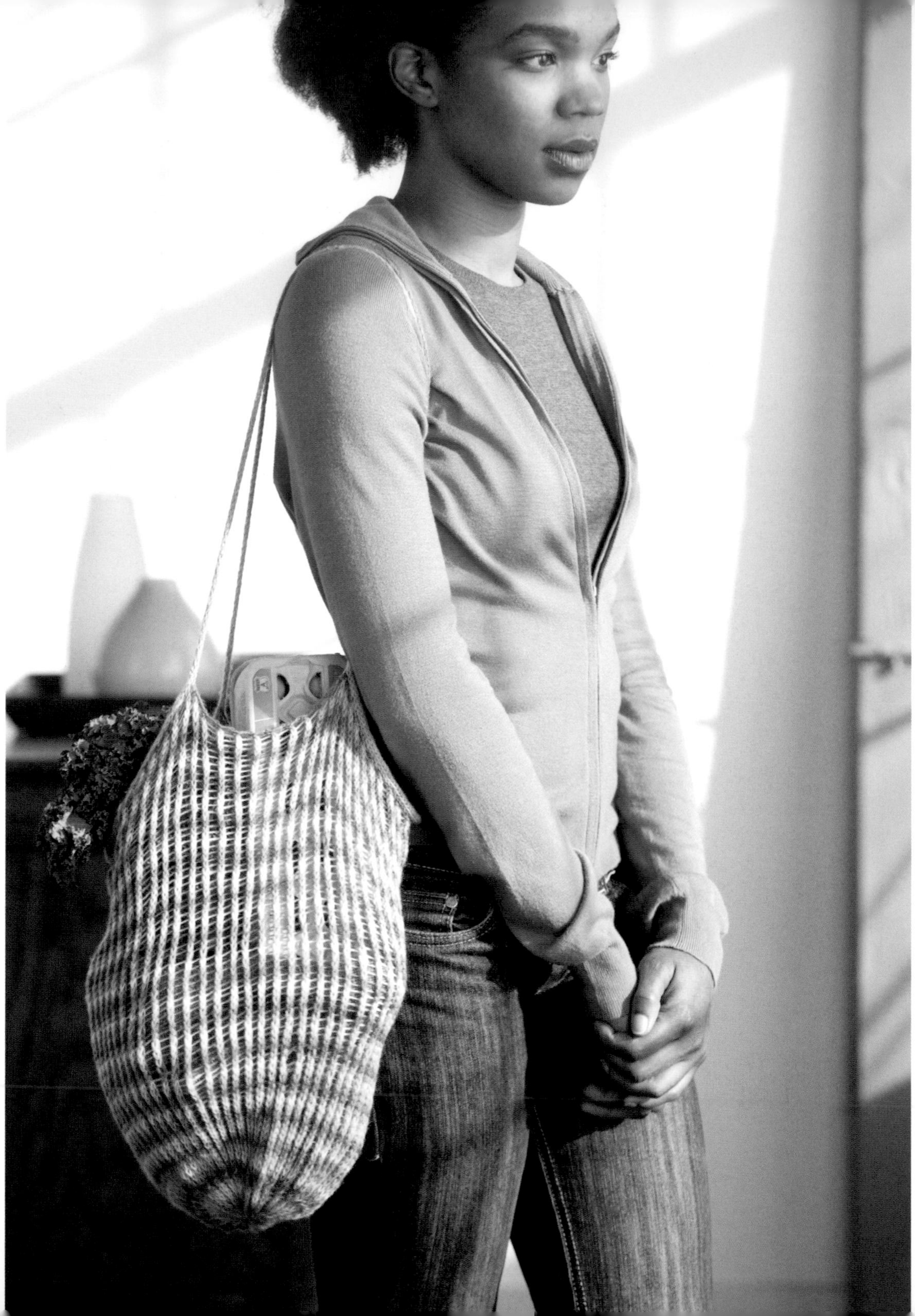

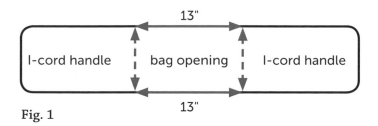

13"

I-cord handle | bag opening | I-cord handle

13"

Fig. 1

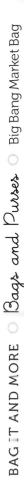

Pattern Essentials

BELLA MESH

Round 1 (WS): *Yo, K2, pass yo over 2 knit stitches; repeat from * to end of round.

Repeat Round 1 for pattern.

Knitting the Handles

○ With 2 double-point needles, cast on 4 stitches. Following the instructions on page 277, work 4-stitch I-cord for 74"/188 cm. Bind off. Sew ends of cord together.

○ Place cord loop on flat surface so that cords are parallel to each other. Use safety pins to mark center 13"/33 cm of each side of cord (see diagram above). The 24"/61 cm segments at each end will be the handles, and the bag is picked up and worked from the center segments of the cord. The remainder of the bag is worked with the wrong side facing.

Knitting the Bag

○ With circular needle, cast on 20 stitches. Pick up and purl (see page 280) 40 stitches along one of the 13"/33 cm segments of I-cord. Cast on 20 stitches. Pick up and purl 40 stitches along the other 13"/33 cm segment of I-cord. *You now have* 120 stitches. Join into a round, being careful not to twist the stitches and making sure bag handles are not tangled. (See Fig. 1.)

○ Work Bella Mesh pattern for about 14"/35.5 cm.

DECREASING FOR THE BAG BOTTOM

○ Round 1: *Yo, K2tog, K2tog, pass yo over 2 K2togs; repeat from * to end of round. *You now have* 60 stitches.

○ Rounds 2–7: Work even in Bella Mesh stitch.

○ Change to double-point needles.

○ Rounds 8 and 9: Repeat Round 1.

Finishing

○ Cut yarn, leaving a 6"/15 cm tail. Thread tail onto tapestry needle and draw through remaining stitches. Pull up snug and fasten off on inside. Weave in ends. Turn bag inside out, with ridges on the outside.

Margaret, A Vintage Purse

Designed by Cara Sharpes

With its sloped shape and pleated detail, Margaret is reminiscent of a 1950s evening bag. The antiqued gold hardware and the beaded handle complete the look.

FINISHED MEASUREMENTS	Approximately 10"/25.5 cm wide at base, 4¾"/12 cm deep, and 5½"/14 cm tall
YARN	Colinette Jitterbug, 100% superwash merino wool, 3.5 oz (100g) / 292 yds (267 m), Color 116 Velvet Plum
NEEDLES	US 3 (3.25 mm) circular needles 16"/40 cm and 24"/60 cm long *or size you need to obtain correct gauge*
GAUGE	24 stitches and 36 rounds = 4" (10 cm) in stockinette stitch
OTHER SUPPLIES	Stitch markers (including one of a different color), scrap yarn for holder, reinforcing purse bottom material such as heavyweight interfacing or other flexible and washable craft sheet (optional), cable needle, 6"/15 cm metal purse frame with loops, 325 (approximately 2 g) size 14° seed beads, 18"/45.5 cm beading wire, two crimp beads, two lobster clasps, sewing needle and coordinating thread

Knitting the Purse Bottom

○ With longer needle, cast on 35 stitches.

○ Rows 1–3: Knit.

○ Row 4: Knit.

○ Row 5: K3, purl to last 3 stitches, K3.

○ Repeat Rows 4 and 5 until piece measures 9½"/24 cm from garter-stitch border.

○ Knit 3 rows. Bind off.

○ *Note:* Pick up stitches around bottom of purse between garter-stitch border and stockinette-stitch bottom so that the garter stitch folds to the inside of the bag. This flap will be used later to secure the reinforcement.

○ With same needle, *pick up and knit (see page 280) 30 stitches along short side of bag, pick up and knit 48 stitches along long side of bag; repeat from * along remaining two sides. *You now have 156 stitches.*

Knitting the Body

○ Join to work in the round.

○ Next Round: K30, place marker, K48, place marker, K30, place marker, K48, place marker (use different color marker here for beginning of round).

○ Work even in stockinette stitch for 1"/2.5 cm.

INSERTING THE REINFORCED BOTTOM (OPTIONAL)

○ Cut reinforcing material into a 10" × 4¾"/25.5 × 12 cm rectangle. Turn the purse inside out and sew rectangle under the garter-stitched flap. Weave in ends and turn purse right side out.

SHAPING THE BODY

○ Round 1: *K1, ssk, knit to 3 stitches before marker, K2tog, K1; repeat from * three more times. *You now have 148 stitches.*

○ Rounds 2 and 3: Knit.

○ Round 4: Repeat Round 1.

○ Repeat Rounds 2–4 four more times, changing to shorter needle when there are too few stitches for the longer needle. *You now have* 108 stitches: 18 stitches on each side and 36 stitches each on front and back.

Dividing for Front and Back

○ K9, place previous 9 left-side stitches, 36 back stitches and 9 right-side stitches, including markers, on holder. Continuing on remaining 54 stitches, work back and forth for front as follows:

○ Row 1 (RS): Slip 1 purlwise, knit to end of row.

○ Row 2: Slip 1 purlwise, purl to last stitch, K1.

○ Row 3: Repeat Row 1.

○ Row 4: Repeat Row 2.

○ Row 5: Slip 1 purlwise, *knit to 3 stitches before marker, K2tog, K1, slip marker, K1, ssk; repeat from * once, knit to end of row.

○ Repeat Rows 2–5 two more times. *You now have* 42 stitches.

Making the Pleats

○ Row 1 (WS): Slip 1 purlwise, purl to last stitch, K1.

○ Row 2: Slip 1 purlwise, knit to 3 stitches before marker, K2tog, K1, slip marker, K5, slip next 5 stitches to cable needle and hold in back, (K1 from left-hand needle together with 1 from cable needle) five times, slip next 5 stitches to cable needle and hold in front, (K1 from cable needle together with 1 from left-hand needle) five times, K5, slip marker, K1, ssk, knit to end of row.

○ Row 3: Repeat Row 1.

○ Row 4: Slip 1 purlwise, knit to end of row.

○ Row 5: Repeat Row 4, creating a folding ridge on outside.

○ Row 6: Repeat Row 4.

○ Row 7: Repeat Row 1.

○ Repeat Rows 6 and 7 once more. *You now have* 30 stitches: 20 stitches for front and 5 stitches for each side. Bind off.

○ Place 54 held stitches on needle and repeat shaping for back of purse.

Finishing

○ Weave in ends. Stitch top of bag to purse frame. String beads onto beading wire, following manufacturer's directions for using crimp beads to secure the ends and attach to lobster clasps, snipping off any extra wire. Attach lobster clasps to purse frame.

Tosh Purse

Designed by Judith Durant

This lovely monochromatic green yarn cried out to be something leafy. The purse is knit in five squares, and in order to prevent any striping, each square is made up of four triangular leaf motifs. The optional beads, reminiscent of dewdrops, can move around slightly on their slipped stitches.

FINISHED MEASUREMENTS	Each panel is approximately 6"/15 cm square
YARN	Madelinetosh Tosh Sock, 100% superwash merino wool, 3.5 oz (100 g)/395 yds (361 m), Jade
NEEDLES	Set of five US 1.5 (2.5 mm) double-point needles *or size you need to obtain correct gauge*
GAUGE	20 stitches = 4" (10 cm) in stockinette stitch
OTHER SUPPLIES	80 (approximately 2 g) size 8° seed beads (optional), big eye beading needle (optional), tapestry needle, scrap yarn for holders, ¼ yd/23 cm lining fabric, sewing needle and coordinating thread
SPECIAL ABBREVIATIONS	**SS1B (slip stitch 1 bead)** *Working on the wrong side:* With yarn in back (toward right side of work), slide 1 bead up to needle, slip 1 stitch purlwise, bring the yarn to the front, leaving a bead on the right side of the work.

Pattern Essentials

SEED STITCH

Row 1: *P1, K1; repeat from * to last stitch, P1.

Repeat Row 1 for pattern.

Preparing the Yarn

○ Thread the yarn through the big eye needle and string 80 beads. *Note:* Push the beads down along the yarn, bringing one up to the needles when necessary.

Knitting the Panels (make 5)

○ Cast on 1 stitch. K1, P1, K1 in this stitch. *You now have 3 stitches.*

○ Following the chart on page 230, work Rows 1–38 of Leaf Triangle pattern. *You now have 41 stitches.* Bind off loosely. Repeat three more times for a total of four triangles.

JOINING THE TRIANGLES

○ With yarn threaded in tapestry needle and right sides facing, join four triangles into a square.

Joining the Panels

○ With yarn threaded in tapestry needle and right sides facing, join one square to each of the four sides of the fifth square. Join the four squares together along the side seams.

Knitting the Top of the Bag

○ Setup: With right side facing, onto Needle 1 pick up and knit (see page 280) 37 bound-off stitches along the top of one panel as follows: (pick up 6 stitches, skip 1 stitch) two times, pick up 13 stitches, (skip 1 stitch, pick up 6 stitches) two times. Onto Needle 2 pick up and knit 23 stitches along the top of the next panel as follows: pick up 1 stitch at the top of the seam, (pick up 1 bound-off stitch, skip 1 stitch) 20 times, pick up 1 bound-off stitch, pick up 1 stitch at the top of the seam. Onto Needle 3 pick up and knit 37 bound-off stitches along the top of the next panel as before, then onto Needle 4 pick up and knit 23 stitches along the top of the last panel as before.

○ Round 1:

  ○ Needles 1 and 3: Work K1, P1 rib as follows: *K1, P1; repeat from * to last stitch, K1.

  ○ Needles 2 and 4: Work seed stitch as follows: P2tog, *K1, P1 to last 3 stitches, K1, P2tog. *You now have* 21 stitches on Needles 2 and 4.

○ Round 2:

  ○ Needles 1 and 3: Work K1, P1 rib as follows: *K1, P1; repeat from * to last stitch, K1.

  ○ Needles 2 and 4: Work Seed Stitch as follows: *K1, P1; repeat from * to last stitch, K1.

○ Round 3:

  ○ Needles 1 and 3: Repeat Round 1.

  ○ Needles 2 and 4: K2tog, *P1, K1; repeat from * to last 3 stitches, P1, K2tog. *You now have* 19 stitches on Needles 2 and 4.

○ Round 4:

  ○ Needle 1: Bind off 37 stitches.

  ○ Needle 2: *P1, K1; repeat from * to last stitch, P1. Place these 19 stitches on scrap yarn to hold.

  ○ Needle 3: Bind off 37 stitches.

  ○ Needle 4: *P1, K1; repeat from * to last stitch, P1.

Knitting the Strap

○ Work Seed Stitch back and forth on 19 stitches on Needle 4 until piece measures 11"/28 cm. Place the other 19 stitches from holder onto a needle and work Seed Stitch until piece measures the same as the first strap. With wrong sides together, join tops of strap with three-needle bind off (see page 282). Weave in all ends.

Making the Lining

○ Cut five 7½"/19 cm squares. Using ½"/1.3 cm seams, sew squares together so there are four sides and one square on the bottom. Press ½"/1.3 cm of top edges to wrong side. Sew a long running stitch along the tops of two opposite sides. Slip the lining into the bag with wrong sides together. Use small stitches to sew the lining to the picked-up stitches inside the bag, adjusting the running stitch to ease in fullness on the strap ends of the bag.

LEAF TRIANGLE

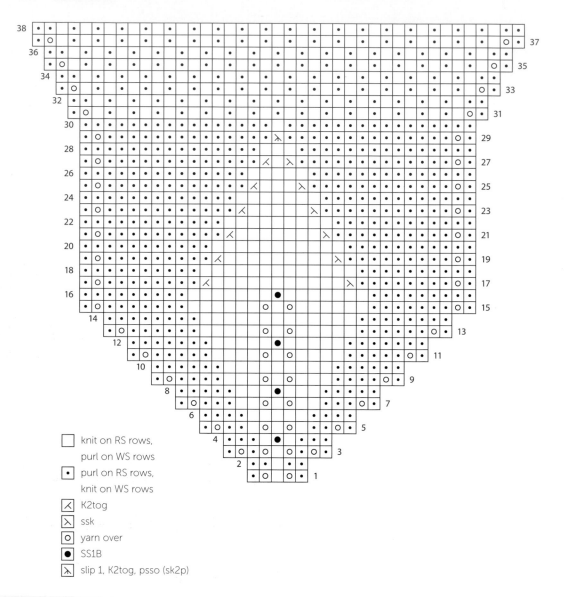

knit on RS rows,
purl on WS rows

• purl on RS rows,
knit on WS rows

K2tog

ssk

○ yarn over

● SS1B

slip 1, K2tog, psso (sk2p)

Ira Garber / John Tavares

Reading Glasses Case

Designed by Edie Eckman

Hang your reading glasses around your neck, and you'll never have trouble finding them again. If you prefer, make the cord shorter for a more traditional look. You can make several cases from one skein of yarn.

FINISHED MEASUREMENTS	Approximately 4½"/11.5 cm) circumference and 6"/15 cm long
YARN	Claudia Hand Painted Yarns Fingering, 100% merino wool, 3.5 oz (100 g)/175 yds (160 m), Poppy
CROCHET HOOK	US G/6 (4 mm) hook *or size you need to obtain correct gauge*
GAUGE	18 stitches and 16 rounds = 4" (10 cm) in Texture Stitch
OTHER SUPPLIES	Tapestry needle
ABBREVIATIONS	**FPtr** front post treble crochet (see page 232)

Knitting the Case

○ Ch 20. Join with a slip stitch to form a ring, being careful not to twist chain.

○ Ch 3 (counts as dc), dc in each ch to end of round, join with slip stitch to top of chain — 20 dc.

○ Work Rounds 1–4 of Texture Stitch until piece measures 6"/15 cm or desired length, ending with Round 2 or 4.

Finishing

○ Flatten tube and with wrong sides of bottom edges together, sc through both layers to seam bottom edge. Fasten off. Make a chain 36"/91.5 cm long, or desired length. Sc in second chain from hook and in each ch to end. Fasten off. Weave in ends. Thread chain through second round of post stitches at top of bag and tie.

Pattern Essentials

FRONT POST TREBLE CROCHET

Yo twice, insert hook from front to back to front around post of stitch indicated, draw up a loop, (yo, pull through 2 loops) three times.

TEXTURE STITCH

Round 1: Ch 1, sc in each stitch to end of round, join with slip stitch to first sc.

Round 2: Ch 3 (counts as dc), FPtr around dc below next sc, *dc in next sc, FPtr around dc below next sc; repeat from * to end of round, join with slip stitch to top of chain.

Round 3: Repeat Round 1.

Round 4: Ch 1 loosely and draw up to level of next round (does not count as a stitch), FPtr around chain below first sc, dc in next sc, *FPtr around dc below next sc, dc in next sc; repeat from * to end of round, join with slip stitch to first FPtr.

Repeat Rounds 1–4 for Texture Stitch pattern.

Ruby Begonia Sunglasses Sock

Designed by Debbie Haymark

This snug little sock will protect your favorite sunglasses from the nicks and scratches they love to attract. Accented with glass seed beads, the top of the bag stays closed to keep the glasses from escaping.

FINISHED MEASUREMENTS	Approximately 5½"/14 cm circumference and 9"/23 cm long, including ruffle
YARN	OnLine Supersocke 100 Holiday Color, 75% superwash wool/25% polyamide, 3.5 oz (100 g)/455 yds (420 m), Color 998 Red
NEEDLES	Set of five US 1.5 (2.5 mm) double-point needles *or size you need to obtain correct gauge*
GAUGE	32 stitches and 48 rounds = 4" (10 cm) in stockinette stitch
OTHER SUPPLIES	Stitch marker, tapestry needle, big eye beading needle, 23 (approximately 3 g) size 4 mm square beads, 69 (approximately 6 g) size 6° seed beads, crochet hook size US C/2 (2.75 mm)

Knitting the Ruffle

○ Cast on 180 stitches and divide evenly onto four double-point needles. Place marker and join into a round, being careful not to twist the stitches.

○ Row 1: Knit.

○ Row 2: Purl.

○ Row 3: Knit.

○ Row 4: *K2tog; repeat from * to end of round. *You now have* 90 stitches.

○ Rows 5 and 6: Knit.

○ Row 7: *K2tog; repeat from * to end of round. *You now have* 45 stitches.

○ Row 8: Knit.

Knitting the "Sock"

○ Work K3, P2 rib for 1½"/4 cm.

○ Work even in stockinette stitch for 6½"/16.5 cm.

Decreasing for the "Toe"

○ Row 1: *K2tog; repeat from * to last stitch, K1. *You now have* 23 stitches.

○ Row 2: *K2tog; repeat from * to last stitch, K1. *You now have* 12 stitches.

○ Cut yarn, leaving a 6"/15 cm tail. Thread tail onto tapestry needle and draw through remaining stitches twice. Pull up snug and fasten off.

Beading the Ruffle Edge

○ Thread yarn onto big eye beading needle and string beads as follows: *1 square bead, 3 size 6° seed beads; repeat from * until all beads are strung. Make a slipknot at the end of the yarn, leaving a 6"/15 cm tail. With right side of ruffle facing, use the crochet hook to pull the slipknot through a cast-on stitch, from inside to outside.

○ *Slip stitch into next stitch, slide a bead up against the slip stitch, chain 1 above the bead to secure it, skip 1 stitch. Repeat from * to end of round, omitting 4 skipped stitches evenly spaced, then slip stitch into the first slip stitch of the round.

Finishing

○ Cut yarn and weave in ends.

Beady Necklace

Designed by Judith Durant

The small amount of elastic in this yarn makes it ideal for knitting choker-style necklaces. This one is knitted in two pieces, and beads are incorporated into the cast-on rows.

FINISHED MEASUREMENTS	Approximately 14"/35.5 cm circumference
YARN	Crystal Palace Panda Soy, 49% bamboo/ 33% soy/ 18% elastic nylon, 1.75 oz (50 g)/ 185 yds (171 m), Fudge Brownie
NEEDLES	US 2 (2.75 mm) straight needles and two US 2 (2.75 mm) double-point needles *or size you need to obtain correct gauge*
GAUGE	28 stitches = 4" (10 cm) in garter stitch
OTHER SUPPLIES	Big eye beading needle, 320 (approximately 9 g) size 8° seed beads in dark brown, 160 (approximately 14 g) size 6° seed beads in silver-lined copper, scrap yarn for holders, one ¾"/2 cm button, small tapestry needle

Preparing the Yarn

○ With yarn threaded in big eye beading needle, *string one size 8° seed bead, one size 6° seed bead, one size 8° seed bead; repeat from * 79 more times for a total of 240 beads.

Knitting the Large Ruffle

○ Using the long-tail method (see page 278), cast on 2 stitches, *slide three beads up to needle, cast on 2 stitches; repeat from * 79 more times. *You now have 162 stitches.*

○ *Note:* Be careful not to allow the beads to go through the cast-on stitches. They should rest between the stitches. Try casting on the stitch immediately following a group of beads by holding the beads in place with your pinky while casting on the stitch; casting on the next stitch will tighten everything up.

○ Row 1 (RS): Knit.

○ Rows 2–4: Knit.

○ Row 5: K1, *K2tog; repeat from * to last stitch, K1. *You now have 82 stitches.*

○ Rows 6–10: Knit.

○ Row 11: Repeat Row 5. *You now have 42 stitches.*

○ Rows 12–16: Knit.

○ Place stitches on scrap yarn to hold.

Knitting the Small Ruffle

○ Prepare yarn and cast on as for first ruffle.

○ Row 1 (RS): Knit.

○ Row 2: Knit.

○ Row 3: K1, *K2tog; repeat from * to last stitch, K1. *You now have 82 stitches.*

○ Rows 4–6: Knit.

○ Row 7: Repeat Row 3. *You now have 42 stitches.*

○ Rows 8–10: Knit.

Joining the Ruffles

○ Place held stitches of large ruffle on a needle with right side facing and needle pointing to the right. Place needle holding small ruffle on top of first ruffle, also with right side facing and needle pointing to the right. Use a double-point needle to join stitches together with the three-needle bind off (see page 282). The bind off will form a decorative ridge along the outside edge of the ruffles.

Finishing

○ Hold the ruffles open with the bind off in the center. On right side of necklace, use a double-point needle to pick up and knit (see page 280) 2 stitches along the edge of the large ruffle, 1 stitch in the bind off, and 2 stitches along the edge of the small ruffle. Work 5-stitch I-cord (see page 277) for 4"/10 cm. Bind off and sew button to end of I-cord. On left side of necklace, use a double-point needle to pick up and knit 2 stitches along the edge of the small ruffle, 1 stitch in the bind off, and 2 stitches along the edge of the large ruffle. Work 5-stitch I-cord for 5"/12.5 cm. Bind off. Fold I-cord back to form a ¾"/2 cm buttonhole loop and secure with yarn end. Weave in all ends.

Möbius Necklace and Earrings

Designed by Grace (Maggie) Covey

The crossed-stitch design is a great way to show off a subtly variegated yarn, and this light and airy necklace is as fun to knit as it is to wear. Complete with matching earrings.

FINISHED MEASUREMENTS	Approximately 3¾"/9.5 cm wide and 34"/86.5 cm long, blocked
YARN	Crystal Palace Panda Superwash, 51% bamboo/39% superwash wool/10% nylon, 1.75 oz (50 g)/186 yds (170 m), Color 0441 Chocolates
NEEDLES	US 3 (3.25 mm) straight needles for necklace; US 0 (2 mm) straight needles for earrings *or sizes you need to obtain correct gauge*
GAUGE	26 stitches = 3¼"/8.5 cm in pattern
OTHER SUPPLIES	Tapestry needle, two French hook ear wires

KNITTING THE NECKLACE

○ Cast on 26 stitches.

○ Rows 1–4: Knit.

○ Row 5: K1, *insert needle into next stitch knitwise, wrap the yarn around needle three times, then finish the stitch, leaving all three wraps on the needle; repeat from * to last stitch, K1.

○ Row 6: K1, *slip next 8 stitches with yarn in back, dropping the extra wraps. *You now have* 8 elongated stitches on right-hand needle. Slip the first 4 of these stitches over the second 4 stitches but do not drop them from the needle. Return all 8 stitches to left-hand needle and knit them, keeping the crossed order; repeat from * to last stitch, K1.

○ Rows 7 12: Knit.

○ Row 13: Repeat Row 7.

○ Row 14: K1, slip 4 stitches with yarn in back, dropping the extra wraps, then cross the first 2 stitches over the second 2 stitches and knit these 4 stitches in the crossed order, *slip 8 stitches and cross 4 over 4 as in Row 4; repeat from * to last 5 stitches, slip 4 stitches and cross 2 over 2, K1.

○ Rows 15 and 16: Knit.

○ *Note:* To change the direction of a cross, work an odd number of knit rows between the pattern repeats.

○ Repeat Rows 1–16 of pattern until piece measures 26"/66 cm, ending with Row 16. Bind off.

Finishing

○ Block to desired measurements. To create a Möbius loop, place strip on flat surface and flip top right corner down to create a half twist in the strip. Fold strip in half and line up ends, maintaining twist. Sew the ends together. Weave in ends.

KNITTING THE EARRINGS

○ Cut a length of yarn about 4 yards (3.7 m) long and separate the plied strands. Use two strands to knit the earrings.

○ Cast on 10 stitches.

○ Rows 1–6: Knit.

237

○ Row 7: Knit 1, knit 8 stitches with three wraps as for Row 3 of scarf, K1.

○ Row 8: K1, work 8-stitch cross pattern as for Row 4 of scarf, K1.

○ Rows 9 and 10: Knit.

○ Rows 11–17: Bind off 1, knit to end of row.

○ After completing Row 17, you have 3 stitches remaining. Knit 2 rows. Bind off and cut yarn, leaving a 4"/10 cm tail.

Finishing

○ Pin into shape on pressing board and steam well. Allow to dry before removing. Use tail to attach to ear wires. Weave in ends.

French Press Snuggly

Designed by Beverly Vasquez

This is just the thing to keep your coffee cozy and warm while you linger after lunch. Sized for a large (six- to ten-cup) French coffee press, the snuggly works up quickly with yarn used doubled throughout.

SIZES AND FINISHED MEASUREMENTS	To fit large (6- to 10-cup) French coffee press, approximately 14½"/37 cm circumference and 12"/30.5 cm tall
YARN	Conjoined Creations Flat Feet, 80% superwash wool/20% nylon, 3.5 oz (100 g)/400 yds (366 m), One-of-a-kind color
NEEDLES	Set of five US 5 (3.75 mm) double point needles *or size you need to obtain correct gauge*
GAUGE	22 stitches and 34 rounds = 4" (10 cm) in stockinette stitch
OTHER SUPPLIES	Four stitch markers (including one of a different color), two 2¾"/7 cm buttons, tapestry needle

Knitting the Top

○ *Note:* Yarn is used doubled throughout.

○ Cast on 40 stitches and divide evenly onto four double-point needles. Place different-colored marker and join into a round, being careful not to twist the stitches.

○ Knit for 1"/2.5 cm.

○ Picot Round: *K2tog, yo; repeat from * to end of round.

○ Knit for 1"/2.5 cm.

○ Joining Round: Fold at Picot Round and *knit 1 stitch from the needle together with 1 cast-on stitch; repeat from * to end of round.

○ Knit for 1"/2.5 cm.

○ Eyelet Round: *K6, yo, K2tog; repeat from * to end of round.

○ Knit 1 round.

Increasing for the Body

○ Round 1: *Kfb, K9, place marker; repeat from * to end of round. *You now have* 44 stitches.

○ Round 2: Knit.

○ Round 3: *Kfb, knit to marker; repeat from * to end of round.

○ Round 4: Knit.

○ Repeat Rounds 3 and 4 until you have 80 stitches. Remove all markers except beginning-of-round (different-color) marker.

Knitting the Body

○ Rounds 1 and 2: Knit.

○ Round 3: Purl.

○ Rounds 4–9: Knit, ending last Round 3 stitches before marker.

○ Round 10: P1, K1, P1, slip marker, (K1, P1) two times, knit to 3 stitches before marker.

DIVIDING FOR THE OPENING

○ Next Round: K1, P1, K1, bind off 1, K1, P1, K1, knit to 3 stitches before bind off, P1, K1, P1. Turn work.

○ *Note:* The remainder of the snuggly is worked back and forth.

○ Row 1: Work 3 stitches in established Seed Stitch (knit the purls and purl the knits), purl to last 3 stitches, work last 3 stitches in established Seed Stitch.

○ Continue working stockinette stitch between Seed Stitch borders, for 2"/5 cm, ending with a wrong-side row.

○ Button-Loop Row: Cast on 12 stitches, then bind them off loosely. Knit the first bound-off stitch together with first stitch on needle to form a loop. Continue in Seed Stitch and stockinette stitch as established.

○ Continue in patterns as established for 3"/7.5 cm.

○ Make second button loop.

○ Work 4 rows in patterns as established.

○ Work 4 rows in Seed Stitch on all stitches.

○ Bind off in pattern.

Finishing

○ Following the instructions on page 277, knit a 3-stitch I-cord 16"/40.5 cm long. Weave I-cord through eyelets. Attach buttons to border opposite loops. Weave in ends.

Posy Cozy

Designed by Rebecca Mercier

This is for the girlie girls out there. Dress up your lotions, perfumes, even soda cans with this delightful cozy of many petals. You could also adapt the design to adorn the top of a sock!

○ ○ ○ ○ ○ ○ ○ ○ ○ ○ ○ ○ ○ ○ ○ ○ ○ ○

Pattern Essentials

ADDING PETALS

Place a petal on a spare needle with right side facing (the first stitch is a purl). Hold the needle in front and parallel to your work. *Purl 1 base stitch together with 1 petal stitch; knit 1 petal stitch together with 1 base stitch; repeat from * to end of petal.

○ ○ ○ ○ ○ ○ ○ ○ ○ ○ ○ ○ ○ ○ ○ ○ ○ ○

Knitting the Petals

○ Cast on 6 stitches.

○ Row 1 (WS): *K1, P1; repeat from * to end of row.

○ Row 2 (RS): (P1, K1) into first stitch, (P1, K1) to last stitch, (P1, K1) into last stitch. *You now have 8 stitches.*

○ Row 3: (K1, P1) into first stitch, (K1, P1) to last stitch, (K1, P1) into last stitch. *You now have 10 stitches.*

○ Row 4: Repeat Row 2. *You now have 12 stitches.*

FINISHED MEASUREMENTS	Approximately 7"/18 cm circumference and 4½"/11.5 cm tall
YARN	Crystal Palace Panda Cotton, 59% bamboo/25% cotton/16% elastic nylon, 1.75 oz (50 g)/182 yds (167 m), Color 0432 Strawberries-Limes
NEEDLES	Set of five US 1.5 (2.5 mm) double-point needles *or size you need to obtain correct gauge*
GAUGE	32 stitches = 4" (10 cm) in stockinette stitch
OTHER SUPPLIES	Scrap yarn for holders, tapestry needle

242

Row 5: Repeat Row 3. *You now have 14 stitches.*

Row 6: Repeat Row 2. *You now have 16 stitches.*

Rows 7–12: Work even in established rib.

Cut the yarn and place stitches on holder. Repeat for 24 petals.

Knitting the Base

Loosely cast on 64 stitches and divide evenly onto three double-point needles. Join into a round, being careful not to twist the stitches.

Rounds 1–10: *P1, K1; repeat from * to end of round.

Round 11: Add four petals.

Rounds 12–15: Repeat Round 1.

Round 16: (P1, K1) four times, add four petals. *Note:* The last 8 stitches from the fourth petal are the first 8 stitches of the next round.

Rounds 17–21: Repeat Round 1.

Round 22: Repeat Round 11.

Rounds 23–28: Repeat Round 1.

Round 29: Repeat Round 16.

Rounds 30–36: Repeat Round 1.

Round 37: Repeat Round 11.

Rounds 38–46: Repeat Round 1.

Round 47: Repeat Round 16.

Rounds 48–56: Repeat Round 1.

Bind off in pattern.

Finishing

Weave in ends.

Moso Netbook Sock

Designed by Kendra Nitta

This pattern uses almost every bit of the skein — you'll have to unravel your gauge swatch and use that yarn too!

SIZES AND FINISHED MEASUREMENTS	To fit a Netbook, approximately 13"/33 cm circumference and 11"/28 cm long
YARN	Knit Picks Stroll, 75% superwash merino wool/25% nylon, 1.75 oz (50 g)/231 yds (211 m), Ash
NEEDLES	US 2 (2.75 mm) circular needle 16"/40 cm long and set of four US 2 (2.75 mm) double-point needles *or size you need to obtain correct gauge*
GAUGE	30 stitches and 44 rounds = 4"/10 cm in stockinette stitch; 27 stitches – 4"/10 cm in pattern
OTHER SUPPLIES	Four split-ring stitch markers, cable needle, tapestry needle
SPECIAL ABBREVIATIONS	**C6B** slip next 3 stitches to cable needle and hold in back, knit 3 from left needle, knit 3 from cable needle **LT** knit second stitch tbl and leave on needle, knit first stitch, slip both stitches off needle **RT** knit 2 together but leave stitches on needle, knit the first stitch, slip both stitches from needle

Knitting the Body

With circular needle, cast on 88 stitches. Place marker and join into a round, being careful not to twist the stitches.

Setup Round: *K1, P2, (K2, P2) ten times, K1 (44 stitches worked), place marker; repeat from * to end of round.

Work K2, P2 rib pattern as established for 2"/5 cm.

Following the Netbook Cable chart on page 245, work pattern Rounds 1–12 seven times.

Knitting the "Heel" Flap

○ Setup Round: K6, turn.

○ Row 1 (WS): Slip 1, P11, leaving end-of-round marker in place, turn.

○ Row 2: (Slip 1, K1) six times, turn.

○ Repeat Rows 1 and 2 ten more times.

Turning the "Heel"

○ Row 1 (WS): P6, P2tog, slip 1, turn.

○ Row 2: K2, ssk, slip 1, turn.

○ Row 3: P3, P2tog, slip 1, turn.

○ Row 4: K4, ssk, slip 1, turn.

○ Row 5: P5, P2tog, turn.

○ Row 6: K5, ssk. *You now have* 6 stitches.

Knitting the Gussets

○ Pick up and knit (see page 280) 12 stitches along side of flap. Place split-ring marker in last stitch at bottom of flap. Work Round 1 of Netbook Cable chart to next marker. Remove marker and work second "heel" as first, including picking up 12 stitches along side of flap and marking last stitch. Work Round 1 of chart to first heel flap, then pick up and knit 12 stitches along other side of first heel flap, marking the first stitch. Knit to original end-of-round marker.

○ *Note:* Move stitch markers up each round as you work the decreases.

○ Work 1 round even, following Round 2 of chart and working in stockinette stitch for the heels and picking up and knitting 12 stitches along second side of second flap, marking the first stitch. *You now have* 124 stitches.

○ Decrease Round: *Knit to stitch before marked stitch, s2kp, work established chart pattern to stitch before marked stitch, s2kp; repeat from * once more, knit to marker. *You now have* 116 stitches.

○ Next Round (Even Round): Work even in pattern.

○ Repeat these 2 rounds, following the chart for the center stitches, for one full pattern repeat. Work 1 more Decrease Round and 1 more Even Round following Round 2 of chart for *both* rounds.

○ Next Round: Work Decrease Round following Round 2 of chart.

○ Next Round: Work Decrease Round following Round 4 of chart. *You now have* 60 stitches.

○ Continue decreasing every round in stockinette stitch, changing to double-point needles when you have too few stitches for the circular needle. When 12 stitches remain, remove markers, arrange stitches onto two double-point needles and graft together with Kitchener stitch (see page 278).

Finishing

○ Weave in ends. Block to fit your Netbook.

NETBOOK CABLE

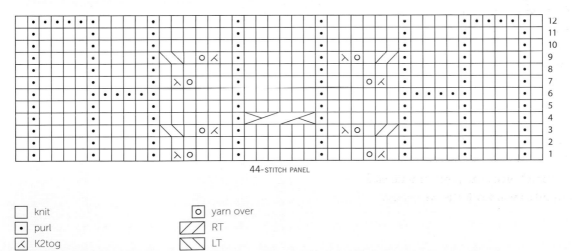

44-STITCH PANEL

	knit			yarn over
•	purl			RT
	K2tog			LT
	ssk			C6B

Umbrella Lamp Shade

Designed by Irina Poludnenko

This unique lamp shade will change the character of any room! It is knitted in eight sections worked off a crocheted base. The frame is a rice-paper parasol lamp shade, 24"/61 cm in diameter, from which the paper has been removed.

FINISHED MEASUREMENTS	Approximately 24"/61 cm in diameter
YARN	Noro Kureyon Sock, 70% wool/30% nylon, 3.5 oz (100 g) 459 yds (420 m), Color 240
NEEDLES	US 5 (3.75 mm) and US 8 (5 mm) straight needles *or size you need to obtain correct gauge*
CROCHET HOOK	Size C/2 (2.75 mm)
GAUGE	14 stitches and 23 rows = 4" (10 cm) in stockinette stitch on larger needle
OTHER SUPPLIES	24"/61 cm-diameter parasol lamp-shade frame, tapestry needle, two or three plastic drinking straws

Crocheting the Top

o *Note:* If you are unfamiliar with crochet terms, see Glossary in the Appendix.

o Chain 30 and join with a slip stitch to form a round. Work 3 rounds of single crochet.

o Increase Round: *2 sc in next stitch, sc in next 2 stitches; repeat from * to end of round. *You now have* 40 stitches.

o Work 8 rounds of single crochet.

Knitting the Panels

o With smaller needles and right side facing, pick up and knit (see page 280) in 5 single crochets at the edge of the top. Purl 1 row.

o Row 1 (RS): K2, M1, K1, M1, K2. *You now have* 7 stitches.

o Rows 2–6: Work even in stockinette stitch.

o Row 7: K2, M1, K3, M1, K2. *You now have* 9 stitches.

o Rows 8–12: Repeat Rows 2–6.

o Continue in this manner, increasing 1 stitch at each end of every sixth row, working stockinette stitch between the increase rows, and changing to larger needles after third increase row, until you have 27 stitches.

o Work even in stockinette stitch until piece measures 11"/28 cm from base. Bind off loosely. Make seven more panels.

Finishing

o Seam the sections together. Cut the plastic straws into twenty-four ½"/1.3 cm lengths. Wrap yarn around the straws, passing through the straw with each wrap. Fasten off and use the tail to sew one end shut to form a cone. Attach the cones to the edge of the panels with open ends facing the center, placing one cone at each seam and two cones equally spaced between each pair of seams. Slip base over top of parasol frame and fit cones over ends of parasol pegs.

Nevermore Window Panel

Designed by Debra Swinski

Thread a dowel through the top row and
hang this in a window or on the wall —
it will attract attention wherever it lives!
The piece is worked "sideways," from the
right-hand side of the motif through the
left-hand side. Dimensions may be varied
with blocking for a perfect fit.

FINISHED MEASUREMENTS	Approximately 26"/66 cm wide and 20"/51 cm tall
YARN	Malabrigo Sock, 100% superwash merino wool, 3.5 oz (100 g)/440 yds (402 m), Côte D'Azure
CROCHET HOOK	US F/5 (3.75 mm) hook *or size you need to obtain correct gauge*
GAUGE	7 edc Spaces = 4" (10 cm)
OTHER SUPPLIES	Tapestry needle
SPECIAL ABBREVIATIONS	**edc** extended double crochet (see box at right)

Crocheting the Panel

○ *Note:* In this project, extended double crochet stitches and chain stitches are combined to create Blocks and Spaces as indicated on the chart. Each Block is made up of 3 edc per square, and each Space is made of 2 ch and 1 edc per square. Edcs worked over a space are worked into the chain *stitch* and not into the ch-2 space.

○ Loosely ch 110. Referring to chart (see page 250), work as follows:

○ Row 1: Edc in 8th ch from hook (counts as edc and 1 Space), *ch 2, skip next 2 ch, edc in next ch; repeat from * across, turn. *You now have* 35 Spaces.

○ Row 2: Ch 3 (counts as edc), work 35 Spaces across row.

○ Row 3: Ch 3 (counts as edc), 2 Spaces, 4 Blocks, 5 Spaces, 5 Blocks, 12 Spaces, 5 Blocks, 2 Spaces.

○ Continue in this manner, following chart for placement of Blocks and Spaces, until chart is complete. Do not fasten off.

Finishing

○ Rotate piece so that you are now working across the bottom of the image. Working into chain-*spaces* along lower edge, ch 1. 2hdc in first Space, ch 3, *2 hdc in next Space, ch 3; repeat from * across, ending last repeat 2hdc in last space. Fasten off. Weave in ends. Block.

Pattern Essentials

EXTENDED DOUBLE CROCHET

Yo, insert hook, draw up a loop, yo, pull through 1 loop, (yo, pull through 2 loops) two times.

BLOCK

Edc in next 3 stitches.

SPACE

Ch 2, skip next 2 stitches, edc in next ch (or edc).

NEVERMORE
WINDOW
PANEL

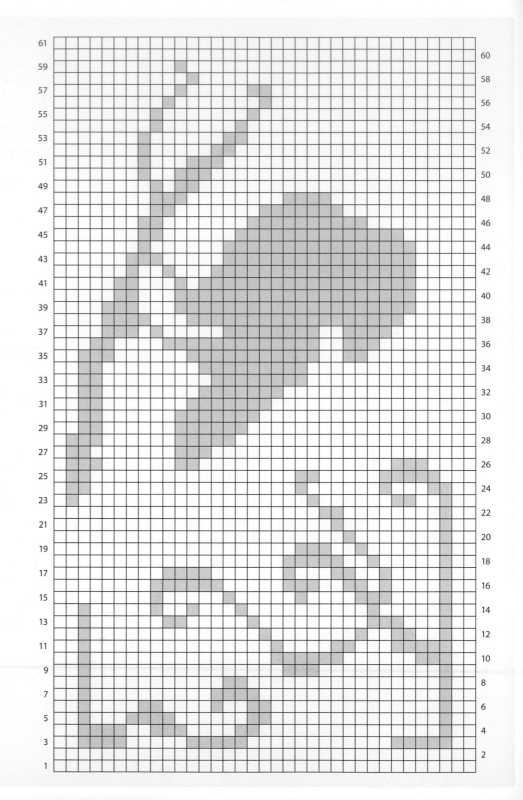

■ block
□ space

Heirloom Holiday Ornament

Designed by Terry Liann Morris

Short rows do the shaping here. The ornament is knitted back and forth, then seamed and stuffed.

Pattern Essentials

BOBBLE

(K1, P1, K1) in next stitch, turn; P3, turn; slip 2, K1, p2sso.

Knitting the Body

○ *Note:* When working Rows 1, 10, 11, and 18 (on last three chart repeats), work the wraps together with the stitches they wrap.

○ Using a provisional method (see page 280), cast on 38 stitches.

○ Work Rows 1–18 of Chart A three times, then work Rows 1–16 once more.

○ Work Row 1 of Chart B. Cut yarn, leaving a 24"/61 cm tail.

○ Block the ornament.

FINISHED MEASUREMENTS	Approximately 5½"/14 cm circumference and 4"/10 cm tall, excluding tail
YARN	Knit Picks Palette, 100% wool, 1.75 oz (50 g)/231 yds (210 m), Cream
NEEDLES	US 1 (2.25 mm) straight needles *or size you need to obtain correct gauge*
GAUGE	32 stitches = 4" (10 cm) in stockinette stitch
OTHER SUPPLIES	Scrap yarn for cast on, cable needle, tapestry needle, roving or polyester fiberfill for stuffing, crochet hook (optional)
SPECIAL ABBREVIATIONS	**C3B** slip 1 stitch to cable needle and hold in back, knit 2 from left-hand needle, purl 1 from cable needle **C3F** slip next 2 stitches to cable needle and hold in front, purl 1 from left-hand needle, knit 2 from cable needle **C4B** slip next 2 stitches to cable needle and hold in back, knit 2 from left-hand needle, knit 2 from cable needle **kfbf** knit into the front, back, and front of stitch (2 stitches increased) **WT** wrap and turn (see page 282)

251

Knitting the Corkscrew Tail

○ Cast on 38 stitches.

○ Row 1: *Kfbf; repeat from * to end of row. *You now have* 114 stitches.

○ Row 2: Bind off.

Finishing

○ Carefully remove the provisional cast on and place stitches onto needle. Use the tail to graft beginning and ending stitches together with Kitchener stitch (see page 278), filling the ornament with roving or fiberfill before closing.

○ Thread a length of yarn onto tapestry needle. Pick up 8 stitches along lower edge and gather them together. Pull up snug and fasten off. Repeat on other end.

○ Use the crochet hook to make a chained loop on top of the ornament for hanging. Sew tail to opposite end. Weave in all ends.

CHART A

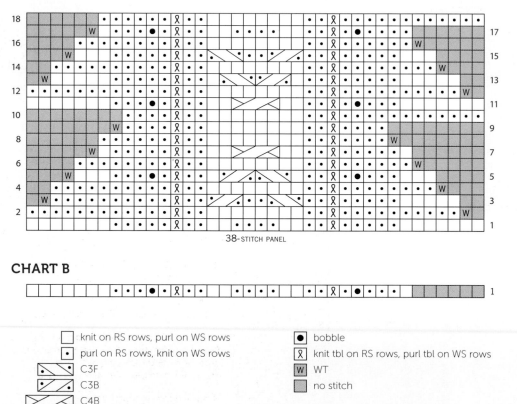

38-STITCH PANEL

CHART B

	knit on RS rows, purl on WS rows		bobble
•	purl on RS rows, knit on WS rows	⅄	knit tbl on RS rows, purl tbl on WS rows
C3F		W	WT
C3B			no stitch
C4B			

Beaded Bauble Ornament

Designed by Terry Liann Morris

Here's a great use of left-over bits of sock yarn. The ornament is knit in two stages — from the center to the top, then from the center to the bottom. The beads are prestrung and added to the knitting as you go.

Preparing the Yarn

○ Thread yarn onto big eye beading needle and string 190 beads. As you work, you'll push the beads down along the yarn, bringing up one at a time as instructed.

FINISHED MEASUREMENTS	Approximately 2"/5 cm wide and 2"/5 cm tall, excluding tassel
YARN	Lisa Souza Dyeworks Sock!, 75% superwash wool/25% nylon, 4 oz (113 g)/450 yds (411m), Pumpkin
NEEDLES	Set of four US 1 (2.25 mm) double-point needles *or size you need to obtain correct gauge*
GAUGE	32 stitches = 4" (10 cm) in stockinette stitch
OTHER SUPPLIES	Big eye beading needle, approximately 190 (approximately 16 g) size 6° glass beads, scrap yarn for cast on, tapestry needle, roving or polyester fiberfill for stuffing
SPECIAL ABBREVIATIONS	**SB** slide bead up next to needle

253

Knitting the Bauble

○ Using a provisional method (see page 280), cast on 95 stitches and divide onto three double-point needles. Join into a round, being careful not to twist the stitches.

○ Work Rounds 1–18 of Bauble Chart. Cut yarn, leaving a 6"/15 cm tail. Thread tail onto tapestry needle and draw through remaining stitches. Pull up snug and fasten off. Make a small loop for hanging. Weave in tail.

○ Carefully remove provisional cast on and place stitches onto three double-point needles. Attach yarn and work Rounds 1–15 of chart. Stuff the bauble with roving or fiberfill. Work remaining rounds and finish as for other end, omitting the loop for hanging.

Finishing

○ Lightly steam the ornament and mold into shape. Following the instructions on page 281, make a tassel and attach to the bottom point.

BAUBLE

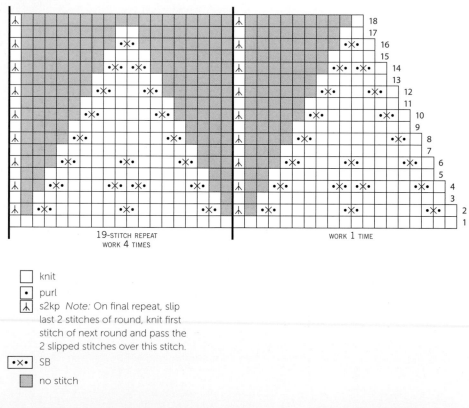

19-STITCH REPEAT
WORK 4 TIMES

WORK 1 TIME

	knit
•	purl
⋏	s2kp *Note:* On final repeat, slip last 2 stitches of round, knit first stitch of next round and pass the 2 slipped stitches over this stitch.
•×•	SB
▨	no stitch

Ira Garber/John Tavares

Asphodel Lace Coasters and Centerpiece

Designed by Kirsten Hipsky

You don't need circular knitting skills or super-fine yarn to make special lace table linens. One 50-gram skein of sock yarn, a pair of needles, and an interesting lace stitch are all you need. This set is fast and inexpensive to knit and makes a fantastic gift. It's named for the asphodel plant, which has a spiderlike flower.

FINISHED MEASUREMENTS	Approximately 4"/10 cm square coasters, 9½" × 11"/24 × 28 cm centerpiece
YARN	Valley Yarns Huntington, 75% wool/25% nylon, 1.75 oz (50 g)/218 yds (199 m), Natural
NEEDLES	US 5 (3.75 mm) needles *or size you need to obtain correct gauge*
GAUGE	20 stitches = 4" (10 cm) in pattern, blocked
OTHER SUPPLIES	Tapestry needle, blocking wires or scrap yarn

Pattern Essentials

SPIDER LACE

Row 1 (RS): Slip 1 wyif, K2, *K2tog, yo, K1, yo, K2tog, K1; repeat from * to last 2 stitches, K2.

Row 2: Slip 1 wyif, K1, K2tog, yo, K3, yo, *sk2p, yo, K3, yo; repeat from * to last 4 stitches, K2tog, K2.

Row 3: Slip 1 wyif, K2, *yo, K2tog, yo, sk2p, yo, K1; repeat from * to last 2 stitches, K2.

Row 4: Slip 1 wyif, K1, *K1, yo, K2tog, k1, K2tog, yo; repeat from * to last 3 stitches, K3.

Row 5: Slip 1 wyif, K2, *K1, yo, sk2p, yo, K2; repeat from * to last 2 stitches, K2.

Row 6: Slip 1 wyif, K2, K2tog, yo, K1, yo, K2tog, *yo, sk2p, yo, K1, yo, K2tog; repeat from * to last 3 stitches, K3.

Repeat Rows 1–6 for pattern.

SPIDER LACE

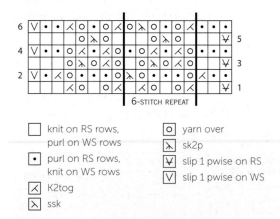

6-STITCH REPEAT

	knit on RS rows, purl on WS rows			yarn over
·	purl on RS rows, knit on WS rows			sk2p
	K2tog			slip 1 pwise on RS
	ssk			slip 1 pwise on WS

Knitting the Centerpiece

○ Cast on 59 stitches.

○ Rows 1–5: Slip 1, knit to end of row.

○ Work Rows 1–6 of Spider Lace pattern eight times, then work Rows 1–5.

○ Knit 5 rows, slipping the first stitch of every row.

○ Bind off.

Knitting the Coasters

○ Cast on 23 stitches.

○ Rows 1–5: Slip 1, knit to end of row.

○ Work Rows 1–6 of Spider Lace pattern twice, then work Rows 1–5 once.

○ Knit 5 rows, slipping the first stitch of every row.

○ Bind off.

Finishing

○ Weave in ends. Block pieces to desired measurements, using blocking wires or strong, thin scrap yarn held taut to help keep edges straight.

Southwest Cactus Tea Cozy

Designed by Sonda Lee

Designed to fit an assortment of teapots, this cozy will keep your tea warm even if you're not in the Southwest. The cozy begins in the round, is divided to make openings for a handle and a spout, and is embellished with cactus tassels.

FINISHED MEASUREMENTS	Approximately 24"/61 cm circumference at base and 6"/15 cm tall
YARN	Fortissima Colori Socka Yarn, 75% superwash wool/25% polyamid, 3.5 oz (100 g)/459 yds (420 m), Color 9044 Veracruz Fair Isle
NEEDLES	US 2 (2.75 mm) circular needle 24"/60 cm long and set of four US 2 (2.75 mm) double-point needles or size you need to obtain correct gauge
GAUGE	32 stitches and 44 rounds = 4" (10 cm) in stockinette stitch
OTHER SUPPLIES	Stitch markers, scrap yarn for holders, tapestry needle

Knitting the Base

○ Cast on 192 stitches. Place marker and join into a round, being careful not to twist the stitches. Work K1, P1 rib until piece measures 1"/2.5 cm.

○ Work Rounds 1–13 of Float Stitch chart.

○ Purl 2 rounds.

Dividing for the Openings

○ P80, bind off 16, P96, turn; bind off 16, P80. Working back and forth on the 80 stitches just worked, place remaining 80 stitches on hold.

Knitting the Front

○ Row 1: Knit.

○ Row 2: K5, P70, K5.

○ Repeat Rows 1 and 2 until piece measures 6"/15 cm from cast-on edge. Cut yarn.

Knitting the Back

○ Place held stitches on needle. With wrong side facing, attach yarn and work as for front, beginning with Row 2.

Knitting the Top

○ P80, cast on 16, P80 from holder, cast on 16. Place a marker and join into a round.

○ Purl 2 rounds.

○ Knit 2 rounds.

DECREASING FOR THE TOP

○ Round 1: *P6, P2tog; repeat from * to end of round. *You now have 168 stitches.*

○ Round 2: Purl.

○ Round 3: *P5, P2tog; repeat from * to end of round. *You now have 144 stitches.*

○ Rounds 4 and 5: Knit.

○ Round 6: *P4, P2tog; repeat from * to end of round. *You now have 120 stitches.*

○ Round 7: Purl.

○ Round 8: *P3, P2tog; repeat from * to end of round. *You now have 96 stitches.*

○ Rounds 9 and 10: Knit.

○ Round 11: *P2, P2tog; repeat from * to end of round. *You now have* 72 stitches.

○ Round 12: Purl.

○ Round 13: *P1, P2tog; repeat from * to end of round. *You now have* 48 stitches.

○ Rounds 14 and 15: Knit.

○ Round 16: *P2tog; repeat from * to end of round. *You now have* 24 stitches.

○ Round 17: Purl.

○ Round 18: *P2tog; repeat from * to end of round. *You now have* 12 stitches.

○ Round 19: Knit.

WORKING THE EYELETS

○ Round 1: *K1, yo, K2tog; repeat from * to end of round.

○ Rounds 2–6: Knit.

○ Cut yarn, leaving a 6"/15 cm tail. Thread tail onto tapestry needle and draw through remaining stitches. Pull up snug and fasten off.

Knitting the Cacti

○ Cast on 8 stitches.

○ Rows 1–4: Knit.

○ Row 5: Bind off 4, K4.

○ Rows 6–8: Knit.

○ Row 9: Cast on 8, K12.

○ Row 10: Cast on 8, K20.

○ Rows 11–14: Knit.

○ Row 15: Cast on 1, K21.

○ Row 16: Knit.

○ Row 17: K2tog, knit to end of row.

○ Rows 18–20: Knit.

○ Row 21: Bind off 12, K8.

○ Row 22: Bind off 4, K4.

○ Rows 23–26: Knit.

○ Row 27: Cast on 8, K12.

○ Rows 28–31: Knit.

○ Bind off. Repeat to make four cacti. With wrong sides together, sew two cacti together.

Finishing

○ Following the instructions on page 277, make a 3-stitch I-cord 9"/23 cm long. Weave cord through eyelet round and attach a cactus to each end.

FLOAT STITCH

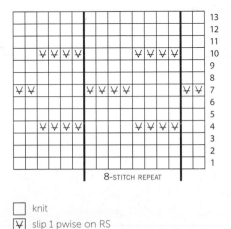

8-STITCH REPEAT

☐ knit
Ⓥ slip 1 pwise on RS

Antique-Style Valance

Designed by Beverly Vasquez

The valance is knit side to side, then stitches are picked up along the side and knit horizontally to form the rod sleeve. Picots accent the folding line. The natural-color yarn lends an antique look to the piece.

FINISHED MEASUREMENTS	Approximately 30"/76 cm wide and 11"/28 cm deep
YARN	Cherry Tree Hill Supersock Solids, 100% merino wool, 4 oz (113.5 g)/420 yds (384 m), Natural
NEEDLES	US 6 (4 mm) straight needles *or size you need to obtain correct gauge*
GAUGE	22 stitches and 22 rows = 4" (10 cm) in garter stitch
OTHER SUPPLIES	Scrap yarn for cast on, coilless safety pin, tapestry needle

Knitting the Valance Body

○ Using a provisional method (see page 280), cast on 42 stitches.

○ Work Rows 1–40 of chart (see page 262) seven times, binding off on Row 40 of last repeat. Leave last stitch on safety pin to hold. Cut yarn.

Knitting the Rod Sleeve

○ *Note:* Slip all stitches purlwise with yarn in front.
○ With held stitch on the left and right side facing, pick up and knit (see page 280) 141 edge stitches along what is now the top of the valance. Slip held stitch onto needle.

You now have 142 stitches. Turn work, slip 1, P141 tbl.

○ Rows 1–4: Slip 1, knit to last stitch, K1 tbl.

○ Rows 5–14: Slip 1, *yo, K2tog, K1, P1; repeat from * to last stitch, K1 tbl.

○ Rows 15–19: Repeat Row 1.

○ Row 20 (Picot Row): Slip 1, *yo, K2tog; repeat from * to last stitch, K1 tbl.

○ Rows 21–25: Repeat Row 1.

○ Rows 26–35: Slip 1, *yo, K2tog, K1, P1; repeat from * to last stitch, K1 tbl.

○ Row 36: Repeat Row 1.

○ Last Row: Slip 1, K1, *K2tog; repeat from * to last 2 stitches, K1, K1 tbl. *You now have* 73 stitches.

Finishing

○ Break yarn leaving a 50"/127 cm tail. Thread tail onto tapestry needle, fold rod sleeve in half with wrong sides together, and sew live stitches to slip-stitched edge of valance body. Make sure you keep the columns aligned, skipping edge stitches as necessary, and keep this seam nice and loose. Wash and block.

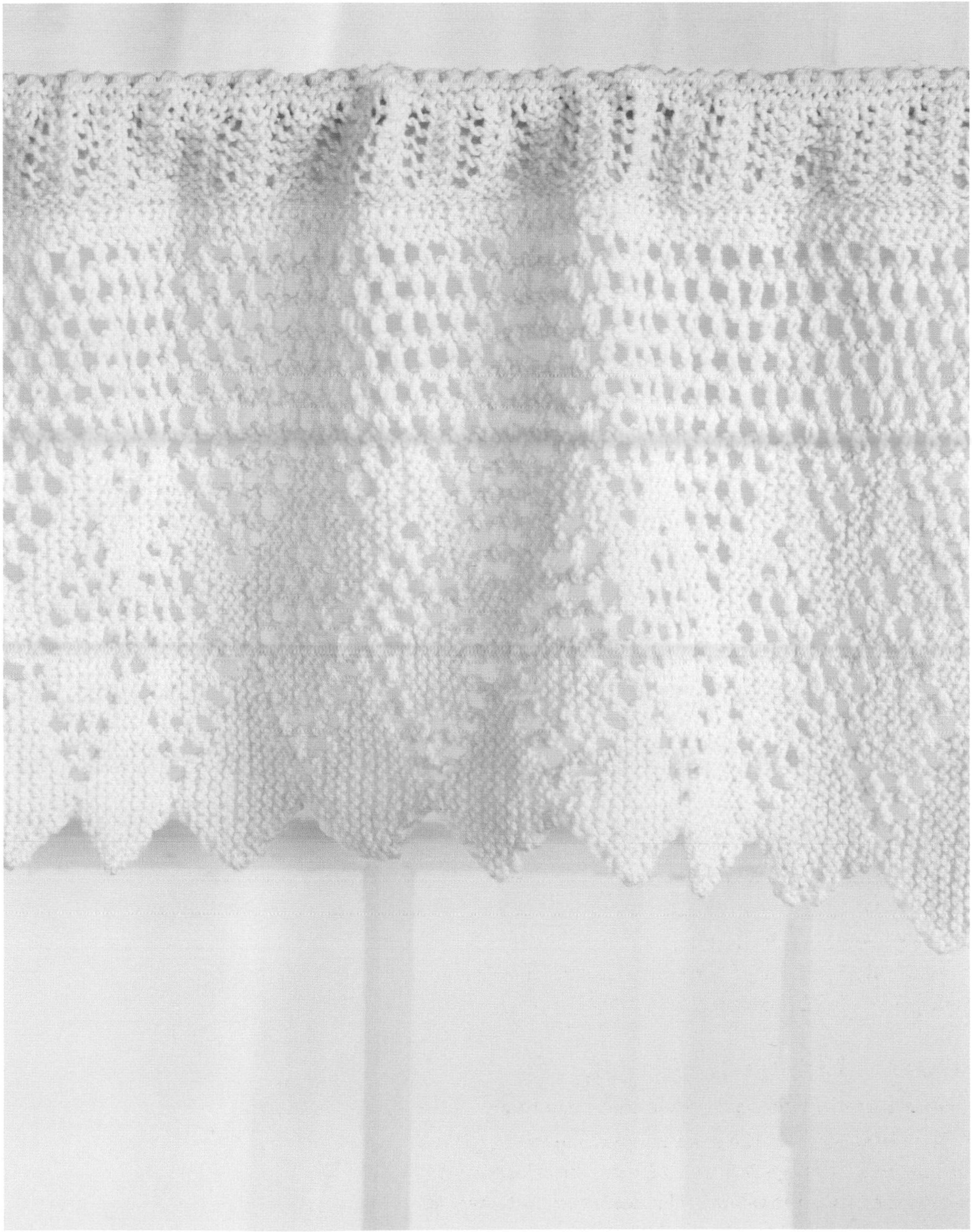

ANTIQUE-STYLE VALANCE

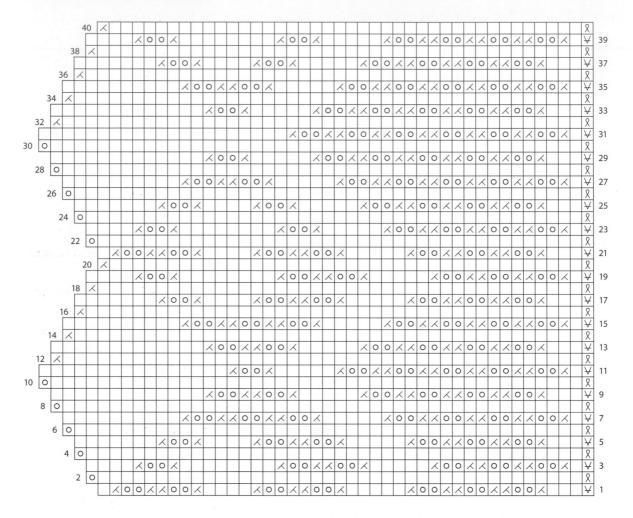

	knit
⟋	K2tog
○	yarn over
⩘	slip pwise wyif
⟁	K tbl

The Manwell

Designed by Stephanie Michaud

This turtleneck dog sweater has an opening at the back for a leash and a pocket to hold a little treat!

SIZES AND FINISHED MEASUREMENTS	To fit a small dog, approximately 13¾"/35 cm circumference and 13½"/34.5 cm long
YARN	J. Knits Creative Hand-Dyed Superwash Me Sock, 75% superwash wool, 25% nylon, 3.7 oz (105 g)/420 yds (384 m), Mesa
NEEDLES	US 1.5 (2.5 mm) straight needles and set of five US 1.5 (2.5 mm) double-point needles *or size you need to obtain correct gauge*
GAUGE	34 stitches and 40 rounds = 4" (10 cm) in stockinette stitch
OTHER SUPPLIES	Stitch marker, tapestry needle

Knitting the Collar

o Cast on 91 stitches and divide onto four double-point needles. Place marker and join into a round, being careful not to twist the stitches.

o Round 1: *K5, P2; repeat from * to end of round.

o Repeat Round 1 until piece measures 2¾"/7 cm.

Knitting the Leash Opening

o Next Round: (K5, P2) six times, bind off 7 stitches, (K5, P2) six times. *You now have* 84 stitches.

o Row 1: Work pattern as established to bound-off stitches, turn.

o Repeat Row 1 five times more.

o Next row (RS): Work to marker.

Increasing for the Body

o Round 1: Continuing in the round, (K1, M1, K4, P2) six times, cast on 8 stitches, (K1, M1, K4, P2) six times. *You now have* 104 stitches.

o Rounds 2 and 3: *K6, P2; repeat from * to end of round

o Round 4: *K6, M1, P2; repeat from * to end of round. *You now have* 117 stitches.

o Round 5: *K7, P2; repeat from * to end of round.

o Round 6: *K1, M1, K5, M1, K1, P2tog; repeat from * to end of round. *You now have* 130 stitches.

o Round 7: *K9, P1; repeat from * to end of round.

o Round 8: *K8, K2tog; repeat from * to end of round. *You now have* 117 stitches.

Knitting the Body

o Work stockinette stitch in the round until piece measures 4½"/11.5 cm.

Shaping the Legs

o Round 1: K10, bind off 14 stitches, K69, bind off 14 stitches, K10. *You now have* 89 stitches.

o Row 2: K10, turn.

o Row 3: P20, turn.

o Round 4: K20, cast on 15 stitches, K69, cast on 15 stitches, K10. *You now have* 119 stitches.

○ Round 5: K10, K2tog, K95, K2tog, K10. *You now have 117 stitches.*

○ Rounds 6–11: Knit, ending last round 5 stitches before marker. Slip next 5 stitches to right-hand needle, remove marker, slip same 5 stitches back to left-hand needle and place marker to indicate new beginning of round.

Decreasing the Back

○ Round 1: (K1, P1) ten times, knit to last 11 stitches, (P1, K1) five times, P1.

○ Rounds 2–4: Work established Seed Stitch (knit the purls and purl the knits) over 20 stitches, knit to last 11 stitches, work established Seed Stitch to end of round.

○ Round 5: Bind off 9 stitches, work in established pattern to end of round. Turn to work back and forth. *You now have 108 stitches. Change to straight needles.*

○ Maintaining Seed Stitch and stockinette stitch as established, bind off 4 stitches at the beginning of the next two rows, then 3 stitches at the beginning of the following two rows. *You now have 94 stitches.*

○ Decrease Row (RS): Slip 1 knitwise wyib, work established Seed Stitch over next 3 stitches, ssk, knit to last 6 stitches, K2tog, work established Seed Stitch over next 3 stitches, P1. On remaining rows, slip the first stitch of every row knitwise wyib and purl the last stitch.

○ Repeat Decrease Row every fourth row seven times more, then every other row 21 times. *You now have 36 stitches. Work 1 wrong-side row.*

○ Next Row: Work in established Seed Stitch to last 5 stitches, K2tog (or P2tog) to maintain pattern, work established Seed Stitch over last 3 stitches.

○ Work 3 more rows in Seed Stitch.

○ Next row: Ssk, work in Seed Stitch to last 2 stitches, K2tog. Work 1 row even.

○ Bind off remaining stitches.

Knitting the Leg Cuffs

○ Pick up and knit (see page 280) 42 stitches around the leg opening onto three double-point needles.

○ Round 1: *K5, P2; repeat from *.

○ Repeat Round 1 until cuff measures 1"/2.5 cm.

○ Bind off in pattern.

Knitting the Pocket

○ *Note:* Pocket will be formed with mitered decreases, with the pocket opening at the side.

○ Measure down 2½"/6.5 cm from collar ribbing and about 1"/2.5 cm to the right of center back. With collar at bottom and tail end at top, pick up and knit 12 stitches from one row of knitting onto one double-point needle, rotate piece 90° and with a second double-point needle pick up and knit 12 stitches in a straight line along 12 rows of knitting, rotate piece 90° again and with a third double-point needle, pick up and knit 12 stitches along one row of knitting. *You now have 36 stitches divided evenly onto three double-point needles.*

○ Row 1: K1, (P9, slip 1, P2tog, psso) twice, P10, K1. *You now have 32 stitches.*

○ Row 2: Knit.

○ Row 3: K1, (P8, slip 1, P2tog, psso) twice, P8, K1. *You now have 28 stitches.*

○ Row 4: K9, K2tog, K6, K2tog, K9. *You now have 26 stitches.*

○ Row 5: K1, P7, slip 1, P2tog, psso, P4, slip 1, P2tog, psso, P7, K1. *You now have 22 stitches.*

○ Row 6: K7, K2tog, K4, K2tog, K7. *You now have 20 stitches.*

○ Row 7: K1, P5, slip 1, P2tog, psso, P2, slip 1, P2tog, psso, P5, K1. *You now have 16 stitches.*

○ Row 8: K5, K2tog, K2, K2tog, K5. *You now have 14 stitches.*

○ Row 9: K1, P3, (slip 1, P2tog, psso) twice, P3, K1. *You now have 10 stitches.*

○ Cut yarn and use Kitchener stitch (see page 278) to graft two sets of 5 stitches together.

Knitting the Leash Opening Cuff

○ Pick up and knit 28 stitches around leash opening.

○ Rounds 1 and 2: *K1, P1; repeat from * to end of round.

○ Bind off in pattern.

Finishing

○ Weave in ends. Block.

Appendix

About the Designers

Abbreviations

Glossary

Index

About the Designers

JEAN AUSTIN

Jean is an office worker by day and a musician by night. You can see her knitting during breaks, during lunch, during meetings, etc. She teaches intermediate classes on Saturdays at Never Enough Knitting in Wheaton, Illinois. She wants to thank Stan for his support and is glad he finally got his sweater.

MARY ALICE BAKER

Mary Alice learned to knit as a child from a wonderfully diagrammed pamphlet long since loaned away. Her true teacher was her mother, who patiently counted stitches and rows. Thank you, Mom! Many years later she is completing the Master Knitter Certificate through WEBs, proving that knitting is a craft that takes minutes (and great diagrams) to learn and a lifetime to master. She is known as forthebirds on Ravelry and ForTheBirdsFibers on Etsy.

BETTY BALCOMB

After four wonderful years at Knitty City, Betty Balcomb has moved to Santa Monica, California. Please follow her knitting adventures on Ravelry at her group Bi Coastal Betty. She plans to return to New York and Knitty City at least a couple of times each year.

RENEÉ BARNES

Reneé Barnes (aka Crochet Reneé) lives amidst yarn, fibers, and Angora bunnies with her infinitely tolerant husband, David, and two beagles. She spins, crochets, knits, and dyes yarn to the point of obsession. Her designs have been published in *Crochet!* magazine, Crochet World online magazine, and *Luxury Yarn One-Skein Wonders* (Storey, 2008). Find out what she's up to at *www.crochetrenee.com*.

TONIA BARRY

Tonia has her own independent line of patterns, Tonia Barry Designs, available at Ravelry. Her patterns range from accessories to coats, with pieces intentionally crafted to become timeless wardrobe staples. Tonia is a member of the design team at Classic Elite Yarns, and over the years she has created designs for several knitting publications, including Lorelei and Goose Rocks for *www.twistcollective.com*. Tonia lives in New Hampshire with her husband, two teenage daughters, and a beagle. She blogs about her knitting endeavors at *http://toniabarrydesigns.wordpress.com*.

HELEN BINGHAM

Helen's knitting passion began when her mom taught her to knit to help her quit smoking in 1992. She quickly fell in love with the art of knitting. Helen teaches people of all ages the basics and creative ways to manipulate stitches at Fresh Purls in Providence, Rhode Island. Over the last seven years, Helen has developed a large number of published patterns for such companies as Nashua, Misti International, Sheep Shop, Swarovski Crystals, and GorMae Handknits. Helen currently lives in Rehoboth, Massachusetts, with her husband of 17 years and their two children.

MARCI BLANK

Knitting since she was in the third grade, Marci has turned her love of the craft into a full-time career. As owner of Th'Red Head, she designs, knits, and markets garments for art fairs, galleries, and shops. She also dyes and spins yarns that she sells or makes into fabulous one-of-a-kind garments. You can see her work at *www.thredhead.com*.

SUSAN BOYE

Sue has been knitting for more than 25 years and designing for more than 20. She has sold her patterns through retail outlets and has designed and knit numerous commissioned works. Sue resides with her family in the greater Toronto area.

CHRISTIANE BURKHARD

The love for knitting, crocheting, and fashion has a long tradition in Christiane's family. Since moving to the United States from Switzerland, Christiane spends a lot of her time designing and teaching knitting and crochet. She is Lismi on Ravelry and blogs at *www.lismiknits.blogspot.com*.

LINDA BURT

Linda Burt is customer service manager for WEBS, America's Yarn Store. In her spare time she can be found in the vineyard and winery she owns with her husband in Hatfield, Massachusetts.

JANICE BYE

Janice has a bachelor's degree in mathematics and is a Canadian master knitter. She left her career as a systems analyst to spend time knitting while her three sons enjoyed the playgrounds. (The boys are now in college.) Janice has taught knitting classes in New Hampshire and Massachusetts and worked for the distributor of Manos Yarns for many years. Janice continues to knit and quilt and edit patterns for yarn companies and designers.

VICKI K. BYRAM

Vicki K. Byram of Red Oak Designs is a 60-year-old 55-year knitter. During her knitting career, Vicki co-owned a yarn shop with her mother, then owned it solo for 20 years after her mother's death. She established a design company with her sister Karla called Red Oak Designs. They had over 60 designs and sold both wholesale and retail kits and patterns. Now Vicki is retired, and her knitting is inspired by skeins of yarn from Ellen's 1/2 Pint Farm, which tell her what they want to be knitted into, and she also draws inspiration from her husband, three children, and six grandchildren. She can be reached at *vmbyram@embarqmail.com*.

CATHLEEN CAMPBELL

Cathy Campbell began knitting several years ago to occupy her hands while commuting by subway from Brooklyn to Manhattan. She officially began her career in the yarn business at Crystal Palace Yarns/Straw into Gold in northern California. She has designed for both Crystal Palace Yarns and O-Wool Hand Knitting Yarns and now offers patterns on Ravelry. Her work has been featured in *101 Designer One-Skein Wonders* (Storey, 2007) and *50 Socks - 50 States (Crystal Palace)*, and she has appeared on the DIY Network show *Knitty Gritty*. Cathy now lives at the Jersey Shore with her husband, Gerry, but still spends some of her time as promotional assistant for Crystal Palace Yarns.

JENNIFER CHASE-RAPPAPORT

As a New Englander transplanted to the Pacific Northwest, Jennifer draws design inspiration from both of her home places. After many years working and designing in a local yarn shop, she now designs independently. More of Jennifer's designs can be found on Ravelry.

ANDI CLARK

Andi lives outside of Boston with her husband. She works for Classic Elite Yarns, and her designs have been featured in their pattern books. Andi's also been published in *Interweave Knits*.

PATRICIA COLLOTON-WALSH

Patricia organizes and teaches knitting and crocheting classes at Loop Yarn Shop in Milwaukee. Loop customers inspire her to create patterns that are doable, functional, and fun. With Caitlin, owner of Loop, and its teaching staff, she promotes crocheting as well as knitting, with classes and sampling and yarn selection.

MARIE R. CONNOLLY

Casual knitter since 1965, knitting fanatic since 2001.

KIMBERLY CONTERIO

Kim learned to knit when she was a wee lass and has never really stopped. She co-owns Bella Yarns in Warren, Rhode Island, and endeavors to teach as many people to knit as possible. Since her daughter's conception in '07, she's been obsessed with designing and knitting adorable things for her to wear. With another daughter due any minute, we're afraid her obsession has only deepened. If she doesn't knit something for herself soon, an intervention may become necessary!

GRACE (MAGGIE) COVEY

Maggie has been creating with fibers for many, many years. Quilting, weaving, dyeing, and spinning her own yarn with the help of her fiber bunnies, Flopsy and Benjamin, are just some of her interests. Knitting is a favorite. You might find Maggie at charity knitting groups, teaching at Fiberworks in Beavercreek, Ohio, or with Knit & Nibble friends at the shop on Tuesday or Sundays. She especially enjoys knitting for family and special friends.

Kerin Dimeler-Laurence

Kerin holds a degree in communications design and worked as a graphic designer before becoming a full-time pattern writer for Knit Picks. Though knitting is her primary craft, she also sews, makes jewelry, and spins, and she is trained as a fine artist. She is an avid cook and gardener and spends as much time as possible outdoors, exploring the state of Oregon.

Judith Durant

Judith Durant is editor of the One-Skein Wonders series and author of several books on knitting and beadwork including *Knit One, Bead Too*. Judith studied theatrical costume design in college and took a circuitous route to a career in publishing. She currently writes, designs, edits, knits, and beads in Lowell, Massachusetts, and teaches classes at Ewe'll Love It in Nashua, New Hampshire, and online at CraftEdu. She wishes she could knit while riding her motorcycle. Visit Judith at *http://judithdurant.com*.

Laura Hein Eckel

Laura Hein Eckel is a fiber artist whose design expertise spans several fields, including knitting, sewing, and gardening. Her work combines her love of color, texture, and pattern with her deep love of nature. She is a busy wife and mother of two, who wears many hats, including designer, knitting instructor, gardener, and working in her local yarn shop. Laura has studied knitting with Lucy Neatby and Charlene Schurch and also holds a master's degree in landscape architecture. She has been knitting, sewing, and gardening since she was a child and enjoys sharing her love of all things creative with both children and adults.

Edie Eckman

Edie Eckman likes to knit, crochet, sew, embroider, teach, design, write, and edit. (She doesn't like to cook or clean, but she will iron.) She is a nationally published designer and is the author of several best-selling books, including *Around the Corner Crochet Borders*, *Beyond the Square Crochet Motifs*, and *The Crochet Answer Book* (all Storey). She can be found on the Web at *www.edieeckman.com*.

Erin Elkins

Erin Elkins is an avid sock knitter, crocheter, and spinner from Nashville, Tennessee. She loves to share her enthusiasm for yarn with other knitters and crocheters. Look for her work on Ravelry under the name putasockonit.

Katherine Eng

Katherine started crocheting at the age of nine and did many projects just as a hobby for several years. For the past 25 years she's worked as a designer for a number of yarn companies and almost all of the crochet publications. Her hobby now is dancing Argentine tango.

Bonnie Evans

Bonnie, a lifelong knitter and seamstress, is delighted to have two designs in this book. Her designs have previously been published in *Luxury Yarn One-Skein Wonders*, *Knit It!* magazine, and *Knitting Fun for Everyone* (Leisure Arts). Bonnie maintains a shop on Etsy, under the name Sewbizgirls's Originals.

Lynne A. Evans

Lynne's mother taught her the basics of knitting when she was a child, but she didn't do much with them until after she married, when she was fortunate enough to take a workshop with Elizabeth Zimmerman that changed her knitting life. Then after working through the sampler in Jacqueline Fee's book, *The Sweater Workshop*, she fell in love with knitting. A few years ago she began the Master Knitters Program with the Knitting Guild Association and now designs a line of hand knitting patterns under the name Knits Charming.

Diana Foster

Diana Foster is owner and designer for Lowellmountain Wools LLC, a farm shop, with sheep, in the Northeast Kingdom of Vermont, offering classes in knitting, spinning, and natural dyeing. She is a member of the Knitting Guild Association and knitting instructor at The Old Stone House Museum.

Patti Ghezzi

Patti Ghezzi melts when, just before naptime, her three-year-old daughter points to a chair and says, "Mommy, knit while I sleep." She lives in Avondale Estates, Georgia.

LISE A. GILL

Lise has been knitting, crocheting, sewing, quilting, and crafting most of her life. When not working at WEBs as the color card coordinator or sales associate, she can be found in the garden or with her grandchildren. Lise enjoys all crafting.

ANNE CARROLL GILMOUR

Anne Carroll Gilmour owned and operated Wildwest Woolies, a full spectrum textile arts shop in Evanston, Wyoming, for nearly six years. She now lives in the beautiful Wasatch Mountains near Park City, Utah, where she works in her studio and teaches workshops in spinning, weaving, and knitting. Her work has been featured in various textile publications and many galleries, museums, and private collections worldwide. A first-generation American, she readily admits that her Celtic roots show up frequently in her designs. When not elbow-deep in wool, she enjoys her family, pets, the great outdoors, reading, music, and dancing. Many of her knitwear patterns are available on her website, *www.wildwestwoolies.com*.

REBECCA HATCHER

Rebecca Hatcher has been making up her own designs almost as long as she's been knitting. Her first published designs were for Schaefer Yarn, and she continues to work with them, as well as self-publishing patterns through her blog and Ravelry (where she is Archiknist). She blogs about her knitting, spinning, and designing (and running, and biking, and rowing) at *http://archiknist.blogspot.com*.

DEBBIE HAYMARK

A freelance designer living in Texas with husband, Lee, and a little Boston terrier named Bella, Debbie's passion for sock knitting has led to a love of sock yarns. She is Dlhaymark on Ravelry.

NAOMI HERZFELD

Naomi Herzfeld learned to knit only ten years ago. She now co-owns Bella Yarns in Warren, Rhode Island, where she also has a small fiber-arts studio and teaches rigid heddle weaving. Naomi writes, "In almost every culture, the world begins with an intentional act of creation. I think that's a reflection of our human passion for making things, an instinctive need to reshape chaos into beauty and purpose. And so, in each act of creation, however small or imperfect, we connect with all humanity and with the divine."

KIRSTEN HIPSKY

Kirsten learned to knit almost as soon as her fingers could hold needles, and she hasn't put them down since. She's now the design coordinator for WEBs and continues struggling to knit down her own stash at home. As a designer, she loves breathing new life into classic shapes and uncommon stitch patterns and performing daring experiments in simplicity.

ELIZABETH HOOD

Beth works part time at Halcyon Yarn in Bath, Maine, while she studies for the ministry. She knits, weaves, and crochets for fun and relaxation. Beth has a recently discovered passion for designing and has created several patterns for Halcyon (*www.halcyonyarn.com*).

GINA HOUSE

Gina House (SleepyEyes) is a new designer whose most popular pattern, the Amanda Hat, has been knit over 1,600 times. She has recently published her first book of designs, *Sleepy Eyes Knits: Dreamscape*, which is a collection of her favorite past and present patterns. For more information and for links to purchase *Dreamscape*, please visit her blog (*http://sleepyeyesknitting.blogspot.com*).

CARLA KISIELNICKI

Carla's knitting skills are half self-taught and half taught by the best knitters around. She has been teaching knitting in the Pittsburgh area since 2006. Working and teaching at Natural Stitches (*www.naturalstitches.com*) keeps her busy, but she still finds time to design. You can find her on Ravelry as knitteach.

MARJI LaFRENIERE

For 22 years, Marji has owned and managed Marji's Yarncrafts in Granby, Connecticut. She squeezes the shop, a husband, three kids, and a funny little dog into one 150-year-old historic home. Marji's designs have been published in *Interweave Knits*, *Knitter's Stash* (Interweave, 2004), and *One-Skein Wonders* (Storey, 2006), and by Berroco and Cascade. She also has her own line of knitting patterns.

BRIGITTE LANG

Brigitte Lang learned to knit at age five and has been a passionate knitter since her early teenage years. She always loved to design and create and now owns and operates Rainbow Yarn & Fibers, a successful yarn store in Germantown, Tennessee. She is about to move to the San Francisco Bay area.

SONDA LEE

Sonda recommends that if you wish to expand your craft, get together with other knitters. They will encourage you to expand your abilities while having a lot of fun. She enjoys her passion for knitting at her local yarn shop, Stitch 'N Hook, in Shorewood, Illinois (*www.stitchnhook.com*).

LION BRAND DESIGN TEAM

The Lion Brand Design Team creates stylish garments and classic designs inspired by everyday living. Currently this team of in-house designers creates almost 1,000 designs a year to support 50+ yarn lines from Lion Brand Yarn Company. A family-owned and -operated business, Lion Brand has been a beloved American brand since 1878. As the fifth generation of Blumenthals joins the business, it is a true passion for yarn, shared by all our associates, that is the secret to Lion Brand's success.

DOREEN L. MARQUART

Doreen taught herself to knit when she was nine years old. In 1993, she opened Needles 'n' Pins Yarn Shoppe, the largest shop in the Delavan, Wisconsin, area devoted exclusively to the needs of knitters and crocheters. With three books published, *Saturday Sweaters*, *Top Down Sweaters*, and *Saturday Style* (all Martingale), she's working on a fourth: *Grammie's Favorite Knits of Baby*, due in March, 2011. Doreen has done design work for Cascade Yarns, Simply Shetland, and Farmhouse Yarns. She is a TKGA Master Knitter, Canadian Master Knitter, and Canadian Master Designer.

BETSY MCCARTHY

Betsy McCarthy is the author of *Knit Socks! 15 Cool Patterns for Toasty Feet* (Storey, 2004). An expanded and revised version of that book, *Knit Socks! 17 Classic Patterns for Cozy Feet*, will be published in September 2010. Betsy teaches nationally, as well at home in Vancouver, Washington. She blogs at *www.betsymccarthyknits.com*.

ANN MCCLURE

Ann McClure is a professional writer and editor who has been crocheting since she was a child and knitting since 2001. When she isn't playing with yarn, she enjoys spending time with her husband, Brian, and their two golden retrievers. Her patterns have also appeared in *Luxury Yarn One-Skein Wonders* (Storey, 2008) and *Sock Club: Join the Knitting Adventure* (Martingale, 2010). Ann blogs about her crafts and her dogs at *www.travelingann.blogspot.com*.

PATRICIA MCGREGOR

Patricia learned to knit during college, and in all the years since she has yet to put her needles down. She likes small projects that give instant gratification and just can't seem to pass up a pretty skein of sock yarn.

MARY MCGURN

Mary is co-owner of Colorful Stitches in Lenox, Massachusetts, and the online store. Her store was recognized by Vogue Knitting International in fall 2007 as "the most inspirational yarn store in the nation" (*www.colorful-stitches.com*).

MARIN J. MELCHIOR

Marin is a product manager for Vermont Organic Fibers Co., manufacturers of O-Wool hand knitting yarns. She lives in Vermont on land her family has owned since the mid-1970s. Although there used to be many animals around, especially dairy goats, there are now only dogs, cats, Angora rabbits, and chickens. She hopes the menagerie increases in the future — cashmere goats would be nice. She has been a knitter since her mom, Lois, taught her to knit. Her first project was a one-skein rectangle that became an awful purse, given to Ruth, her grandmother. The piece was never seen again. Undaunted, she has been an avid knitter for many years since. She loves to knit and share the craft with anyone who can hold needles.

REBECCA MERCIER

Rebecca began knitting for what may seem an unusual reason. Living with severe, chronic pain and nearing her wit's end, she hoped and prayed for something that she could physically do that would both occupy her time *and* take her mind off the pain. Then she saw a television show with knitting and decided to give it a try — that was August 2004! She's been knitting since that day and is very happy to report that knitting does help with the pain. Rebecca blogs at
www.whimsicalknitting.blogspot.com (personal) and
www.whimsicalknittingdesigns.blogspot.com (design).

STEPHANIE MICHAUD

More of Stephanie's designs can be found at
www.mychawd.blogspot.com.

MELISSA MORGAN-OAKES

Melissa Morgan-Oakes, author of the best-selling *2-at-a-Time Socks* and *Toe up 2 at a Time Socks* (both Storey), was taught to sew, crochet, and tat by women who encouraged her to work without commercial patterns. Knitting she learned on her own and hasn't looked back! She lives, works, and writes in beautiful western Massachusetts on a farm she shares with her husband.

BOBBE MORRIS

Bobbe works and designs for Haus of Yarn in Nashville, Tennessee. She describes the shop as cozy, comfortable, and full of wonderful and beautiful yarns — a great place to work. She feels fortunate to be doing exactly what she loves to do and hopes that her knitting enables others to smile, escape, and reminisce. Bobbe believes knitting should be relaxing and fun. "Everyday life, past and present, is a part of my knitting process." She once owned Bandywood Knit Shop, where she specialized in custom-written patterns, and has participated in the Tennessee Association of Craft Artist shows. Bobbe has designs in all of the books in the One-Skein Wonders series. Color and expression dominate her knitting.

TERRY LIANN MORRIS

Terry Liann Morris knits and designs knitting patterns aboard her 50-foot sailboat while she cruises the seas full time, currently along the Caribbean coasts of Central America. A CYCA Certified Knitting Instructor, Terry has taught hundreds of people how to knit or advance their skills. Wherever she travels, she loves to share her passion for knitting and the personal joy that is experienced when making beautiful knitted items. Her original designs are often inspired by the historic or tropical locations she visits and can be seen on her SailingKnitter Liann Originals website at *www.liannoriginals.com*.

LIZ NIELDS

A freelance designer living in Carlisle, Massachusetts, Liz has had designs in *Knit Simple* and *Interweave Knits*; she's also designed for Manos and Nashua Handknits. When not knitting, she's out in the garden, New England weather permitting.

KENDRA NITTA

Kendra Nitta's work has appeared in many books and magazines including *Luxury Yarn One-Skein Wonders* (Storey, 2008) and *Knitting in the Sun* by Kristi Porter (Wiley, 2009), and Knitty, Yarn Forward, and Knitcircus online magazines. She designs mostly with silk and plant-based fibers. Follow along at *www.missknitta.com*.

CHERYL OBERLE

Cheryl Oberle loves color and has been designing knitwear with hand-dyed yarns for over 20 years. She is the author of three popular knitting books and has designed for yarn companies and magazines. At her studio in Colorado she hand-dyes her line of yarns while she expands her catalogue of exclusive knitting patterns.

SARAH-HOPE PARMETER

Sarah-Hope Parmeter teaches composition at the University of California, Santa Cruz, and knits whenever she can. She and her wife, the artist Melissa West, serve as "staff" to a large, demanding — and delightful — family of cats. She blogs (sometimes erratically) about her knitting adventures at *www.whatifknits.com*.

CAROLINE PERISHO

Caroline, former owner of Wild & Wooly yarn shop, continues to develop her artistic nature as a knitwear designer. Caroline creates patterns for books, websites, and several yarn companies.

IRINA POLUDNENKO

Born in Russia, Irina learned to knit at age seven. She graduated from art college as an industrial designer and has been a freelance knitwear designer since 1993. Her designs have been seen in *Vogue Knitting* magazine and in collections for Berroco and recently for Tahki Stacey Charles.

DOROTHY T. RATIGAN

Dorothy T. Ratigan's career in fiber arts spans 35 years, and in that time she's done it all. From bargello to beadwork, crewelwork, crochet, cross-stitch, embroidery, knitting, needlepoint, tatting, and weaving, Dorothy has designed, stitched, edited, and taught it all. This adventure with needlework began with the skills that her mother, Peg, and her aunts, Nell and Delia, brought from Ireland and passed on to her. Dorothy has designed or edited for many major fiber magazines, craft book publishers, and yarn companies. As president and co-owner of Pine Tree Knitters, she designed knitted skiwear, oversaw a production staff, and marketed finished items to L.L. Bean, Eddie Bauer, and others. Dorothy has finally gotten to the bottom of her love of fiber with her recently published *Knitting the Perfect Pair: Secrets to Great Socks* (Krause, 2009).

NICHOLE REESE

Nichole is a designer and an accountant. She enjoys working part time at her local yarn shop, Knot Another Hat. Her designs can be found in books and magazines, as well as in her very own pattern line, bluegirl knits. Check out the full line at *www.bluegirlknits.com*.

HÉLÈNE RUSH

Hélène Rush launched her career in the knitting world in 1979 when she sold her first design. She has since authored five knitting books, was editor of *McCall's Needlework & Crafts* and *Cast On* magazines, has designed over 1,000 patterns, and now owns Knit One, Crochet Too, the yarn company. She loves her job.

CAROL SCOTT

A professor of fashion design and merchandising for 26 years, Carol recently retired to pursue her passion for knitting and sewing. She began knitting and sewing at an early age when she decided that creating unique garments and looking different was a good thing. Carol continues to teach knitting and sewing, as well as designing knit garments under her own label, TrueThreads.

KERRI A. SHANK

Kerri owns the Dragonfly Yarn Shop. Open since 2004, the shop offers a variety of wool and luxury yarns, Louët spinning wheels, fiber, Addi Turbo needles, and dyes. It is the only yarn shop in Janesville, Wisconsin. Monthly classes in addition to classes by the hour are also offered. Stop in for open knitting on Thursday afternoons all year and open spinning on Sundays during the fall and winter months. Visit the website at: *www.dragonflyyarnshop.com*.

CARA SHARPES

Cara Sharpes taught herself to knit 6 years ago and is just beginning to design patterns. She lives in New England with her partner and two small animals. When she is not ferociously knitting and crafting, she's hanging out at WEBS for pay and lots of yarn.

HANNAH SIX

Hannah Six is a knitwear designer, knitting instructor, and spinner. She lives with her husband and two cats in the Washington, D.C.–Metro area, where inspiration abounds.

CAROL J. SORSDAHL

Carol learned to knit while living in Ketchikan, Alaska, in the early 1970s. Knitting brought Carol through the tough times of her life — caring for her son Clint, who battled brain tumors. Since the loss of her son in 2004, Carol has knitted hundreds of hats and other items for charity in his memory. She also enjoys quilting, reading, playing keyboard, and singing with her church music team. Carol sold her baby and children's knits in gift shops, boutiques, and online for many years. She has designed for Coats & Clark and translated Japanese patterns for a yarn company. Her patterns have appeared in several machine- and hand-knitting publications, including *Creative Knitting*.

GWEN STEEGE

A confirmed knitter since childhood, Gwen has edited more than two dozen knitting and crochet books and has contributed designs to several of them. She has her own sheep and spins and dyes their wool for her woven and knitted projects. She also enjoys gardening and watercolor painting and has recently become interested in surface design. She lives in Williamstown, Massachusetts.

DEBRA SWINSKI

A self-described "craft-tastic," Deb Swinski also studied both fine art and graphic design in school. Her mother, Evelyn, passed down her skills and love of crochet to her. Deb shares her knowledge where she works, at WEBS, America's Yarn Store.

KATHLEEN TAYLOR

Kathleen Taylor is a wife, mother, grandmother, knitter, writer, and designer. She's the author of six Tory Bauer Mysteries and four knitting books.

KRISTINA TAYLOR

Kristina Taylor is a self-taught knitter and former local yarn-store employee. This is her first published pattern.

BEVERLY VASQUEZ

Beverly has been knitting for about 55 years, starting with a teddy bear scarf. Her current efforts to spread the joy of knitting go through her yarn shop, Ewe'll Love It! in Nashua, New Hampshire. Knitting is a passion she has carried throughout her life. Beverly's mantra is "In the rhythm of the knitting needles there is music for the soul."

RENÉ E. WELLS

René's grandmother taught her to embroider, cross-stitch, crochet, knit, and sew on a treadle sewing machine when she was very young. Her first knitted sweaters were for her bear and dolls; her grandmother rewarded her efforts with chocolate. Wells and her grandmother started Granny an' Me Designs, knitting baby clothes for boutiques. While raising her family, she designed and knit custom art-to-wear sweaters. René enjoys knitting, spinning on her drop spindle, and designing for the special people in her life. She is a member of TNNA, TKGA, and the Tea Time Knitters w/Chocolate; is published in *Luxury Yarn One-Skein Wonders* (Storey, 2008) and *Vogue Knitting* magazine (Fall/2009); and has patterns available through Buffalo Gold Premium Fibers, Sporfarm Handspun Just for EWE, or *grannyanme@comcast.net*.

SHARON A. WINSAUER
AURORA ALPACAS

Sharon and her husband have lived in several states over the years, spending many years in the snow country of the Upper Peninsula of Michigan. In 1989, they moved to mid-Michigan with two Briards. Shortly thereafter they added a cat and a Newfoundland. With three long-haired dogs, Sharon felt compelled to do something with all that hair, so she made a drop spindle and started spinning. This led her to alpacas, and it was love at first sight. She traded dog hair for alpaca, the drop spindle for a wheel, and as they say, "The rest is history" — Aurora Alpacas was born. Handspun black alpaca inspired Sharon to try her hand at designing lace, which has become a passion. Her designs are unique, including picture shawls such as "Heere Be Dragons" and shaped shawls like "Just a Butterfly." She currently designs for the Alpaca with a Twist yarn company and teaches lace knitting. Her designs can be seen on Ravelry under CrazyLaceLady and at *www.auroraalpacas.etsy.com*.

JESSICA X. WRIGHT-LICHTER

Jessica's mother taught her to knit when she was eight years old, and she's been knitting ever since. It's how she processes her world. These days, Jessica's knitting world includes working with Classic Elite Yarns, where she knits, proofreads, and designs. For her, there are always new techniques to learn, different ways to see things, and, most importantly, amazing ways to put colors and stitches together to create magic!

Abbreviations

beg	begin, beginning
ch	chain
dc	double crochet
dec	decrease
hdc	half double crochet
inc	increase
K	knit
K2tog	knit 2 stitches together (1 stitch decreased)
K3tog	knit 3 stitches together (2 stitches decreased)
kfb	knit into the front and back of stitch (1 stitch increased)
kwise	knitwise, as if to knit
M1	make 1 stitch (see page 279)
M1L	make 1 stitch, left leaning (see page 279)
M1LP	make 1 purl stitch, left leaning (see page 279)
M1R	make 1 stitch, right leaning (see page 279)
M1RP	make 1 purl stitch, right leaning (see page 279)
P	purl
P2tog	purl 2 stitches together (1 stitch decreased)
P3tog	purl 3 stitches together (2 stitches decreased)
Pfb	purl into the front and back of stitch (1 stitch increased)
psso	pass slipped stitch over last stitch on needle
p2sso	pass 2 slipped stitches over
pwise	purlwise, as if to purl
RS	right side
s2kp	slip 2 stitches together knitwise, knit 1, pass 2 slipped stiches over knit stitch
sc	single crochet
sk2p	slip 1, knit 2 together, pass slipped stitch over knit together stitches
skp	slip 1, knit 1, pass slipped stitch over knit stitch
sp	space
ssk	slip 1 knitwise, slip 1 knitwise, place left needle into front of slipped stitches and knit them together
ssp	slip 1 knitwise, slip 1 knitwise, place left needle into back of slipped stitches and purl them together
st(s)	stitch(es)
tbl	through back loop
tr	treble crochet
WS	wrong side
WT	wrap and turn
wyib	with yarn in back
wyif	with yarn in front
yo	yarn over needle

Glossary

Backward-loop cast on. Hold the end of the yarn and a needle in your right hand. Hold the working yarn in your left hand. Bring your left thumb over the top, down behind, and up in front of the yarn creating a loop. Insert needle into loop on thumb as if to knit and slide loop onto needle. You may also use the backward-loop cast on to add stitches to the end of a row of knitting or to increase stitches mid-row.

Cable cast on. Make a slipknot and place it on your left-hand needle. Follow steps 1 and 2 for knitted-on cast on (see page 278), then proceed as follows:

○ Place the second needle between the two stitches on the first needle (see Fig. 1).

○ Knit a new stitch between the two stitches, and place it on the first needle (see Fig. 2).

Continue in this manner, knitting between the last two stitches on the first needle, until you have the required number of stitches.

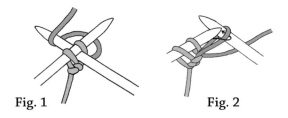

Fig. 1   **Fig. 2**

Chain (crochet). Begin with a slipknot on the hook. Wrap yarn over hook and pull the loop through the slipknot. Yarn over hook, pull loop through loop on hook to make second chain. Repeat for the required number of chain stitches.

Double crochet. Yarn over hook. Insert hook through both loops of next stitch or into next space. Draw loop through stitch. Yarn over and draw loop through first two loops on hook. Yarn over hook and draw loop through two loops on hook.

Figure-8 cast on.

1. Hold two double-point needles parallel. Leaving a 4"/10 cm tail, and holding the tail against the needles with your left hand, *bring the yarn over the top needle from front to back, then bring the yarn between the needles and under the bottom needle from front to back. Repeat from * until you have the desired number of stitches, with the same number on each needle.

2. With a third needle, knit the stitches from the top needle. Turn the work 180° and, with another needle, knit the stitches from the bottom needle.

Garter stitch. When knitting back and forth in rows, knit all rows. When knitting circularly, knit one row, purl one row.

Half double crochet. Yarn over hook. Insert hook through both loops of next stitch or into next space. Yarn over and draw loop through stitch. Yarn over hook and draw through all three loops on hook.

I-cord. Use two double-point needles to make I-cord. Cast on the required number of stitches. *Knit all stitches. Without turning work, slide the stitches to the other end of the needle. Pull the working yarn across the back. Repeat from * until cord is desired length. Bind off.

K2P2 buttonhole. This technique places a buttonhole in a purl section of K2, P2 rib.

Row 1 (RS): Work in pattern to one knit stitch before the two purls, ssk, yarn over twice, K2tog.

Row 2: Work in pattern to double yarn over, K1, P1 in double yarn over, continue in pattern.

Kitchener stitch. This grafting technique is used to join two sets of live stitches invisibly. It is most often used for sock toes but can be used to join shoulder seams or two halves of a scarf.

1. Place the two sets of live stitches to be bound off on separate needles. Hold the needles parallel in your left hand with wrong sides of the knitted fabric together.

2. Insert the tapestry needle into the first stitch on the front needle as if to knit, and slip the stitch off the needle.

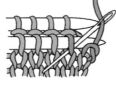

Then insert the tapestry needle into the next stitch on the front needle as if to purl, and leave the stitch on the needle.

3. Insert the tapestry needle into the first stitch on the back needle as if to purl, and slip the stitch off the needle.

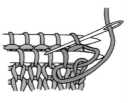

4. Insert the tapestry needle into the next stitch on the back needle as if to knit, and leave the stitch on the needle.

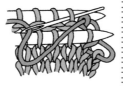

Repeat steps 2, 3, and 4 until all stitches have been joined.

Knitted-on cast on. Make a slipknot and place it on your left-hand needle.

1. Knit a stitch into the slip-knot, leaving the slipknot on the needle.

2. Place the new stitch onto left-hand needle by inserting the left-hand needle into the front of the new stitch.

3. Tighten stitch and continue until you have the required number of stitches.

Knitwise. When a pattern says "slip the next stitch knitwise" or "slip the next stitch kwise," insert your needle into the next stitch from front to back as if you were going to knit it, then slip it to the right-hand needle without knitting it.

Long-tail cast on. Leaving a tail long enough to cast on the desired number of stitches (a generous guess would be one inch per stitch), make a slipknot and place it on the needle.

1. Wrap the tail thread around your thumb and the ball around your index finger. Hold the tails with your other three fingers.

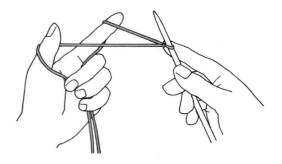

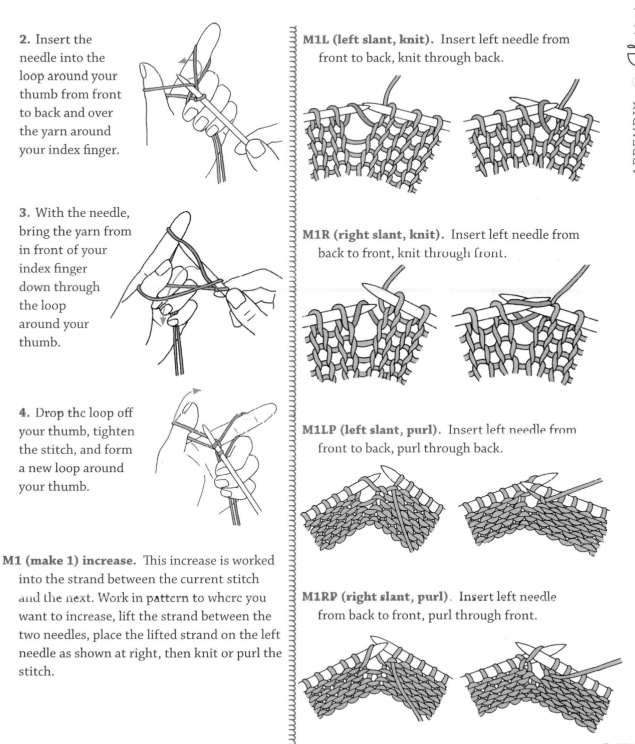

2. Insert the needle into the loop around your thumb from front to back and over the yarn around your index finger.

3. With the needle, bring the yarn from in front of your index finger down through the loop around your thumb.

4. Drop the loop off your thumb, tighten the stitch, and form a new loop around your thumb.

M1 (make 1) increase. This increase is worked into the strand between the current stitch and the next. Work in pattern to where you want to increase, lift the strand between the two needles, place the lifted strand on the left needle as shown at right, then knit or purl the stitch.

M1L (left slant, knit). Insert left needle from front to back, knit through back.

M1R (right slant, knit). Insert left needle from back to front, knit through front.

M1LP (left slant, purl). Insert left needle from front to back, purl through back.

M1RP (right slant, purl). Insert left needle from back to front, purl through front.

279

Mattress stitch. For a half-stitch seam allowance, work through the horizontal bar at the base of the stitches in every other row (Fig. 1). For a full-stitch seam allowance, work through two horizontal bars on either side of the stitches (Fig. 2).

Fig. 1   **Fig. 2**

Pick up and knit.

1. With right side facing, insert the needle under both strands of the edge stitch.

2. Wrap the yarn around the needle.

3. Knit the picked-up stitch.

Pick up and purl.

1. With wrong side facing, insert the needle under both strands of the edge stitch from back to front.

2. Wrap the yarn around the needle.

3. Purl the picked-up stitch.

Provisional cast on (crochet over needle).

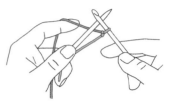

1. With scrap yarn, make a slipknot and place it on a crochet hook. Hold your knitting needle on top of the ball end of the yarn.

2. *With the crochet hook, draw the yarn over the needle and through the loop on the hook. To cast on another stitch, *bring yarn behind knitting needle into position as for step 1*, and repeat from *. *Note:* If you find it awkward to cast on the first couple of stitches, work a few crochet chain stitches before casting on to the needle so you have something to hold on to.

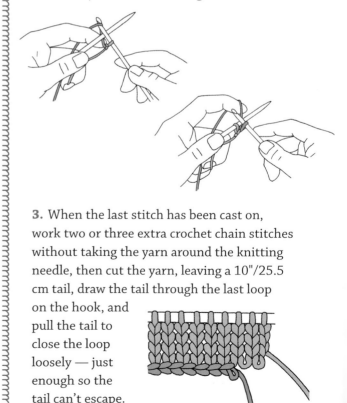

3. When the last stitch has been cast on, work two or three extra crochet chain stitches without taking the yarn around the knitting needle, then cut the yarn, leaving a 10"/25.5 cm tail, draw the tail through the last loop on the hook, and pull the tail to close the loop loosely — just enough so the tail can't escape.

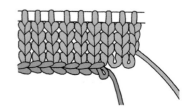

To remove the scrap yarn when you've finished the knitting, pull the tail out of the last loop and gently tug on it to "unzip" the chain and carefully place the live stitches on a needle, holder, or separate length of scrap yarn as they are released.

Provisional cast on (crochet chain).

1. Make a crochet chain with scrap yarn that is at least six chains longer than the number of stitches to be cast on.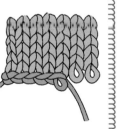

2. Cast on by knitting with the project yarn into the purl bumps on the back of the chain.

3. To remove the scrap yarn when you've finished the knitting, pull out the crocheted chain and carefully place the live stitches on a needle.

Purlwise. When a pattern says "slip the next stitch purlwise" or "slip the next stitch pwise," insert your needle into the next stitch from back to front as if you were going to purl it, then slip it to the right-hand needle without purling it.

Single crochet. Insert hook into next stitch, wrap yarn over hook and draw the loop through the stitch. *You now have* two loops on the hook. Yarn over hook and draw loop through both loops on hook.

Slip-stitch crochet. Insert hook into next stitch, wrap yarn over hook, and draw the loop through the stitch and the loop on the hook.

Stockinette stitch. When knitting back and forth in rows, knit the right-side rows, purl the wrong-side rows. When knitting circularly, knit all rounds.

Tassel.

1. Cut a piece of cardboard about 4"/10 cm wide and a little longer than you want your tassel to be. Wrap the yarn lengthwise around the cardboard to desired thickness of tassel. Cut the yarn even with the bottom edge of the cardboard.

2. Cut a piece of yarn 24"/ 61 cm long. Fold the piece in half, insert it between the cardboard and the wrapped yarn, and slide it up the top edge of the cardboard. With the edges even, tie the piece tightly around the wrapped yarn.

3. Cut through the wrapped yarn opposite the tie.

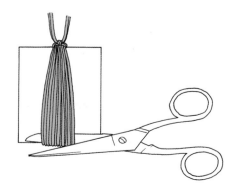

281

4. Cut a 12"/30.5 cm length of yarn and wrap it tightly around the tassel two or three times, about 1"/2.5 cm from the top. Tie it securely. Using a yarn needle, pull the ends through to the inside of the tassel so they hang down inside. Shake out the tassel and trim any uneven ends.

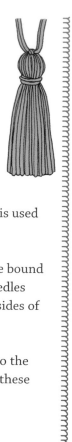

Three-needle bind off. This technique is used to join two sets of live stitches.

1. Place the two sets of stitches to be bound off on separate needles. Hold the needles parallel in your left hand with right sides of the knitted fabric together.

2. Insert the tip of a third needle into the first stitch on both needles and knit these two stitches together.

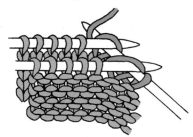

3. Repeat step 2. *You now have* two stitches on the right needle. With one of the needles in your left hand, lift the first stitch on the right-hand needle over the second and off the needle as for a regular bind off. Repeat until all stitches are bound off.

Twisted cord. Adding one-third to the desired length of the cord, cut a piece of yarn that is four times this measurement. Fold the yarn in half and make a knot at each end. Secure the folded end so that it remains stable and twist the yarn tightly, keeping it stretched taut. Pinch the yarn at the center, then fold it in half, keeping it stretched taut. Slowly release a few inches at a time, starting from the folded end, allowing the cord to twist back on itself.

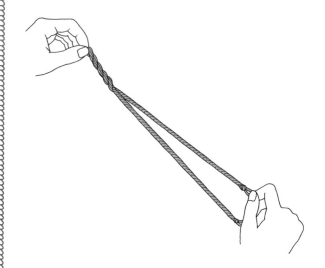

Wrap and turn. Work number of stitches specified. Bring yarn forward and slip next stitch purlwise. Bring yarn back and slipstitch back to left-hand needle. Turn the work. The first stitch on the right-hand needle now has the working yarn wrapped around its base.

Index

Page numbers in *italics* indicate photographs or illustrations. Page numbers in **bold** indicate charts.

The Series with Endless Wonders!

The One-Skein Wonders

books feature portable, stylish, gift-worthy knitting patterns submitted by yarn shops, designers, and fiber artists from all corners of North America. Buy them all, and you'll always have a ready selection of quick and simple projects that show off your beautiful single skeins.

One-Skein Wonders
The book that started it all!
ISBN 978-1-58017-645-3
$18.95

"Stylish, fun-to-knit projects that require little yarn, but deliver big results."
— *Crafts 'n Things*

101 Designer One-Skein Wonders
Knitwear designers contributed the patterns for this exciting collection.
ISBN 978-1-58017-688-0
$18.95

"If she loves to knit, but she's too busy, then *101 Designer One-Skein Wonders* is the book for her."
— *The Star-Ledger Newark*

Luxury Yarn One-Skein Wonders
Fine cashmeres, alpacas, and other natural fibers are the secret ingredients for these 101 posh projects.
ISBN 978-1-60342-079-2
$18.95

These and other books from Storey Publishing are available wherever quality books are sold or by calling 1-800-441-5700.
Visit us at www.storey.com and www.oneskeinwonders.com.